Italian
grammar handbook

Derek Aust

Berlitz Publishing Company, Inc.
Princeton Mexico City London Eschborn Singapore

Italian Grammar Handbook

Published by Berlitz Publishing Company, Inc.
400 Alexander Park, Princeton, NJ 08540 USA
9-13 Grosvenor St., London W1X 9FB UK

Reprinted August 2000

Printed in Canada

ISBN 2-8315-6393-3

The Author:

Derek Aust is an experienced teacher and examiner.

The Series Editor:

Christopher Wightwick is a former UK representative on the Council of Europe Modern Languages Projekt and principal Inspector of Modern Languages for England.

CONTENTS

C Actions and States: Verbs and Their Uses

How to Use This Handbook

This Handbook can be used in two ways.

- If you want to get a general picture of some aspects of Italian grammar, start with the Contents. You can then read through the relevant sections of the text. The many cross-references will lead you to other, related topics.

- If you want to find out more about a specific grammatical point or about the use of particular Italian words or expressions, consult the extensive Index at the end of the book. The Index has many subheadings, and in addition, items are frequently referenced under more than one heading. The Index will point you to individual paragraph numbers.

The Handbook gives a great deal of information about grammatical forms and structures, but above all is designed to show how they fit in with what you want to say or write.

- Grammatical terms are treated as convenient labels and used whenever necessary, but the Handbook does not assume that you already know what they mean. All the sections of this book include explanations of grammatical terms.

- A key feature is the number of examples, drawn from a wide stock of Italian in current use. Wherever it makes sense to do so, these examples are linked together into a short dialogue, topic or narrative. If you do not understand a grammatical explanation, the example will help you to recognize the feature.

- This Handbook is intended for people who want to use their Italian. Where constructions are used only in formal contexts, this is made clear in the text.

Finally, as a safety net, there are special warning sections wherever you see this sign, to help you avoid the more obvious traps and pitfalls.

A

PUTTING IDEAS INTO WORDS

1 Classes of Words: Parts of Speech

1a What Kind of Word Is It?

It is often impossible to say what class a word belongs to (what *part of speech* it is) until it is used in a sentence. On the other hand, understanding a sentence may well depend on knowing what part of speech a word is, so it is useful to be able to recognize grammatical classifications. In this Handbook, we define each part of speech mainly by what it does—what it refers to and its function and position in a sentence. If you can also recognize it by its form, for example from its endings, then this is described as well.

The following paragraphs will refer briefly to the main classes of words, give their English and Italian names, some examples, and references to the paragraphs of the book where they are first defined.

1b Content Words

Four classes of words (the *content words*) contain most of the meaning of the sentence.

(i) *Verbs* (i verbi)

Quest'estate *spero* di andare in Italia. *Penso* di andare a giugno. *Voglio* fare un giro della Toscana.	This summer *I hope* to go to Italy. *I am thinking* of going in June. *I want* to do a tour of Tuscany.

[For more on verbs ➤7–19.]

(ii) *Nouns* (i sostantivi)

Durante il mio *soggiorno* vorrei visitare molti *musei, castelli* e *chiese.*	During my *stay* I would like to visit lots of *museums, castles,* and *churches.*

[For more on nouns ➤20.]

(iii) *Adjectives* (gli aggettivi)

Preferisco una vacanza *culturale* e mi piace visitare i monumenti *storici* e le chiese *antiche*. Per me, questa è la vacanza *ideale*.	I prefer a *cultural* vacation / holiday, and I like to visit *historical* monuments and *ancient* churches. For me, this is the *ideal* vacation / holiday.

[For more on adjectives ➤ 22.]

(iv) *Adverbs* (gli avverbi)

Alcuni miei amici vanno *spesso* in questa regione e mi dicono *sempre* che è *veramente* interessante.	Some of my friends *often* go to this area, and they are *always* telling me that it is *very* interesting.

[For more on adverbs ➤ 26.]

1c *Structure Words*

Structure words do of course add to the meaning, but they do it mainly by the way they relate to the content words.

(i) *Auxiliary Verbs* (i verbi ausiliari)

The verbs **avere** and **essere** are used with other verbs to create a range of compound tenses.

***Sono stato* in Italia tre volte. L'ultima volta, a Pasqua, *ho trascorso* due giorni in Sardegna.**	*I have been* to Italy three times. The last time, at Easter, *I spent* two days in Sardinia.

[For more on auxiliary verbs ➤ 7c.]

(ii) *Pronouns* (i pronomi)

Pronouns take the place of nouns, often to avoid unnecessary repetition.

Ho parecchi amici italiani. Purtroppo, non *li* vedo molto spesso. Per restare in contatto, scrivo *loro* oppure telefono *loro* ogni tanto. Forse alcuni verranno a trovar*mi* a Natale.	I have several Italian friends. Unfortunately, I do not see *them* very often. To stay in touch, I write to *them* or telephone *them* every now and then. Perhaps some of them will come and see *me* at Christmas.

[For more on pronouns ➤23.]

(iii) *Determiners* (i determinativi)

Determiners include some of the most common words in any language, such as the possessives (**il mio, la mia, i miei, le mie**), the demonstratives (**questo, quello**), and indefinites (**alcuni, pochi**).

***I miei* amici di Cuneo verranno negli Stati Uniti per *alcuni* mesi per fare un corso d'inglese.**	*My* friends from Cuneo will be coming to the United States for *a few* months to take an English course.

[For more on determiners ➤21.]

(iv) *Prepositions* (le preposizioni)

Prepositions are connecting words placed in front of nouns or their equivalent. They include words like **con** 'with'; **su** 'on'; **prima di** 'before'; **in** 'in.'

Verranno *in* aereo. Purtroppo, non li potrò vedere *prima della* mia partenza per l'Italia.	They will be coming *by* plane. Unfortunately, I shall not be able to see them *before* my departure for Italy.

[For more on prepositions ➤25.]

(v) *Conjunctions* (le congiunzioni)

Conjunctions are used to join sentences, phrases, or words. Some of the most frequently used conjunctions are **e** 'and'; **ma** 'but'; **quando** 'when'; **perché** 'because.'

Li potrò vedere *quando* tornerò dalle vacanze *perché* si fermano per due mesi.	I shall be able to see them *when* I get back from vacation / holiday, *because* they are staying for two months.

[For more on conjunctions ➤5a.]

(vi) *Exclamations* (gli esclamativi)

Exclamations express sudden emotions — surprise, relief, joy — in reaction to a situation. For example: **Che bello! Che peccato! Bravo!**

***Che peccato* che io non ci sia quando arrivano!**	*What a pity* that I am not here when they arrive!

[For more on exclamations ➤24.]

2 Getting It Down on Paper: Spelling and Punctuation

This chapter describes the basic features of Italian spelling and punctuation. It does not deal directly with pronunciation, as attempts to describe sounds on paper are more likely to be a hindrance than a help.

2a *The Italian Alphabet*

(i) There are twenty-one letters in the Italian alphabet. To these are added **J, K, W, X,** and **Y,** which appear in Italian in words of foreign origin. It is important to know the twenty-six letters, and it is essential to be able to use the Italian alphabet when spelling names and addresses on the telephone, and so forth. Alongside each letter of the alphabet below is the name of the letter in Italian.

A a	**H** acca	**O** o	**V** vu
B bi	**I** i	**P** pi	**W** doppia vu
C ci	**J** i lunga	**Q** cu	**X** ics
D di	**K** cappa	**R** erre	**Y** ipsilon
E e	**L** elle	**S** esse	**Z** zeta
F effe	**M** emme	**T** ti	
G gi	**N** enne	**U** u	

Some examples of words commonly used in Italian that contain the letters **J, K, W, X, Y**:

scarpe da jogging, jazz, judo, kg, km (abbreviations for **chilogrammo** and **chilometro), karatè, bikini, walkman, whisky, windsurf, western** (film), **xenofobia, ex presidente, mixer, maxiprocesso** (the letter **x** is rarely used at the beginning of a word), **yacht, yoga, yogurt**.

• When spelling aloud it is also useful to know the following words:

A maiuscola	capital A
b minuscola	small b

and the expression

Come si scrive?	How is it written?

H as an initial letter is rarely used in Italian. When it is used, for the most part in words of foreign origin, it is nearly always silent. Its use in certain words is to distinguish them from other words similarly pronounced but with entirely different meanings, such as: **ho** 'I have' and **o** 'or,' **hai** 'you have,' and **ai** 'to the,' **ha** 'he / she / it has' and **a** 'to,' **hanno** 'they have' and **anno** 'year.'

- Care should be taken in the pronunciation of double consonants. One should, for example, hear the double **m** in **mamma** (**mam-ma**) and the double **b** in **babbo** (**bab-bo**). This is particularly important in words where failure to articulate the double consonant results in a change of meaning, as illustrated by the following examples:

nono	ninth	**sera**	evening	**sete**	thirst
nonno	grandfather	**serra**	greenhouse	**sette**	seven

(ii) *Capital letters*

Capital letters are used less often in Italian than in English. Sentences always begin with a capital letter. They are not used in the following cases:

- Days of the week and months of the year [▶ 30a, 30b]:

giovedì 10 aprile	Thursday, April 10th

- Adjectives of nationality, including names of languages:

Un amico spagnolo.	A Spanish friend.
Mi piace scrivere in italiano.	I like writing in Italian.

It is common practice to use a small letter for nouns denoting nationality:

I tedeschi	the Germans

- Points of the compass:

il nord, il sud, l'ovest, l'est, il sudovest

But **il Settentrione** 'the North,' **il Mezzogiorno** 'the South,' **l'Oriente** 'the East,' and so forth, when the reference is to a geographical area.

- Personal status and profession in titles:

la signora Martini	Mrs. Martini
il dottor Gamberini	Doctor Gamberini
il colonnello Becchio	Colonel Becchio

(iii) *Stress patterns*

It would not be helpful to go into great detail about stress patterns in Italian. This is best acquired through experience of speaking and listening to native speakers of the language. As a general rule, however, the stress falls on the next-to-the-last vowel and on the end of the word if marked by an accent.

amico, **banca**, **macelleria**, **universitá**, **benché**

As there are so many exceptions, it makes more sense to learn by using the language. Many dictionaries indicate stress, and it would be wise to consult such a dictionary when in doubt. The importance of putting the stress in the right place, however, is best illustrated by the examples quoted below, where a misplaced stress gives rise to another meaning. The stress is underlined in the examples quoted.

l'ancora della nave	the ship's anchor
non è ancora arrivata	she still hasn't arrived
che cosa desideri?	what do you want?
questi sono i miei desideri	these are my wishes
un numero impari	an odd number
così impari	in this way you learn
i principi	the princes
i principi morali	moral principles
lo faccio subito	I'll do it straightaway
ha subito un'operazione	he underwent an operation
gli uccelli volano	birds fly
il gioco del volano	the game of badminton

(iv) *Accents*

In Italian there are two main accents: the acute accent (**accento acuto**) and the grave accent (**accento grave**). The circumflex is rarely used. Both accents are commonly placed on the final vowel, where they have three main functions:

- On words of two or more syllables, to show that the stress falls on the last syllable:

lunedì, **andrò**, **quaggiù**, **ventitré**, **cordialità**

- On the following monosyllables:

ciò, **già**, **giù**, **può**, **più**

- To distinguish between words that have the same spelling but different meaning:

è	'he / she / it is' (verb)
e	'and' (conjunction)
dà	'he / she / it gives' (verb)
da	'from,' 'by' (preposition)
là	'there' (adverb of place)
la	'the,' 'her' (article, pronoun)
lì	'there' (adverb of place)
li	'them' (pronoun)
né	'nor' (conjunction)
ne	'of it,' 'from there' (pronoun, adverb)
sì	'yes' (adverb)
si	'himself,' 'herself,' 'one' (pronoun)
sé	'himself,' 'herself,' 'oneself' (pronoun)
se	'if,' 'whether' (conjunction)
tè	'tea' (noun)
te	'you' (pronoun)

The acute and grave accents are used as follows:

- Acute on closed **e**: **né**, **sé**, **perché**, **poiché**, **ventitré**, **vendé** (third person singular, past definite of regular **-ere** verbs);

- Grave on open **e** and, usually, on the other vowels (**caffè**, **però**, **perciò**, **già**, **più**, **così**).

If the rules regarding the use of accents were rigidly adhered to, then there should be an acute accent on closed vowels (**e**, **i**, **o**, **u**) and a grave accent on open vowels (**a**, **e**, **o**). However, modern usage tends to prefer the grave accent, particularly on **à, ò, ù**, and **ì**. The grave accent, therefore, will be used on these vowels throughout this Handbook.

2b Punctuation

(i) Punctuation marks

The main punctuation marks in Italian are:

	Italian	English
.	**punto**	period / full stop
,	**virgola**	comma
;	**punto e virgola**	semicolon
:	**due punti**	colon
?	**punto interrogativo**	question mark
!	**punto esclamativo**	exlamation mark
-	**trattino**	hyphen
—	**lineetta**	dash
<<...>> or "..." or '...'	**virgolette** (**basse** or **alte**)	guillemets, quotation marks / inverted commas
( )	**le parentesi tonde**	parentheses / round brackets
[ ]	**le parentesi quadre**	square brackets
/	**la sbarretta**	slash
'	**apostrofo**	apostrophe

(ii) Quotation marks

Quotation marks (**le virgolette**) are used to report what someone else has said or to highlight a word or expression used in a particular way, for example, metaphorical or ironic. Although three types of quotation marks exist in Italian, **le virgolette basse** (<<...>>) are the ones most commonly used in newspapers and books, whereas **le virgolette alte** (". . .") are used in handwritten letters. The single inverted comma ('. . .') is normally used to highlight a particular word or phrase within a sentence.

Cosa intendi dire per la 'riforma' del sistema scolastico?	What do you mean by the 'reform' of the school system?

(iii) The dash

The dash (**la lineetta**) can be used to introduce direct speech. A common use within direct speech when reference is made to the speaker.

A differenza degli altri partiti — ha detto il deputato — il nostro ha preso provvedimenti per risolvere il problema.	"Unlike the other parties," said the member of Parliament / Deputy, "ours has taken steps to solve the problem."

(iv) The hyphen

The hyphen (**il trattino**) is used in the following cases:

- To separate two numbers:

Bisogna pagare intorno al 5–7 per cento.	You have to pay around 5 to 7 percent.

- Between two nouns:

la linea Milano-Roma	the Milan-Rome line
il derby Juventus-Torino	the Juventus-Torino derby
i rapporti studenti-professori	student-teacher relationships

- When splitting a word at the end of a line:

simpa- **tico**	nice, pleasant

The word must end the line on a complete syllable. It would be wrong, therefore, to end the line with **simpat-**, as the **t** forms part of the next syllable **-ti**. Never end the line with a double consonant, for example, **intell-igente.** You should usually split the double consonant thus: **intel-ligente.**

[For other uses of the hyphen ➤3a(ii).]

(v) Brackets

Parentheses / round brackets (**le parentesi tonde**) are more frequently used than square brackets (**le parentesi quadre**). They serve to introduce into the sentence a comment made by the writer.

Il vantaggio (se qualche vantaggio c'è) sta nel fatto che ...	The advantage—if there is some advantage—lies in the fact that . . .

These brackets are often replaced by commas or dashes.

(vi) The apostrophe

The main uses of the apostrophe are:

- For elision: ***un'amica, l'aeroporto*** [➤21e(ii), 21c(iv), (vi)].
- With the imperative forms ***da', fa', sta', va', di'*** [➤15b].
- With the abbreviated form ***un po'*** for ***un poco*** 'a little.'
- When the first two numbers are omitted from the year:

negli anni '80	in the '80s

(vii) The comma

The use of the comma (**la virgola**) is for the most part the same as in English. However, in presenting numbers, there are important differences [▶ 28a(G)]. In Italian a comma is used in decimals where in English there would be a decimal point or a period / full stop:

L'inflazione è scesa al 4,7%.	Inflation has gone down to 4.7%.

A comma is used with large numbers in English. A period / full stop (**il punto**) is used in Italian.

100.000 abitanti	100,000 inhabitants

Linking Words

3a *Compound Words or Phrases?*

All languages need ways of combining word meanings so as to express more complex ideas. This may be done either by joining two words together to form one (occasionally hyphenated) compound word or by linking separate words to form phrases.

(i) *Compound words without a hyphen*

Italian has a large number of compound words. There are quite a few comprising verb + noun:

l'apribottiglie	bottle opener
l'apriscatole	can opener
l'asciugamano	towel
l'aspirapolvere	vacuum cleaner
il cacciavite	screwdriver
il cavalcavia	overpass / fly-over
il grattacielo	skyscraper
la lavastoviglie	dishwasher
il parabrezza	windshield / windscreen
il paraurti	bumper (*on vehicle*)
il portacenere	ashtray
il portachiavi	key ring
il portafoglio	wallet
il portavoce	spokesperson
il salvagente	lifebelt
lo stuzzicadenti	toothpick

• Other combinations include noun + noun, preposition + noun, noun + adjective:

la banconota	banknote
il capostazione	stationmaster
la cassaforte	safe
il cavolfiore	cauliflower
i senzatetto	the homeless
il sottopassaggio	underpass / subway
la terraferma	mainland

[For the formation of the plurals of compound nouns ➤20h(viii).]

(ii) Compound words with a hyphen

The hyphen [▶2b(iv)] is rarely used with compound words in Italian, but two places where it does occur are as follows:

- Where two nouns are linked together and the second one describes or defines the first:

la busta paga	pay envelope / packet
una notizia lampo	a news flash
le vacanze-studio	study vacation / holidays

It is difficult to give a hard-and-fast rule as you will certainly come across **busta paga** without the hyphen.

- In compound adjectives such as the following:

socioeconomico	socioeconomic [▶22a(ii)]

3b Phrases Expressing a Complex Idea

In English the words 'tea' and 'cup' are both nouns, but in the expression 'tea cup' the noun 'tea' describes 'cup.' The Italian language also makes use of nouns (and the infinitive form of verbs) in this way, but the wordings are different. When one noun is used to describe another, it generally requires a linking preposition such as **da** or **di**:

un bicchiere da vino*	a wineglass
una bottiglia da vino*	a wine bottle
la carta da lettere	writing paper
una macchina da cucire	a sewing machine
una macchina da scrivere	a typewriter
una sala da ballo	a dance hall
una sala da pranzo	dining room
una tazza da tè*	a tea cup

The **da** in these examples is being used to convey the notion of purpose or function. Thus **un bicchiere da vino** is a glass for the purpose of drinking wine.
Note the distinction in meaning between the examples marked with an asterisk above and the following where the preposition **di** indicates the contents:

un bicchiere di vino	a glass of wine
una bottiglia di vino	a bottle of wine
una tazza di tè	a cup of tea

- **Di** is also generally used to indicate 'made of':

una giacca di cuoio	a leather jacket
un sacchetto di plastica	a plastic bag
un tavolo di legno	a wooden table

- **Di** or **di** + the definite article [▶ 21c(vii)] is the most widely used link in noun phrases:

una casa di campagna	a country house
una festa di compleanno	a birthday party
una partita di calcio	a soccer match / football game
la fermata dell'autobus	bus stop
l'orario dei treni	train schedule
le previsioni del tempo	weather forecast

There are many instances, however, where an adjectival structure is used instead of a noun phrase:

il bollettino meteorologico	weather report
un incidente stradale	a road accident
la stazione ferroviaria	railroad / railway station
la vita familiare	family life

This is only possible of course if the describing noun can be converted into an adjective. Even then, it is still current usage that determines whether the adjective is preferable, or whether **di** + the noun, or either can be used. To attempt, therefore, to provide a rule would in no way be helpful.

3c Suffixes

Suffixes are endings that you add to a word to modify its meaning or sometimes to convert it to another part of speech. Italian uses a large number of them.

(i) Making adjectives from nouns

A descriptive adjective is often formed by adding **-oso** to a noun. It often corresponds to the English suffixes '-y' and '-ous.'

l'avventura	adventure	**il rumore**	noise
avventuroso	adventurous	**rumoroso**	noisy
la fama	fame	**la sabbia**	sand
famoso	famous	**sabbioso**	sandy
la furia	fury	**lo spazio**	space
furioso	furious	**spazioso**	spacious
la nuvola	cloud		
nuvoloso	cloudy		

Abito in un quartiere molto rumoroso.	I live in a very noisy area.
Il mio appartamento è abbastanza spazioso.	My apartment/flat is quite spacious.

(ii) *Making verbs from nouns or adjectives*

A number of verbs are formed in Italian by adding the suffixes **-eggiare, -izzare,** and **-ificare** to nouns and adjectives:

l'analisi	analysis	**festeggiare**	celebrate
analizzare	analyze	**identico**	identical
bianco	white	**identificare**	identify
biancheggiare	whiten	**moderno**	modern
la costa	coast	**modernizzare**	modernize
costeggiare	run along (the side of) the coast	**nazionale**	national
		nazionalizzare	nationalize
elettrico	electrical	**la nota**	note
elettrificare	electrify	**notificare**	notify
la festa	party, celebration	**privato**	private
		privatizzare	privatize

(iii) *Diminutives and augmentatives*

Italian has a great variety of suffixes that are added to nouns and adjectives to indicate smallness and largeness, but that often also contain other nuances. They normally take their gender according to that of the original noun or, in the case of adjectives, the noun they describe.

(A) One of the most widely used diminutives is **-ino**, which indicates both smallness and endearment.

La tua *sorellina* è molto *carina*.	Your *little sister* is very *sweet.*
I miei parenti abitano in un *paesino* in piena campagna.	My relatives live in a *little village* in the heart of the countryside.

(B) Other diminutives are **-etto** and **-ello**.

Hanno una *casetta* vicino al mare.	They have a *little house* (cottage) near the sea.

Almeno adesso si può respirare con questo *venticello*.	At least you can breathe now with this *little breeze*.

[For more detail on suffixes with nouns and adjectives ➤20k(i) and 22g(ii). Adverbs are occasionally modified by suffixes ➤26c.]

3d *Prefixes*

Italian also uses a considerable number of prefixes, particularly before verbs, nouns, and adjectives. Reference will be made to some of these prefixes in the relevant chapters. [For verbs ➤18e; for nouns ➤20k(ii); for adjectives ➤22g(i).]

3e *Side by Side: Words in Apposition*

Sometimes we add a phrase immediately after the names of people or things, giving further information about them. This explanatory phrase is said to be *in apposition* to the name.
In Italian, a noun in apposition is not normally preceded by either the definite article [➤21c] or the indefinite article [➤21e].

Mia sorella, *infermiera* all'ospedale da più di otto anni, ha deciso di dimettersi.	My sister, *a nurse* at the hospital for more than eight years, has decided to resign.

B

PUTTING A SENTENCE TOGETHER: SYNTAX

Recognizing Sentences

4a *What Is a Sentence?*

A sentence is a spoken or written utterance that has a subject and a predicate. When talking, we often say things that are not sentences (for example, exclamations [➤24] or isolated phrases that make perfect sense because we know the context), but in writing we usually try to use complete sentences. The way a sentence is put together is known as its *syntax.*

4b *The Subject of a Sentence*

(i) *What is a subject?*

Generally speaking, the subject is the word or phrase whose action or state the sentence is describing:

L'*aereo* parte da Londra alle otto.	The *plane* leaves London at eight o'clock.

The subject of the sentence is **l'aereo,** and the main verb is **parte**.

In Italian, subject pronouns (such as **io**, 'I,' **tu** '[familiar] you,' **lui** 'he,' **lei** 'she,' etc.) [➤23b(i)] are often not used, since the subject is expressed by the verb ending.

A che ora *devi* partire di casa per prendere questo aereo?	At what time *do you have to* leave home to catch this plane?

The impersonal subject 'it' is also often contained in the verb in Italian [➤8g].

Se *piove,* è meglio stare a casa.	If *it is raining, it is* better to stay at home.

(ii) *Passive sentences*

The verb may be used in a form known as *passive* [➤17a], which means that the subject of the verb, instead of doing the action of the verb, becomes the receiver of the action:

La famiglia **è stata accolta a braccia aperte dai miei amici italiani.**	*The family* was welcomed with open arms by my Italian friends.

The subject of the sentence is **la famiglia** and the verb is **è stata accolta,** which is the passive form of **accogliere**. The welcoming is not done by the subject but by **i miei amici italiani**.

(iii) *Omission of the subject*

In command forms [➤15] the subject is nearly always omitted but clearly understood because each form is distinct in itself.

Vieni a trovarmi stasera.	Come and see me this evening.
Stia tranquillo.	Keep calm.

In the first example the main verb is **vieni**, and the subject—understood but not stated—is **tu**. In the second example the verb is **stia**, and the subject—again not stated—is **Lei**.

4c *The Predicate of a Sentence*

The predicate consists of the whole of the rest of the sentence, excluding the subject. It must have at least a main verb, that is, a verb in a tense, usually in the indicative mood [➤18c]. This verb *agrees* with its subject, that is, its form changes to match the subject in person and number. Chapter 7 describes the various types of verb and what they do.

L'aereo arrivò.	The plane arrived.

However, most predicates have more than this bare minimum. Other words and expressions are required to complete the information given about the subject.

L'aereo arrivò a Milano con dieci minuti di ritardo causa vento contrario.	The plane arrived in Milan ten minutes late because of a head wind.

In this case the predicate consists of the verb **arrivò** plus the remainder of the sentence, which is the adverbial expression of place **a Milano** [▶27b(iii)], the expression of time **con dieci minuti di ritardo** [▶27b(i)], and the causal phrase **causa vento contrario**.

Note that the compound preposition for 'because of' is **a causa di** [▶25c(xi)], but **causa** is perfectly acceptable in the above context.

4d *Types of Sentence*

There are three types of complete sentence:

- statements, which are the basic form;
- direct questions [▶6];
- commands [▶15].

All three must have a main clause; they may also have any number of subordinate clauses.

4e *Main Clauses*

A main clause is a sentence that can stand by itself, though of course it may not make sense unless you know what the speaker is talking about. The most common word order is subject + verb + object or complement, although other orders are possible in Italian [▶4g], and object pronouns [▶23b(ii), 23b(iii)] precede the verb in most circumstances.

Mio fratello non capiva.	My brother didn't understand.

4f *Subordinate Clauses*

A subordinate clause is always dependent on a main clause, whose meaning it completes or expands. It is linked to the main clause by one of three types of word:

- a subordinating conjunction [▶5a(ii)];
- a question word [▶6d];
- a relative pronoun [▶23m].

In certain subordinate clauses in Italian, the verb will be in the subjunctive [▶16].

In the following example the main sentence is **Mio fratello non capiva** and the remaining clauses are subordinate to it.

Mio fratello non capiva perché volevo andare a vivere in un posto che dista cinquanta chilometri dalla città più vicina e dove non c'è niente da fare.

My brother didn't understand why I wanted to go and live in a place that is fifty kilometers / kilometres from the nearest town and where there is nothing to do.

4g *The Order of Words*

Word order is very fluid in Italian and is often varied according to the word or part of the sentence that the speaker wishes to emphasize. The following can therefore only be guidelines: there are no hard-and-fast rules.

(i) *Subject + verb + object + adverbials*

This order gives a neutral statement, with no particular emphasis on any element. Adverbials of time tend to come before those of place, although this may also depend on the emphasis the speaker intends.

Mio fratello ha un appartamento in città.

My brother has an apartment / flat in the city.

(ii) *Verb + subject*

However, the subject often follows the verb for reasons of emphasis.

È piccolo *il suo appartamento.* Ha detto *mio fratello* che è comodo per fare le spese.

His apartment / flat is small. *My brother* said that it's convenient for shopping.

(iii) Any element of the sentence that needs to be highlighted may be brought forward to the beginning of the sentence, including the direct or indirect object, which then has to be duplicated by the redundant object pronoun [► 23b(vi)].

***Questo appartamento l'*ha comprato due anni fa.**
***Queste scarpe* le ho messe soltanto una volta.**

He bought *this apartment / flat* two years ago.
I wore *these shoes* only once.

(iv) *Adverbials*

Adverbials [➤27c] tend to be placed immediately before or after the verb they qualify, but the order may be changed to shift the emphasis.

Due anni fa* mio fratello ha comprato questo appartamento.** **Mio fratello ha comprato questo appartamento *due anni fa. **Mio fratello ha comprato *due anni fa* questo appartamento.**	*Two years ago* my brother bought this apartment / flat.

It is particularly in the final example that more emphasis is being placed on **due anni fa** so that it was 'two years ago' and not 'three' for example. The importance of position is much more clearly highlighted in the spoken language through intonation and the tendency to pause at significant moments in the sentence.

(v) *Questions*

In questions without a question word, the order is often verb + object + subject.

Ha comprato un appartamento tuo fratello?	Has your brother bought an apartment / flat?

Here again, no hard-and-fast rule applies; and it would be perfectly acceptable to put the subject, **tuo fratello**, before the verb. As previously explained, however, the change in word order can result in a shift of emphasis. In questions where the subject is contained in the verb, the word order is often the same as in English.

Perché ha deciso di comprare un appartamento in città?	Why did he decide to buy an apartment / flat in the city?

With **essere** 'to be,' the complement — **bello** — is often put before the subject.

È bello l'appartamento?	Is the apartment / flat nice?

The word order for both questions and statements can be the same:

È contento di abitare da solo?	Is he happy to live on his own?
È contento di abitare da solo.	He is happy to live on his own.

In speech the intonation indicates the difference between a question and a statement, whereas in writing the punctuation marks the difference.

[For word order with: adjectives ➤22b(i – iv); object pronouns ➤23b(v); exclamations ➤24a.]

Linking Clauses

5a Clauses with Conjunctions

Conjunction means 'joining.' There are two sorts of conjunction, *coordinating* and *subordinating*. Their names reflect their function in the sentence.

(i) Coordinating conjunctions

Coordinating conjunctions link clauses of equal status: main with main, subordinate with subordinate. They tell us something about how the clauses' meanings relate to each other (reinforcing, contrasting, and so forth), but they do not change the clause structure at all.

These are the common coordinating conjunctions:

anche	also, too
dunque / perciò	so, therefore
e	and
eppure	and yet
infatti	in fact
ma	but
né ... né	neither . . . nor
non solo ... ma anche	not only . . . but also
o ... o	either . . . or
o / oppure	or
però	however
sia ... sia	both . . . and; whether . . . or

L'appartamento di mio fratello è bello *e* comodo.	My brother's apartment / flat is nice *and* comfortable.
C'è *anche* una terrazza.	There's *also* a terrace.
Andrò a vederlo oggi *o* domani.	I shall go and see it today *or* tomorrow.
Mi piace l'appartamento, *ma* non mi piace il quartiere.	I like the apartment / flat, *but* I don't like the area.

***Infatti,* non mi piace *né* il quartiere *né* i suoi vicini.**	*In fact,* I like *neither* the area *nor* his neighbors / neighbours.
È un quartiere *non solo* sporco *ma anche* molto rumoroso.	It's *not only* a dirty area *but also* very noisy.

Ed is frequently used in place of **e** when the following word begins with a vowel.

Mio fratello *ed* io ci vediamo ogni settimana.	My brother *and* I see each other every week.

(ii) *Subordinating conjunctions*

Subordinating conjunctions here link subordinate clauses to the rest of the sentence. Usually the subordinate clause is the equivalent of an adverbial expression [▶ 26]. Many subordinating conjunctions are followed by the subjunctive in Italian [▶ 16], others by an indicative form of the verb [▶ 12–14].

Quando vado a trovare mio fratello, preferisco prendere l'autobus perché è sempre difficile parcheggiare la macchina in città.	When I go to see my brother, I prefer to take the bus, because it's always difficult to park the car in town.

The subordinating conjunctions here are **quando** and **perché**, both followed by the present indicative **vado** and **è**.

Benché l'appartamento sia piccolo, mio fratello invita spesso i suoi amici a cena.	Although the apartment / flat is small, my brother often invites his friends to dinner.

The subordinating conjunction is **benché**, followed in present tense structures by the subjunctive, in this case **sia**.

(iii) In the following list of frequently used subordinating conjunctions, those that normally require a subjunctive are followed by (**S**):

a condizione che (S)	on condition that
affinché (S)	in order that, so that

a meno che (S)	unless
anche se	even if
appena	as soon as
benché (S)	although
caso mai (S)	should, if ever
che	that
chiunque (S)	who(m)ever
come	as, like
come se (S)	as if
comunque (S)	however, in whatever way
da quando	since, ever since
dato che	given that, inasmuch as
dovunque (S)	wherever
dopo che	after
finché	until
in modo / maniera che (S)	so that
in modo / maniera che	with the result that
malgrado (che) (S)	despite the fact that
man mano che	(progressively) as
mentre	while
nel caso che (S)	in the event that
nonostante (che) (S)	despite the fact that
ogni volta che	every time that
ovunque (S)	wherever
perché	because
perché (S)	in order that
per quanto (S)	however (much)
poiché	seeing as, since
prima che (S)	before
purché (S)	provided that
qualunque cosa (S)	whatever
quando	when
se	if
sebbene (S)	although
sempre che (S)	provided that, as long as
senza che (S)	without
siccome	as, since
sino a che	until
una volta che	once
visto che	seeing that, inasmuch as

It is important to remember that some of these words also exist in similar forms as prepositions [➤25]. The essential difference is that a preposition is followed by a noun, or something that has the value of a noun, such as a pronoun, or an infinitive; a subordinating conjunction is followed by a complete clause. The following examples illustrate the difference:

senza il biglietto	without the ticket (preposition + noun)
senza di me	without me (preposition + pronoun)
senza sapere	without knowing (preposition + infinitive)
senza che lo sappiano	without them knowing (subordinating conjunction + subjunctive)

[For more details on prepositions ➤25; on subjunctives ➤16]

5b *Relative Clauses*

Relative clauses are introduced by relative pronouns [➤23m]. They describe or define a noun and thus do much the same job as an adjective [➤22]. The relative clause comes very soon (usually immediately) after the noun it refers to, for which reason the noun is known as the *antecedent*. When **che** is the object of the relative clause, the subject often follows the verb.

L'appartamento che ha comprato *mio fratello* non era molto caro.	The apartment/flat that *my brother* bought was not very expensive.

When a preposition precedes a relative pronoun in Italian, **che** cannot be used and must be replaced by **cui** or the appropriate form of **il quale**, **la quale**, and so forth [➤23m(iv), 23m(vi)].

L'appartamento *in cui* abito io non mi è costato molto.	The apartment/flat (*that*) I live *in* didn't cost me a lot.

In Italian it is not possible to place the preposition at the end of the clause, as is frequently done in English. It is also fairly common practice to omit the relative pronoun in English whereas in Italian this is *not* done.

5c *Direct and Indirect Speech*

There are two ways of reporting what people have said (or perhaps thought). Both are introduced by verbs like **dire** 'say,'

rispondere 'answer,' **affermare** 'state,' **pensare** 'think,' and **credere** 'believe,' 'think.' What is said is, in fact, the direct object of this verb [▶ 8d], it answers the question **Cos'ha detto X?** 'What did X say?'.

(i) *Direct speech*

The first way is simply to repeat word for word what was said or thought. This is called *direct speech*, and in English it is marked by the use of quotation marks or inverted commas. Italian punctuation is somewhat different [▶ 2b]. The subject and 'reporting' verb are always inverted when they follow the words spoken.

—Ho sempre voluto comprare un appartamento in città—ha detto mio fratello.	"I've always wanted to buy a apartment/flat in the city," said my brother.

(ii) *Indirect speech*

The second way is known as *indirect speech* or *reported speech.* What was said is rephrased, usually in a clause introduced by **che** 'that' or a question word [▶ 6d]. You cannot omit **che** in Italian as you can 'that' in English.

Mio fratello ha detto *che* aveva sempre voluto comprare un appartamento in città.	My brother said (*that*) he had always wanted to buy an apartment/flat in the city.

(iii) As you can see, direct speech undergoes certain changes when it is reported in this way.

(**A**) The part of the verb and any pronouns present are changed so that they still refer to the right person (here from the first person—**io**—to the third person—**lui**).
(**B**) Verb tenses are changed, usually as in English, so that in the above example the present perfect is changed to the pluperfect. The following table shows how tenses change from direct to indirect speech, when the speech is subsequently reported:

Direct speech	***Indirect speech***
present tense	imperfect tense
present perfect tense	pluperfect tense
future tense	conditional tense

—Sono da Claudio. Ho lasciato qualcosa da mangiare nel frigorifero. Tornerò fra un'ora.	—I am at Claudio's. I have left something to eat in the refrigerator I shall be back in an hour.

becomes

Ha detto che era da Claudio. Aveva lasciato qualcosa da mangiare nel frigorifero. Sarebbe tornato fra un'ora.	He said he was at Claudio's. He had left something to eat in the refrigerator. He would be back in an hour.

5d *Indirect Questions*

Indirect questions are a form of indirect speech [➤ 5c]. They obey the same rules and are introduced by the same types of verb, followed by the relevant question word. Indirect questions are used for various purposes:

(i) To report a direct question that has been or will be asked

Ho domandato dove erano andati in vacanza.	I asked where they had gone on vacation / holiday.
Domanderò dove vanno in vacanza.	I shall ask where they are going on vacation / holiday.

(ii) To ask more courteously

Potreste dirmi dove andate esattamente?	Could you tell me where you are going exactly?

(iii) To say whether we know the answer to a question

Non so se porteranno con sé il cane.	I don't know whether they are going to take the dog with them.

[For the use of the subjunctive in indirect questions ➤ 16c(v).]

5e *Reported Requests and Commands*

These can often be dealt with in Italian by a construction with the infinitive [▶ 8j(ii)C].

Gli ho detto di chiudere tutto a chiave.	I told him to lock everything up.

Asking for Information: Direct Questions

6a *What Is a Direct Question?*

A direct question is a form of direct speech. It tells us word for word what the person said or thought. The questions in the examples below are all direct questions—these are the actual words used, expecting a direct answer. But we often also talk about questions that have been or are going to be asked. These are indirect questions, which are discussed in paragraph 5d.

6b *True or False? Yes/No Questions*

In this type of question we are asking whether something is true or not, so it is always possible to answer 'Yes' or 'No.' The subject and verb are often inverted in this type of question. See the section on word order [➤4g] for more detailed observations.

***Abita* in città *tuo fratello*?—Sì.**	*Does your brother live* in town? —Yes.
È bello *il quartiere*?—No.	*Is the area* nice?—No.

6c *Checking Up: Tag Questions*

Tag questions are statements with a question tag added to the end that asks for confirmation of the statement. English has a wide variety of tags such as 'isn't it?', 'didn't they?', 'aren't we?', and so forth. In Italian the usual all-purpose one is **vero?** In speech, **no** is often used after a positive statement.

Trovare un appartamento in città è difficile, *vero*?	To find an apartment/flat in the city is difficult, *isn't it*?
È stato fortunato, *no*?	He was lucky, *wasn't he*?

6d Asking for Details: Question-Word Questions

We use these questions when we want to find out more about something we already know. The questions always start with a question word, such as those listed below.

Many of the question words listed here are the same as or closely related to relative pronouns [➤23m] or conjunctions [➤5a(ii), 5a(iii)]. Do not confuse them!

(i) *People:* ***Chi? Di chi?*** *Who(m)? Whose?*

***Chi* viene al cinema con me?**	*Who* is coming to the movies / cinema with me?
***Di chi* sono queste chiavi?**	*Whose* keys are these?
***Con chi* vai al ristorante?**	*With whom* are you going to the restaurant?

Con 'with' and other prepositions [➤25] must always precede the question word.

(ii) *Things:* ***Che? Cosa? Che cosa?*** *What?*

***Cosa* facciamo stasera?**	*What* are we doing this evening?
***Che cosa* vuoi fare?**	*What* do you want to do?

(iii) *Selection:* ***Quale?*** *(plural* ***quali****) Which?*

***Quale* dei due film preferisci vedere?**	*Which* of the two movies / films do you prefer to see?
Dei famosi registi italiani *quali* conosci?	*Which* of the famous Italian movie / film directors do you know?

(iv) *Definition:* ***Che? Che tipo di?*** *What? What kind of?*

***Che* film danno all' Astra?**	*What* movie / film is showing at the Astra?
***Che tipo di* film è?**	*What kind of* movie / film is it?

(v) *Description:* ***Come?*** *What . . . like?*

***Com'*era il film che hai visto sabato sera? — Molto comico.**	*What* was the movie / film *like* that you saw on Saturday evening? — Very funny.

(vi) *Time:* ***Quando? A che ora?*** *When? At what time?*

***Quando* andiamo allora? — Domani sera.**	*When* are we going then? — Tomorrow evening.
***A che ora* ci vediamo? — Alle otto davanti al cinema.**	*At what time* shall we meet?— At eight o'clock outside the movie house / cinema.

(vii) *Place:* ***Dove?*** *Where?*

***Dove* si trova il cinema Astra? — È proprio in centro.**	*Where* is the Astra movie house / cinema? — It's right in the center / centre (of town).

(viii) *Manner (methods and means):* ***Come?*** *How?*

***Come* andiamo? In macchina?**	*How* are we going? By car?

(ix) *Quantity and degree:* ***Quanto, quanta, quanti, quante?*** *How much? How many?*

***Quanto* tempo dura il film? — Non lo so.**	*How* long (*how much* time) does the movie / film last? — I don't know.
***Quanti* vengono al cinema?**	*How many* are coming to the movie house / cinema?

(x) *Reasons:* ***Perché?*** *Why?*

***Perché* non andiamo a mangiare una pizza dopo il film? — Che buon'idea!**	*Why* don't we go and have a pizza after the movie / film? — What a good idea!

C

ACTIONS AND STATES: VERBS AND THEIR USES

What Verbs Do

➤ For extensive treatment of the forms of Italian verbs, see the Berlitz *Italian Verb Handbook.*

7a Actions, Feelings, or States

Verbs are words that define *actions:*

***Leggo* molto.**	I *read* a lot.

or that define *feelings* or *states:*

Mi *piace* leggere.	I *like* reading.
***Sono* studente.**	I'*m* a student.

7b Simple and Compound Verbs

Italian verbs consist either of a single word (*simple* tense form), as in the above examples, or of more than one word (*compound* tense form), made up of the appropriate part of the verb **avere** or the verb **essere** and a past participle:

***Ho* sempre *avuto* una passione per la lettura.**	I *have* always *had* a love for reading.

Verbs may have a compound form in one language but not in another:

Il mio primo insegnante di inglese *è stato* molto bravo e mi *ha aiutato* tanto.	My first English teacher *was* very good and *helped* me so much.

7c Auxiliary Verbs

When **avere** and **essere** are used in this way to create compound forms, they are known as *auxiliary* verbs, and are used in combination with a form of the main verb known as the *past participle* to produce a range of tenses [➤ 11b, 11c, 18]:

Mi *sarebbe piaciuto* imparare l'inglese alla scuola elementare.	I *would have liked* to learn English in elementary school.
Non *ho* mai *studiato* una lingua straniera.	I *have* never *studied* a foreign language.

Most verbs use **avere** to form compound tenses. [For those that use **essere** ➤ 11c(ii) – 11c(viii).]

What Verbs Govern

8a *What Does a Verb Govern?*

(i) *Transitive and intransitive verbs*

All sentences must contain a subject and a predicate [▶4]. The predicate will consist of at least one main verb and, in the majority of cases, further information. In the example below, the predicate consists of the main verb only:

I miei amici *partono.*	My friends *are leaving.*

In the next example, the predicate consists of the verb plus further information:

I miei amici *hanno fatto le valigie ieri sera.*	My friends *packed their suitcases last night.*

Since subject pronouns [▶23b(i)] are often not expressed in Italian, it is possible for the subject and predicate, and therefore a complete sentence, to be contained in one word:

Partono.	They are leaving.

When a verb can stand in a sentence and be meaningful without the need to add further information (as with **partono** in the above examples), it is called intransitive. When a verb requires a direct object in order to complete its sense, it is known as transitive. In the second example, **hanno fatto** on its own would not make sense without the direct object **le valigie**.

(ii)

In many cases, verbs can be used either transitively:

Gianni legge una rivista.	Gianni is reading a magazine.
Perché non mangi l'insalata?	Why don't you eat the salad?
Mi passi il pane per favore.	Can you pass me the bread, please.

or intransitively:

Gianni legge.	Gianni is reading.
Perché non mangi?	Why don't you eat?
Il tempo passa.	Time goes by.

These differences are usually indicated in a dictionary by the abbreviations 'v.i.' (verb intransitive) and 'v.t.' (verb transitive).

(iii) The predicate of a sentence may contain a great deal of additional information that, though useful to clarify or extend the meaning, is not necessary for the verb to perform its grammatical function.

I miei amici hanno fatto le valigie ieri sera prima di andare a letto.	My friends packed their suitcases last night before going to bed.

In the above example, the sentence would be meaningless if the verb **hanno fatto** was not followed by a direct object, in this case **le valigie**. If the remainder of the information were omitted, it would not affect the grammatical completeness of the sentence.

Italian verbs may well be linked to their objects or other parts of the predicate in a different way from their English equivalents [➤ 8h]. For example, a transitive verb in English, taking a direct object, may require a preposition before its object in the equivalent Italian form:

Godono *di* buona salute.	They enjoy good health.

Some verbs that take a direct object in Italian need a preposition in English:

Aspetto l'autobus.	I am waiting *for* the bus.

Some take a preposition, but a different one in each language:

Dipende *dal* giorno.	It depends *on* the day.

[For more details on these differences ➤ 8h.]

8b Reflexive Verbs

(i) Turning the action back on the subject

A reflexive verb is a verb whose action is turned back on the subject. The object is therefore the same person or thing as the subject.

***Mi diverto* sempre quando esco con i miei amici.**	*I* always *enjoy myself* when I go out with my friends.
La mattina non *mi guardo* mai nello specchio per paura di svenire.	In the morning *I* never *look at myself* in the mirror for fear of fainting.
***Si pesa* ogni mattina.**	*He weighs himself* every morning.

(ii)

There are many instances where reflexive verbs in Italian express an action whose reflexive nature is not stated (though it is perhaps understood) in English:

Durante la settimana *mi sveglio* alle sei: *Mi alzo* quasi subito, *mi lavo* e *mi vesto*.	During the week, I wake up at six o'clock: I get up almost immediately, I wash and get dressed.
Quando torno dal lavoro, *mi riposo*. Di solito *mi addormento* in una poltrona.	When I get back from work, I rest. Usually I fall asleep in an armchair.
***Mi corico* abbastanza presto.**	I go to bed quite early.

(iii)

There are a number of instances where the reflexive meaning is absent altogether from the English equivalent:

Ho degli amici benestanti che *si lamentano* sempre del costo della vita, ma non *si rendono* conto che c'è molta gente che ha difficoltà a sbarcare il lunario.	I have some well-off friends who are always complaining about the cost of living, but they don't realize that there are people who have difficulty in making ends meet.

Other similar examples include:

accorgersi	notice, realize	**affrettarsi**	hurry
affidarsi	rely on	**andarsene**	go away

avvicinarsi	approach	**pentirsi**	repent, regret
dimenticarsi	forget	**rammaricarsi**	regret
fidarsi	trust	**recarsi**	go
figurarsi	imagine	**ricordarsi**	remember
girarsi	turn around	**rivolgersi (a)**	speak, turn (to)
immaginarsi	imagine	**sbrigarsi**	hurry
infischiarsi	care nothing (about something)	**scusarsi**	apologize
		servirsi di	use
		stupirsi	be amazed
meravigliarsi	be amazed, wonder at	**trattenersi**	stay, remain
		tuffarsi	dive
mettersi a	begin to	**vantarsi**	boast
opporsi	oppose, be opposed to	**vergognarsi**	be ashamed
		voltarsi	turn around

Many reflexive verbs can be used nonreflexively, as the following examples illustrate:

Mi sono svegliato.	I woke up.
Ci siamo girati per guardare.	We turned around to look.

but

Ho svegliato mio fratello.	I woke up my brother.
Abbiamo girato tutti i negozi.	We went around all the shops.

(iv) *Actions done to each other*

Verbs can be used in the reflexive form to express actions people do to each other. Because of this reciprocal action, it is only possible to use the plural forms **noi, voi,** and **loro**.

Purtroppo, non vedo spesso i miei amici italiani, ma per restare in contatto o *ci scriviamo* o *ci telefoniamo*.	Unfortunately, I don't see my Italian friends often, but (in order) to stay in touch either *we write (to each other)* or *we telephone (each other)*.

(v) *Reflexive instead of English passive*

Reflexive forms are frequently used where a passive form would be used in English [➤ 17e].

Non *si vendono* giornali qui.	Newspapers *are* not *sold* here.

(vi) There are a number of reflexive verbs that convey the meaning of 'becoming' or 'getting into a state,' such as:

abituarsi	get accustomed	**raffreddarsi**	get / catch a cold
abbronzarsi	get tanned	**seccarsi**	get annoyed
annoiarsi	get bored	**stancarsi**	get tired
arrabbiarsi	get annoyed	**stabilirsi**	get settled
innervosirsi	get nervous	**ubriacarsi**	get drunk
preoccuparsi	get worried		

8c *The Verbs* Essere *and* Stare

There are a number of occasions in Italian where the verb 'to be' is not conveyed by **essere** but by **stare**. Pay attention to the use of **stare** in the following examples:

- to inquire about someone's well-being

Come *stai*? — *Sto* molto bene grazie, e tu?	How *are* you? — I *am* very well, thank you, and you?

- to form the progressive tenses

Cosa *stai* facendo? — *Sto* scrivendo una lettera.	What *are* you doing? — I *am* writing a letter.

- in the phrase ***stare per*** 'be about to'

Il pullman *sta per* partire.	The (Pullman) bus / coach *is about to* leave.

- in a number of idiomatic expressions such as:

stare attento	be careful
stare fresco	be in for it
stare sulle spine	be on tenterhooks
stare buono	be good
stare zitto	be / keep quiet
stare in pensiero	be worried

stare tranquillo	be quiet, calm
stare fermo	be / keep still
stare in piedi	stand
stare seduto	be seated
stare in ginocchio	kneel
stare fuori	be outside, be away from home

8d Verbs with One Object: The Direct Object of Transitive Verbs

The majority of transitive verbs take one object, which is a direct object, the person or thing primarily affected by the action of the verb.

Marco scrive *una lettera*.	Marco is writing *a letter*.
Vedo *la mia amica* ogni sera.	I see *my friend* every evening.

The direct object of the verb can be determined by asking the question **Che cosa** 'What?' or **Chi** 'Whom?' In the first example, therefore, the answer to **Marco scrive che cosa?** is **una lettera**. In the second example, in response to the question **Vedo chi?**, the answer is **la mia amica**.

8e Verbs with Two Objects: Direct and Indirect Objects

Some transitive verbs describe the transfer of the direct object to another person (or possibly thing). This person is then the indirect object of the verb. The main uses for indirect objects are described in the following paragraphs.

(i) Transferring something or someone

Verbs that describe the transfer of people, objects, or information normally must have an indirect object if they are to make sense, though sometimes it may be assumed. There are a number of these verbs in Italian, and they include the following:

chiedere	ask	**far vedere**	show
consegnare	deliver	**insegnare**	teach
consigliare	advise	**inviare**	send
dare	give	**mandare**	send
dire	say, tell	**mostrare**	show
domandare	ask	**portare**	bring
far sapere	let know	**presentare**	present, introduce

prestare	lend	**scrivere**	write
promettere	promise	**spiegare**	explain
regalare	give (as gift)	**suggerire**	suggest
restituire	give back		

Cos'hai regalato *a tua sorella* per il suo compleanno? — *Le* ho regalato un compact disc.	What did you give *your sister* for her birthday? — I gave *her* a compact disc.

In Italian, as the above example shows, the indirect object — **tua sorella** — is introduced by the preposition **a**. In the reply, the noun is replaced by the pronoun **le** 'to her.'

In English the indirect object is often not preceded by the preposition 'to'; and it can be mistaken for a direct object, i.e., 'gave her.' English speakers need to pay particular attention to this. It is worth considering learning the above verbs in the following way to try and overcome this problem.

dare qualcosa a qualcuno	give something to someone
spiegare qualcosa a qualcuno	explain something to someone

English speakers have to take similar care when expressing passive constructions. In Italian, indirect objects cannot become the subject of a passive verb [➤ 17f] as they can in English.

(ii) Some verbs in Italian take an indirect object where the English equivalent has a direct object.

Assomiglia molto *a sua madre*.	She resembles *her mother* a lot.

[For other examples ➤ 8h(i).]

(iii) *Doing something for someone*

The indirect object form (generally in this case a personal pronoun) is frequently used in speech to express the idea of doing something for someone:

***Mi* puoi fare un piacere quando vai in città? *Mi* compri un chilo di zucchero?**	Can you do (for) *me* a favor / favour when you go to town? Can you buy (for) *me* a kilo of sugar?

Gli **ho trovato un bell'appartamento proprio in centro.**	I have found (for) *him* a lovely apartment / flat right in the center / centre of town.

The person or thing from which something is removed or taken is often expressed as the indirect object in Italian:

Mi **ha strappato la lettera.**	He snatched the letter away *from me.*
Il ladro ***le*** **ha rubato la borsa.**	The thief stole (*from her*) her handbag.

(iv) Actions to the body or clothes

When an action is performed to a part of someone's body or clothing, the person is the indirect object and no possessive [▶ 21c(viii)H, 21h(vi)] is used.

Il dottore ***mi*** **ha fasciato il braccio.**	The doctor bandaged my arm.
Quella macchia di caffè ***le*** **ha rovinato il vestito.**	That coffee stain has ruined her dress.

(v) Order of objects

When both direct and indirect objects are nouns, the direct usually precedes the indirect if they are of similar length. If one object is significantly longer than the other, then this order is reversed:

Ho regalato ***una giacca*** **a** ***mia madre.***	I gave *a jacket* to *my mother.*
Ho regalato a ***mia madre una bellissima giacca verde.***	I gave *my mother a very beautiful green jacket.*

When both objects are pronouns, the indirect always precedes the direct.

Me l'ha **prestato mio cugino.**	My cousin lent *it* to *me.*

[For the position of object pronouns in relation to the verb ➤23b(iv).]

8f *Objects and Reflexive Verbs*

A great number of reflexive verbs are transitive verbs whose action is 'turned back' on the subject. The object, therefore, refers to the same person or thing as the subject [➤8b(i)]:

Giovanni *si lava*.	Giovanni *washes (himself)*.

In Italian, what is being said is **Giovanni lava Giovanni.**

(i) Many Italian reflexive verbs are the equivalent of English intransitive verbs [➤8b(ii), 8b(iii)].

Il treno *si è fermato* a tutte le stazioni.	The train *stopped* at every station.
Quanti giorni *ti fermi* a Venezia?	How many days *are* you *staying* in Venice?

(ii) The reflexive pronoun as indirect object

The reflexive pronoun can also be the indirect object [➤8e], particularly when the subject is performing an action to a part of his or her own body or article of clothing [➤8e(iv)]:

Mentre riparavo la macchina *mi sono tagliato* il dito.	While I was repairing the car, I cut my finger.

In the above example the direct object is **il dito** and **mi** becomes the indirect object.

(iii) The reflexive pronoun is also used in a reciprocal sense [➤8b(iv)], either as a direct or indirect object:

***Si salutano* ogni volta che *si vedono*.**	They greet *each other* every time they see *each other*.
***Vi scrivete* spesso? — No, ma *ci telefoniamo* una volta al mese.**	Do you write to *each other* often? — No, but we telephone *(to) each other* once a month.

8g *Impersonal and 'Back-to-Front' Verbs*

An impersonal verb in English has the subject 'it,' which has no real meaning by itself but serves to introduce weather phrases and other verbs in sentences such as 'it is snowing,' 'it is difficult to say.' In Italian the subject pronoun 'it' is contained in the verb and not expressed as a separate word. Impersonal verbs in Italian fall into the following categories:

(i) *Verbs referring to the weather and natural phenomena*

Apart from the verbs such as **nevicare** 'snow,' **tuonare** 'thunder,' **piovere** 'rain,' there are a number of expressions that use **fare, essere,** and **c'è**.

piovere	rain	**fare bello**	be nice / fine
piovigginare	drizzle	**fare brutto**	be bad / awful
nevicare	snow	**fare notte**	get dark
gelare	freeze	**fare giorno**	get light
sgelare	thaw	**essere nuvoloso**	be cloudy
grandinare	hail	**essere umido**	be humid
lampeggiare	flash lightning	**essere afoso**	be heavy / sultry / muggy
tuonare	thunder	**essere mite**	be mild
fare caldo	be hot	**c'è il sole**	it's sunny
fare freddo	be cold	**c'è la nebbia**	it's foggy
fare fresco	be cool	**c'è la foschia**	it's misty

Note also

tirare vento be windy

Durante questo periodo il tempo è molto variabile, ma purtroppo fa sempre brutto: c'è la nebbia, fa molto freddo, nevica abbastanza, verso le quattro e mezzo fa già notte ...	During this period of the year the weather is very changeable, but unfortunately it's always awful: it's foggy, it's very cold, it snows a fair amount, it gets dark around four-thirty. . . .
D'estate, però, fa molto caldo, delle volte 32 - 34 gradi. Non piove quasi mai. Si sta meglio la sera quando comincia a fare più fresco.	In summer, however, it's very hot, 32–34 degrees (centigrade). It almost never rains. You feel better in the evening when it begins to get cooler.

(ii) ***C'è, ci sono****: there is, there are*

These forms are used in the full range of tenses in the third person singular and plural:

Se questa nebbia non si dissipa, ci saranno molti incidenti stradali. Stamattina c'è stato un orribile incidente sul tratto di strada che passa davanti a casa nostra.	If this fog doesn't lift, there will be a lot of road accidents. This morning there was a terrible accident on the stretch of road that passes our house.

(iii) The verb **essere** (third person singular) followed by an adjective, adverb, or past participle.

Expressions such as **è facile** 'it's easy,' **è possibile** 'it's possible,' **è necessario** 'it's necessary,' **è bene** 'it's a good thing,' **è male** 'it's a bad thing,' **è meglio** 'it's better,' **è vietato** 'it's forbidden,' **è permesso** 'it's allowed' are usually termed impersonal, because they are introduced by 'it.' However, they are not strictly so in Italian, as the following infinitive or clause is really the subject of the verb. In the examples below, the subject 'it' can be replaced by the following infinitive or clause in Italian (shown in italics).

È impossibile guidare con questa nebbia fitta.	It's impossible to drive in this thick fog.
***Guidare* con questa nebbia fitta è impossibile.**	To drive in this thick fog is impossible.
È bene che non dobbiamo uscire.	It's a good thing that we don't have to go out.
***Che non dobbiamo uscire* è bene.**	That we don't have to go out is a good thing.

(iv) *Verbs expressing need, necessity, appearance*

There are a number of verbs that can be used impersonally in Italian that may be used personally in English. These verbs are either followed by a dependent clause whose verb is in the subjunctive [▶ 16c(iii)] or by an infinitive [▶ 8i]. The following verbs are used in this way:

accadere	happen	**bisognare**	be necessary
avvenire	happen	**convenire**	be fitting / be a good idea
bastare	be enough / sufficient	**costare**	cost

importare	matter, mind	**sembrare**	seem
interessare	be interested in	**servire**	be of use
occorrere	be necessary	**spettare**	be up to, be the duty of
parere	seem, look like	**succedere**	happen
riuscire	be (+ *adjective*)	**toccare**	be up to

Pare che voglia piovere.	It looks like rain.
Non importa, non andiamo lontano, basta portare l'ombrello.	It doesn't matter, we aren't going far, we need only (it's enough to) take the umbrella.
Non serve a niente portare l'ombrello quando tira un vento così forte.	It's no use taking the umbrella when it's so windy.
Riesce difficile tenerlo aperto.	It's difficult to keep it open.
Non bisogna che tu venga con me.	You don't need to come with me. (It's not necessary for you to come with me.)

These same verbs (with the exception of **bisogna**) are used always either in the third person singular or plural and often have an indirect object indicating the person to whom it matters, appears, and so forth.

Non *mi* interessa uscire quando fa così freddo.	I am not interested in going out (it doesn't interest *me* to go out) when it is so cold.
***Ci* pare che le strade siano molto scivolose.**	It seems *to us* that the roads are very slippery.
Gino, non *ti* conviene prendere la macchina. Per una volta *ti* tocca andare a piedi.	Gino, it's not a good idea *(for you)* to take the car. For once *you* must walk.
Prima di andare in macchina su queste strade scivolose, *ci* occorrono delle gomme nuove.	Before going on these slippery roads with the car, *we* need some new tires/tyres.

(v) ***Piacere*** *'like' and similar 'back-to-front' verbs*

There is a group of verbs in Italian that works the opposite way around to their English counterparts: the subject in English (usually a person) is the object in Italian. The verb is usually in the third person. If the object (a person) is a noun, it usually comes first preceded by the preposition ***a***.

A mio fratello **piacciono i piatti vegetariani. Non gli piace affatto la carne.**	My brother likes vegetarian dishes. He doesn't like meat at all.

The main points about this construction are therefore:

- The Italian subject (**i piatti vegetariani**) usually follows the verb, which is plural if the subject is plural: i.e., if you like something plural, the verb is plural. You are saying 'Vegetarian dishes please my brother': 'they please him.'
- A pronoun object is sometimes reinforced by **a** + the disjunctive pronoun [▶23h(ii)], especially for emphasis.

A me **non mi piacciono i piatti vegetariani.**	*I* don't like vegetarian dishes.

- A number of verbs that can work in this way have already been mentioned in the previous section [▶8(iv)].
Below are some others:

andare di	feel like	**mancare**	lack
capitare di	happen	**rimanere**	remain
dispiacere	be sorry	**rincrescere**	be sorry
dolere	hurt	**sfuggire**	escape (one's attention)
far male	hurt		

Anche se mi fa male la schiena, non mi va di andare dal medico.	Even if my back hurts, I don't feel like going to the doctor's.
Per fortuna, mi sono rimasti degli antidolorifici.	Fortunately, I have some painkillers left.
Se ti capita di andare in farmacia, ti dispiace comprarmi delle aspirine?	If you happen to go to the drugstore / chemist's, would you mind buying me some aspirins?

8h Verb + Preposition + Noun

Quite a number of verbs are linked to their object by a preposition — the most common being **a** or **di**. In most cases these verb-preposition combinations are fixed: it would not be possible to leave the preposition out or use a different one without at least changing the meaning or, more, making no sense at all.

The following Italian verbs are either linked to their object by a preposition, which may not necessarily correspond to the English preposition, or are translated in English by a verb that takes a direct object without a preposition.

Mia figlia *bada ai* bambini.	My daughter is taking care of the children.
Non ho potuto *resistere alla* tentazione.	I couldn't resist the temptation.
***Assomiglia* molto *a* sua sorella.**	She looks a lot like her sister.
Dice che *ha bisogno di* soldi ma non *mi fido di* lui.	He says he needs money, but I don't trust him.

*(i) Verbs linked with **a***

accennare a	refer to, mention
affacciarsi a	appear (at), look out (of)
affezionarsi a	become fond of, take a liking to
affidarsi a	trust in, rely on
aspirare a	aspire to
assistere a	witness, be present at, attend
assomigliare a	resemble
avvicinarsi a	approach, get near
badare a	take care of
cedere a	give in to
concedere a	grant, allow
contribuire a	contribute to
credere a / in	believe in
dedicarsi a	devote oneself to
disubbidire a	disobey
giocare a	play (a game)
giungere a	reach, arrive at
interessarsi a / di	be interested in
mirare a	aim at
opporsi a	oppose, be opposed
partecipare a	take part in
pensare a	think about
prepararsi a	prepare, get ready for

provvedere a	provide for, see to
puntare a	aim at
resistere a	resist
ricorrere a	resort to
riferirsi a	refer to
rimediare a	put right, remedy
rinunciare a	give up
rispondere a	answer
rivolgersi a	turn to, speak to
sopravvivere a	survive
sottoporsi a	undergo
sovrintendere a	supervise
sparare a	shoot at
spettare a	be up to, be the responsibility of
telefonare a	telephone
tenerci a	care a lot about, attach importance to
toccare	be up to, be the responsibility of
ubbidire a	obey
voler bene a	be fond of, love

Mio figlio si dedica ai suoi studi. Al momento, pensa solo ai suoi esami. Non gioca più a tennis, che gli piace molto; non telefona ai suoi amici, che faceva quasi ogni sera; non ha risposto all'ultima lettera del suo corrispondente. Non fa altro che studiare.	My son devotes himself to his studies. At the moment, he thinks only about his exams. He doesn't play tennis anymore, which he likes a lot; he doesn't call his friends, which he did almost every evening; he hasn't answered his pen pal's last letter. He does nothing but study.

*(ii) Verbs linked with **di***

accontentarsi di	make do with, be satisfied with
accorgersi di	notice, realize
approfittare di	take advantage of
diffidare di	mistrust
dimenticarsi di	forget
discutere di	talk about, discuss
fidarsi di	trust
godere di	enjoy
informarsi di / su	find out about
innamorarsi di	fall in love with

impadronirsi di	take hold of, master (a language)
intendersi di	know about, be an expert on
lagnarsi di	complain about
lamentarsi di	complain about
mancare di	lack
meravigliarsi di	be amazed at
occuparsi di	look after, take care of
pensare di	think of (opinion)
preoccuparsi di (per)	worry, care about
rendersi conto di	notice, realize
ricordarsi di	remember
ridere di	laugh at
riempire di	fill with
sapere di	taste, smack of
servirsi di	use, make use of
stancarsi di	get tired of
stupirsi di	be amazed at
trattarsi di	be a question of
vantarsi di	boast of / about
vergognarsi di	be ashamed of
vivere di	live on

Mio figlio si rende conto dell'importanza dei suoi studi. Io e mia moglie ci meravigliamo del suo impegno e della sua motivazione. Approfitta di ogni occasione per studiare. Non si lamenta mai della quantità del lavoro che deve fare.

My son realizes the importance of his studies. My wife and I are amazed at his commitment and motivation. He takes advantage of every opportunity to study. He never complains about the amount of work he has to do.

(iii) Verbs linked with ***con***

arrabbiarsi con	be annoyed with
avercela con	have it in for
competere con	compete with
congratularsi con	congratulate
incontrarsi con	meet
prendersela con	be upset with
sposarsi con	get married to
trattare con	deal with

Mi congratulo con te.	I congratulate you.
Si è sposato con una ragazza francese.	He got married to a French girl.

(iv) Verbs linked with ***per***

entusiasmarsi per	be enthusiastic about
lottare per	struggle, fight for
partire per	leave for
passare per	pass through
prendere per	mistake for
scambiare per	mistake for

L'ho preso per tuo cognato.	I mistook him for your brother-in-law.
Sono partiti per l'Italia due giorni fa.	They left for Italy two days ago.

(v) Verbs linked with ***da***

allontanarsi da	go away
avere da	have to
dipendere da	depend on
fare da	act as
giudicare da	judge by / on
guardarsi da	beware of, avoid
provenire da	come from
scendere da	get out of (car, train, etc.)
servire da	serve for, be used as

Non è sempre possibile giudicare dalle apparenze.	It's not always possible to judge by appearances.
Durante il congresso ho fatto da interprete.	During the conference, I acted as interpreter.

(vi) Verbs linked with ***in, su, verso,*** *and* ***contro***

entrare in	enter
tradurre in	translate into
trasformare in	change, transform into

abbattersi su	hit
decidere su	decide on
incidere su	affect
indagare su	investigate
influire su	influence, affect
insistere su	insist on
riflettere su	reflect on, think about
salire su / in	board (bus, train, car)
avviarsi verso	head for
dirigersi verso	head for, make one's way towards
lottare contro	fight against

Siamo entrati in casa.	We went into the house.
La decisione presa dal governo inciderà sul costo della vita.	The decision taken by the government will affect the cost of living.
L'uragano sta per abbattersi sulla costa.	The hurricane is about to hit the coast.

(vii) Conversely, the following verbs, which are linked to their object by a preposition in English, take a direct object in Italian.

approvare	approve of
ascoltare	listen to
aspettare	wait for
commentare	comment upon, talk about
cercare	look for
chiedere	ask for
domandare	ask for
guardare	look at
operare	operate on
pagare	pay for
sfiorare	touch on (a subject)
sfogliare	glance / skim through (book, newspaper)
sognare	dream about

A casa nostra preferiamo ascoltare i dischi o la radio piuttosto che guardare sempre la televisione.	In our house we prefer listening to records or the radio rather than always watching television.

8i Verb + Bare Infinitive

The following are the main verbs that govern a bare infinitive, i.e., without any connecting preposition.

bastare	be enough, sufficient	**lasciare**	leave, allow
bisognare	be necessary	**occorrere**	be necessary
convenire	be fitting / worthwhile	**osare**	dare
desiderare	want, wish	**piacere**	please, like
detestare	hate	**potere**	be able
dispiacere	be sorry	**preferire**	prefer
dovere	have to, must	**rincrescere**	be sorry
importare	matter, be important	**sapere**	know how to
intendere	intend	**sentire**	hear
interessare	interest	**servire**	serve, be of use
		vedere	see
		volere	want, wish

Quest'anno intendo trascorrere le vacanze estive in Italia. Desidero andarci per perfezionare il mio italiano. Naturalmente mi interesserebbe visitare i monumenti antichi.	This year I intend to spend my summer vacation / holidays in Italy. I want to go there to perfect my Italian. Naturally I am (would be) interested in visiting the ancient monuments.

The infinitive construction after verbs expressing wish, preference, regret, and so forth, is possible only when the verb and the infinitive have the same subject. The verb + infinitive construction cannot be used in Italian to convey English sentences of the type 'want / prefer someone to.' To express this idea in Italian, a separate clause must be used with the subjunctive [➤16a, 16c].

Quest'estate voglio *andare* in Italia.	This summer I want *to go* to Italy. (infinitive because the subject is the same)
Non voglio *che* tu *vada* da solo.	I don't want *you to go* on your own. (separate clause introduced by **che** and the verb in the subjunctive because the subject is different)

8j Verb + Preposition + Infinitive

A large number of verbs can be linked to a following infinitive by a preposition. As with verbs linked to nouns [▶ 8h], this is a fixed pairing that cannot be changed.

The most common linking prepositions are **a** and **di**, but some others are also used.

(i) *Verbs + **a** + infinitive*

Verbs linked to an infinitive with **a** include many:

(A) Implying beginning

apprestarsi a	get ready to
cominciare a	begin to
iniziare a	begin to
mettersi a	start, set about + —ing
prendere a	begin to
prepararsi a	get ready to
scoppiare a (ridere)	burst out (laughing)

(B) Implying motion

affrettarsi a	hasten, hurry to
andare a	go to, go and, be going to
correre a	run to
tornare a	return to
venire a	come to, come and, be coming to

(C) Encouraging, inviting, obliging

costringere a	force, compel to
forzare a	force to
incitare a	urge to
incoraggiare a	encourage to
invitare a	invite to
obbligare a	oblige to
persuadere a	persuade to
spingere a	urge, incite to
stimolare a	urge, encourage to

The following verbs also use the linking preposition **a**:

abituarsi a	get used to	**autorizzare a**	authorize to
aiutare a	help to	**azzardarsi a**	dare to
apprendere a	learn to	**continuare a**	continue to

convincere a	convince to	**provare a**	try to
decidersi a	make up one's mind to	**rassegnarsi a**	resign oneself to
divertirsi a	enjoy (doing)	**riuscire a**	succeed in, manage to
esitare a	hesitate to		
imparare a	learn to	**sfidare a**	challenge to, defy to
impegnarsi a	undertake to		
insegnare a	teach to	**tardare a**	delay in + —ing
limitarsi a	limit oneself to	**tendere a**	tend to
portare a	lead to	**tenere a**	be eager to

Ieri sera ho provato ad imparare questi verbi. Ho cominciato a studiare intorno alle sette. Dopo un'ora, ero riuscito ad impararne una trentina. A quel punto, volevo smettere ma un amico mi ha incoraggiato ad andare avanti.	Last night I tried to learn these verbs. I started studying around seven o'clock. After an hour, I had managed to learn about thirty. At that point, I wanted to stop, but a friend encouraged me to go on.

(ii) *Verbs +* ***di*** *+ infinitive*

Verbs linked to an infinitive with **di** include:

(A) Those that indicate the ending or stopping of an action or separation from it:

cessare di	stop, cease
finire di	finish
smettere di	stop
stancarsi di	tire of
stufarsi di	get fed up of / with

(B) Those where **di** translates literally as 'of':

accusare di	accuse of
avere vergogna di	be ashamed of
pentirsi di	repent of
rammaricarsi di	repent of, feel sorry for
trattarsi di	be a question of
vantarsi di	boast of
vergognarsi di	be ashamed of

The following verbs also use the linking preposition **di:**

accettare di	accept	**ammettere di**	admit
accorgersi di	notice, realize	**aspettarsi di**	expect

avere bisogno di	need
avere intenzione di	intend
avere paura di	be afraid
avere voglia di	feel like
badare di	take care to
cercare di	try
chiedere di*	ask
consigliare di*	advise
credere di	believe
decidere di	decide
dichiarare di	declare
dimenticare / -si di	forget
dire di*	say, tell
domandare di*	ask
fare finta di	pretend
fingere di	pretend
giurare di	swear to
immaginare di	imagine
impedire di	prevent
mancare di	fail to
meravigliarsi di	be surprised at
meritare di	deserve
minacciare di	threaten
non vedere l'ora di	look forward to
offrire di	offer
ordinare di*	order
parere di	seem
parlare di	talk (of doing)
pensare di	plan, think of
permettere di*	allow
pregare di	beg, ask
pretendere di	profess, claim
proibire di*	prohibit
promettere di*	promise
proporre di*	propose
rendersi conto di	realize
ricordare / -si di	remember
rifiutare / -si di	refuse
rischiare di	risk, be in danger of
risolvere di	resolve, decide
ritenere di	consider
sapere di	know
scegliere di	choose
sembrare di	seem
sentirsi di	feel
sforzarsi di	try hard to
sognare di	dream
sperare di	hope
suggerire di	suggest
temere di	fear
tentare di	try, attempt
vietare di	forbid, prohibit

Note: The above list includes some *verbal phrases*, such as **avere bisogno di**, which is in fact a verb + noun + preposition. However, they function in the same way as the other verbs listed.

Abbiamo deciso di vendere la macchina perché consuma troppa benzina. Un amico ha offerto di comprarla, e ci ha chiesto di tenerla ancora per qualche settimana mentre cerca di vendere la sua. Abbiamo promesso di aspettare un po'. Ad ogni modo, non pensiamo di comprare un'altra macchina.

We have decided to sell the car because it uses up too much gasoline / petrol. A friend has offered to buy it, and he has asked us to keep it for a few weeks longer, while he tries to sell his. We have promised to wait a while. In any case, we are not thinking of buying another car.

• The verbs in the list marked with an asterisk have a particular structure, i.e., verb + indirect object + **di** + infinitive.

Abbiamo promesso ai nostri amici *di* aspettare un po'.	We have promised (to) our friends to wait a while.

It might be helpful to learn this particular structure in the following way:

promettere a qualcuno di fare qualcosa	promise (to) someone to do something

The **a qualcuno** will help to remind you to use the indirect object and the **di fare** serves as a reminder that you always have to put the preposition **di** before the following infinitive.

[For indirect object pronouns ➤23b(iii).]

(iii) *Verbs + **per** + infinitive*

finire per	end by, finish by	**servire per**	be used for
lottare per	fight for	**stare per**	be about to

Abbiamo finito *per* accettare la sua offerta.	We ended by accepting his offer.

8k *Verb + the Present Participle or 'Gerund' [➤ 10b, 10d]*

This is a very common construction in English, but its use in Italian is limited to the following circumstances.

(i) ***Stare** + gerund*

Stare + gerund is used to form the progressive or continuous tenses [➤10e(ii)], usually the present or imperfect, and occasionally the future. These correspond closely with the English progressive tenses, but care must be taken that the action being referred to is / was actually in progress at the time.

Cosa stai facendo?	What are you doing? (at this very moment)
Sto scrivendo una lettera alla mia corrispondente italiana.	I am writing a letter to my Italian pen pal / penfriend.

Stavo scrivendo una lettera quando ho sentito bussare alla porta.	I was writing a letter when I heard a knock at the door.

In the following example, the present tense is used because the action is not actually in progress at the point of reference.

Non esco stasera perché devo scrivere alcune lettere.	I'm not going out this evening because I have to write some letters.

(ii) ***Andare*** *+ gerund*

Andare is sometimes used to form the progressive tenses when a cumulative progression is indicated.

Andava **parlando di questa corrispondente per ore e ore.**	She went on talking about this pen pal for hours and hours.

[For the use of the gerund standing on its own (= by / while doing) ➤10e(i). For other translations of the English '-ing' ending ➤10e(iii).]

8l ***Verb + the Past Participle***

The verbs that most frequently combine with past participles in Italian are **avere** and **essere** when used as auxiliaries to form compound tenses [➤11c].

The verb **essere** is also used with past participles to form passive constructions, such as:

La lettera *è scritta*.	The letter *is written*.

[For verbs other than **essere** to express the passive ➤17d. To express in Italian the idea conveyed by the English expression 'to have / get something done' ➤9e.]

Attitudes to Action: Modal Verbs

A modal verb seldom carries a full meaning by itself. Instead, as the examples in this chapter will show, a modal verb says something about the relationship between the subject and the full verb, which is in the infinitive [➤10a]. It creates a *mood* for the verb that follows.

Note: Object pronouns may precede the modal verb or be attached to the end of the infinitive [➤23b(iv)].

***Ci* devo andare. / Devo andar*ci*.**	I have to go *there*.
***Te lo* possiamo comprare. / Possiamo comprar*telo*.**	We can buy *it for you*.

The most frequently used modal verbs in Italian are:

dovere	have to, must
potere	be able to, can
sapere	know how to
volere	wish, want

The precise use and variations of meaning of the modal verbs are explained in the sections that follow.

9a Dovere

The verb **dovere** expresses obligation, the idea of having to do something, adding nuance and variation to this central meaning by the use of different tenses. It corresponds to a range of English equivalents, such as 'have to . . . ,' 'must . . . ,' 'should . . . ,' 'ought to . . .,' 'should have. . . .' It is also used (as in English) to express strong supposition such as 'He must be at least forty.'

(i) In the present tense

As the most *immediate* tense, the message conveyed by the present tense of **dovere** is usually fairly strong.

Prima di uscire *devi* mettere in ordine la tua camera.	Before going out *you must* tidy up your room.
***Devo* andare a comprare qualcosa in città. Quando torno tutto *deve* essere al suo posto, altrimenti guai!**	*I have to* go and buy something in town. When I get back, everything *must* be in its place; otherwise look out!

It also expresses strong supposition.

***Devi* arrabbiarti quando i figli lasciano la roba dappertutto.**	*You must* get annoyed when the children leave things everywhere.
***Dev'essere* molto difficile tenere la casa sempre in ordine.**	*It must* be very difficult to always keep the house tidy.

(ii) *In the present perfect tense*

Mia moglie *ha dovuto* comprare qualcosa per la cena.	My wife *had to* (*has had to*) buy something for dinner. (obligation)

Note the following construction:

Mia moglie *dev'essere andata* in città.	My wife *must have gone* to town. (supposition)

(iii) *In the imperfect tense*

Mia moglie *doveva* andare in città per fare la spesa.	My wife *had to* (=*was going to have to*) go to town to do the shopping. (obligation)
Mia moglie *doveva* andare in città per fare la spesa.	My wife *was supposed to* go to town to do the shopping. (supposition)

(iv) *In the present conditional*

The present conditional of **dovere** is widely used, and its equivalent meaning in English is 'ought' or 'should.'

La mia mamma ha ragione. *Dovrei* mettere la mia camera in ordine prima di uscire.	My mother is right. *I should* (ought to) tidy up my room before going out. (obligation)

There are occasions where the idea of compulsion or obligation is expressed by the appropriate tense of **essere** and the past participle of **costringere** or **obbligare**.

Se non mettessi la mia camera in ordine, *sarei costretto* a stare a casa.	If I didn't tidy up my room, *I would have to* stay at home.
***Sono obbligato* a mettere in ordine la mia camera prima di uscire.**	*I have to* (*am obliged to*) tidy up my room before going out.

(v) *In the conditional perfect*

The conditional perfect conveys the equivalent of the English 'ought to have . . . ,' 'should have. . . .'

***Avrei dovuto* mettere la mia camera in ordine ieri sera.**	*I should have (ought to have)* tidied up my room last night. (obligation)

It is occasionally used to convey 'would have had to. . . .'

Se non avessi messo in ordine la mia camera prima di uscire, l'*avrei dovuto* fare al mio ritorno.	If I hadn't tidied up my room before going out, *I would have had to* do it on my return.

(vi) *In the pluperfect tense*

***Aveva dovuto* mettere in ordine la sua camera prima di uscire.**	*He had had to* tidy up his room before going out.

Dovere also exists as an ordinary nonmodal verb, with the meaning 'to owe.'

Quanto ti *devo?*	How much do *I owe* you?

9b *Potere*

(i) *Be able to, can*

Potere conveys the idea of 'being able to . . . ,' 'being physically capable of . . . ,' 'being allowed to . . . ,' 'having permission to . . . ,' and is expressed in English in a variety of ways, such as 'can,' 'could,' 'may,' and 'might.'

***Posso* entrare?**	*May I* (*Can I*) come in? (permission)
Non *possiamo* venire domani sera.	*We can*not come tomorrow evening. (unable to)
Non *posso* chiudere questa finestra.	*I ca*n't close this window. (incapable)

In the third example above, it is possible to use **riuscire a** in place of **potere**.

Non *riesco* a chiudere questa finestra.	*I ca*n't close this window.

Riuscire expresses 'succeed in . . . ,' 'manage to . . . ,' or 'be able to. . . .'

Quando parli in fretta non *riesco a* capire tutto.	When you speak quickly, *I ca*n't understand (*don't manage to understand/don't succeed in understanding*) everything.

Note that it is common practice to omit **potere** with verbs of perception, such as **sentire** 'hear,' 'feel,' and **vedere** 'see.' This possibility also applies to **trovare** 'find.'

Parla più forte per favore perché non ti *sento.*	Speak more loudly please because *I ca*n't *hear* you.
Ho tolto i miei occhiali per fare la doccia, e adesso non li *trovo.*	I took off my glasses to take a shower, and now *I ca*n't *find* them.
Senza gli occhiali, non *vedo* niente.	Without my glasses, *I can*'t *see* anything.

A more formal way of expressing permission is to use **permettere** with the infinitive [▶ 8j(ii)C].

Mi *permette* di dire una parola?	*May I (Will you allow me to)* say a word?

The impersonal phrase **si può** [▶ 17e(ii)] is often used when seeking permission, particularly when the action (the infinitive) is not expressed.

***Si può* (fumare)?**	*May I/May we* (smoke)?

Fumare need not be expressed because in a real life situation the gesture would make it obvious what one is seeking permission to do.

(ii) *Possibility*

Potere also expresses possibility, especially when used in the conditional mood:

***Potrei* telefonare più tardi.**	*I could* (= could possibly) telephone later.
***Avresti potuto* telefonare ieri sera.**	*You could have* called last night.

Great care has to be taken when conveying the English 'could,' which may be a past tense or a conditional. It is important to consider the underlying message and the function of 'could,' i.e., does it mean *possibility* or *ability?* The two examples below, illustrate the point.

***Potrei* uscire domani sera, ma stasera non posso perché sono troppo impegnato.**	*I could* go out tomorrow evening, but this evening I can't because I am too busy.
Non *potevo* uscire perché ero troppo impegnato.	*I could*n't go out because I was too busy.

In the first example the meaning is 'I *could possibly* go out tomorrow evening . . . ' (= conditional) whereas the second example means 'I *was not able* to go out . . . ' (= past tense, in this case the imperfect). It is often a good guide to rephrase the English using 'be able.' If this is done for the first example the meaning becomes nonsense. In the second example, however, 'could' and 'was able' are interchangeable.

Potere can also be used to express indignation.

Avrebbero potuto **dirci che non venivano.**	*They could have* told us that they weren't coming.

(iii) ***Può darsi***

Possibility can also be expressed by using the impersonal reflexive form **può darsi** [> 16c(iii)].

Può darsi **che siano malati.**	*Maybe* (*It's possible that*) they're sick/ill.

9c ***Sapere***

(i) ***Sapere*** *vs* ***potere***

Sapere has only limited use as a modal verb, with the meaning 'know how to.' However, since this idea is frequently expressed in English by the word 'can,' English speakers have to be careful not to confuse the use of **sapere** and **potere**.

Mi ***puoi*** **dare una mano a tradurre questa lettera visto che** ***sai*** **parlare italiano?—Va bene, ma non** ***posso*** **farlo adesso.**	*Can you* give me a hand to translate this letter since you *can* (*know how to*) speak Italian? —Very well, but I *can't* do it now.

Sapere is also used in the sense of 'be in a position to . . . ' or 'be capable of. . . .'

Quando il professore di storia mi ha interrogato sulla lezione precedente, ***ho saputo*** **rispondere a quasi tutte le sue domande.**	When the history teacher questioned me about the preceding lesson, *I could* answer almost all his questions.
Sapresti **riconoscere quella ragazza se la vedessi un'altra volta?**	*Would you* (*Would you be able to*) recognize that girl if you saw her again?

(ii) ***Sapere*** *to know*

Sapere is used much more frequently as a nonmodal verb, meaning 'know a fact.'

***Sai* a che ora chiudono le banche?**	Do *you know* at what time the banks close?

Conoscere must be used when the meaning is 'be acquainted with a person or place.'

Non *conosco* molto bene questa regione.	*I* don't *know* this region very well.
Nella nostra strada *conosciamo* due famiglie.	On / In our street *we know* two families.

9d Volere

(i) Expressing wish

As with other modal verbs [▶ 9a–9c], **volere** has a variety of equivalents in English. It is the basic verb in Italian for expressing wish:

Non *voglio* andare al cinema. — Cosa *vuoi* fare allora?	*I do*n't *want* to go to the movies / cinema. — What do *you want* to do then?

(ii) Expressing willingness and polite requests

Volere is also widely used to express willingness and polite requests:

Non so proprio cosa fare perché mio figlio non *vuole* studiare.	I really don't know what to do because my son *will* not study.
***Vuoi* qualcosa da bere?**	*Would you like* something to drink?
***Volete* stare zitti per favore?**	*Will you* be quiet, please?

(iii) Expressing intention

Volere can convey the idea of 'be going to . . . ,' 'want to . . . ,' 'intend to. . . .'

—Cosa *vuoi* fare quando finisci i tuoi studi universitari?—A dire il vero, non ho la più pallida idea. Quando ero a scuola, *volevo* fare il medico; ma poi ho cambiato idea.	—What *do you want to* do when you finish your university studies? —To tell you the truth, I haven't got the faintest idea. When I was at school, *I wanted* to become a doctor; but then I changed my mind.

(iv) *Should / would like*

To say you *would like* to do something is most frequently expressed by the present conditional form of **volere.**

Quando finisco i miei studi, *vorrei* diventare insegnante.	When I finish my studies, *I would like to* become a teacher.

It is also possible to use the present conditional [▶ 14d] of **piacere.**

Quando finisco i miei studi, *mi piacerebbe* diventare insegnante.	When I finish my studies, *I would like to* become a teacher.

Forms of politeness can also be conveyed in Italian by **gradire.**

***Gradirei* un bicchiere di acqua minerale.**	*I would like* a glass of mineral water.
***Gradiresti* una tazza di caffè?**	*Would you like* a cup of coffee?

(v) *Should have / would have liked*

To say you would like to have done something, use the conditional perfect [▶ 14e] of either **volere** or **piacere.**

A scuola *avrei voluto (mi sarebbe piaciuto)* imparare il tedesco.	At school *I would have liked to* learn German.

When you want or would like someone else to do something, you must use **volere** or **piacere** + **che** + the subjunctive [▶ 16c(i)].

I miei genitori *volevano che (io) imparassi* il francese.	My parents *wanted me to learn* French.

Note the idiomatic use of **volere** in the following expressions:

***Voglio bene* ai miei genitori.**	*I love* my parents.
Tutti gli *vogliono bene.*	*They are* all *fond of* him.
Sembra che *voglia* piovere.	It looks as if *it might* rain.
Quanto *ci vuole* per arrivare all'aeroporto? — Con la macchina *ci vogliono* due ore.	How long *does it take* to get to the airport? — By car *it takes* two hours.
Cosa *vuol dire* questa parola?	What *does* this word *mean*?
Al giorno d'oggi, conoscere le lingue *vuol dire* molto.	Nowadays, a knowledge of languages *means (counts for)* a lot.
Ho sempre dei brutti voti in matematica. — Ma cosa *vuoi* se non studi mai?	I always get bad marks in math / maths. — But what *do you expect* if you never study?

[For the use of the auxiliary **essere** or **avere** with modal verbs ➤11c(vii).]

9e Fare, Lasciare + *Infinitive*

The verbs covered in this section are not modal verbs [➤9a–d], but can be used with infinitives in similar ways, to create new or modified meanings.

(i) *Fare*

(A) To say you are having or getting something done, you use **fare** followed *immediately* by the infinitive.

***Ho fatto aggiustare* la lavastoviglie.**	*I have had* the dishwasher *repaired.*
Quando l'*hai fatta* aggiustare?	When *did you have* it *repaired*?

With **fare** + infinitive constructions, any object pronoun (**l'** in the above example) is placed before **fare**, not attached to the following infinitve as in the majority of verb + infinitive forms.

(B) Fare + infinitive also means 'to get someone to do something.'

***Ho fatto tradurre* la lettera dalla mia amica.**	*I got* my friend *to translate* the letter.

Notice that the word order in Italian is different from that of the English. The Italian word order does not allow you to put either **la lettera** or **dalla mia amica** between **fatto** and **tradurre**.

When both **fare** and the following infinitive have an object, the one relating to **fare** becomes the indirect object

Ho fatto assaggiare questo formaggio *al mio amico.*	I had *my friend* taste this cheese.
Fa*gli* assaggiare questo formaggio.	Have *him* try this cheese.

Both these sentences imply that you are inviting or asking someone to do something, whereas in the previous example you are getting the job done *by* someone.

(C) Fare + reflexive verb in infinitive: if the infinitive following **fare** is reflexive, the reflexive pronoun is omitted.

Quello che mi fa *arrabbiare* è che ho appena comprato questa lavastoviglie.	What makes me *angry* is that I have just bought this dishwasher.

(D) Note also:

far aspettare	keep (someone) waiting
far capire	make (someone) understand
far entrare	show (someone) in
far passare	let (someone) through / by
far vedere	show (to someone)
fare venire	send for (someone)

Scusami se ti *ho fatto aspettare.*	Sorry if *I have kept* you *waiting.*
Mi *hanno fatto capire* che non potevano venire.	They *gave* me *to understand* that they were not able to come.
La *faccio entrare?*	*Shall I show* her *in*?

Mi *ha fatto vedere* la lettera che aveva ricevuto.	*He showed* me the letter he had received.

(ii) Lasciare

With a following infinitive, **lasciare** means 'let someone do something,' or 'let something happen.'

Se vuole andare all'estero con i suoi amici, *lascia*lo *andare.*	If he wants to go abroad with his friends, *let* him *go*.

The special rules relating to pronouns and to reflexive verbs when **fare** is used with an infinitive [➤9e(i) above] also apply to **lasciare** when used in this way.

Note also the following idiomatic uses:

***Lasciamo perdere/andare*!**	*Let's forget about it!*
***Lascia stare* quella radio.**	*Leave* that radio *alone (Hands off* that radio!).

10 Verb Forms Not Related to Time: Nonfinite Forms

10a The Infinitive

The infinitive is the part of the verb most commonly listed in dictionaries. It names a certain activity or state without saying when it happens (a *nonfinite* verb form). It often completes the meaning of the main verb.

(i) *Infinitive endings*

The majority of infinitives in Italian end in **-are** (**trovare**), **-ere** (**vedere**), or **-ire** (**aprire**). There is a small number of verbs that have irregular infinitives, such as **porre** 'put,' **tradurre** 'translate,' and **trarre** 'draw,' 'pull.'

(ii) *Uses of the infinitive*

The main uses of the infinitive are described in these paragraphs:

➤8i bare infinitives;
➤8j verbs + prepositions + infinitives;
➤9 modal verbs + infinitives;
➤15b(i) negative imperative with **tu**;
➤15d(i) as an alternative to the imperative.

(iii) *The infinitive as a noun*

An infinitive often functions like a noun and can serve as a subject, an object, or a predicate. The infinitive used as a subject or object can be preceded by the masculine form of the definite article.

***(Il) viaggiare* mi piace molto.**	I like *traveling.*
Preferisco *andare* in aereo.	I prefer *going* by plane.
Questo è *domandare* troppo alla mia amica che detesta (il) *viaggiare* in aereo.	This is *asking* too much of my friend, who hates *traveling* by plane.

Some infinitives have become nouns in their own right, such as:

l'essere	being	**il dovere**	duty
il dispiacere	displeasure, regret	**il piacere**	pleasure

(iv) *Prepositions + infinitive*

The infinitive is the only part of the verb that can be used after prepositions [➤25b(iii)]. In addition to the prepositions that link the infinitive to a preceding verb, there are certain prepositions that may be followed by an infinitive

al fine di	with a view to, in order to
al posto di	instead of
allo scopo di	for the purpose of, with the aim of
con	with
dopo	after
invece di	instead of
per	(in order) to
senza	without
tra	between, what with

Quest'anno la mia amica ed io abbiamo intenzione di iscriverci a un corso estivo a Firenze *allo scopo di migliorare* il nostro italiano. *Invece di comprare* un biglietto di andata e ritorno, la mia amica preferisce comprare solo il biglietto di andata *per poter* andare in giro finchè vuole alla fine del corso. *Tra il viaggiare, il dormire, il mangiare,* ecc., ci costerà un occhio della testa.

This year my friend and I intend to enroll in a summer course in Florence *with the aim of improving* our Italian. *Instead of buying* a round-trip ticket, my friend prefers to buy a one-way ticket *in order to be able* to travel around as much as she likes at the end of the course. Between *the traveling, the accommodations, the food,* etc., it will cost us an arm and a leg.

Dopo is always followed by the past infinitive, the only permissible exception to this rule being **dopo mangiato** 'after eating.'

Dopo *aver parlato* a lungo dei vari corsi, abbiamo deciso di seguire quello a Firenze.

After talking at length about the various courses, we have decided to take the one in Florence.

10b What Are the Present Participle and the Gerund?

In Italian the *present participle* (**il participio presente**) is distinguished both by its ending and function from the *gerund* (**il gerundio**). The present participle of the majority of verbs is formed by adding **-ante** or **-ente** to the stem of the verb [➤ 10c(i) below]. The gerund is formed by adding the endings **-ando** or **-endo** to the stem [➤ 10d(i) below]. Although the present participle and gerund both convey the English form '-ing,' they have quite separate functions in Italian, and particular care will have to be taken not to confuse them. The functions of both will be explained in the following paragraphs.

10c The Present Participle

(i) Formation

The present participle is formed by adding **-ante** to the stem of **-are** verbs and **-ente** to the stem of **-ere** and **-ire** verbs.

parlare	**parl*ante***	speaking
contenere	**conten*ente***	containing
servire	**serv*ente***	serving

The plural is formed by replacing **-e** with **-i**.

There are a few participles that have irregular formations, such as:

nutriente	nourishing
proveniente	deriving, coming from
ubbidiente	obeying

(ii) Use of the present participle as a verb

The present participle is seldom used with a verbal function in Italian, and it would be advisable to use only the examples you have come across. The present participles listed below are among those that can be used with a verbal function.

appartenente	belonging to
attestante	testifying
concernente	concerning
contenente	containing
indicante	indicating
proveniente	deriving, coming from
rappresentante	representing
riguardante	concerning, regarding

Il treno *proveniente* da Genova è in arrivo sul binario sette.	The train *coming* from Genoa is arriving on track seven.
Durante il viaggio ho letto un articolo *riguardante* il vertice dei paesi *appartenenti* all'ONU (Organizzazione delle Nazioni Unite).	During the journey, I read an article *regarding* the summit meeting of the countries *belonging to* the United Nations.

Whenever you are in any doubt about the use of a present participle, the best solution would be to replace it with a *relative clause.*

Il treno *che proviene* da Genova ...	The train *(that is) coming* from Genoa . . .
Ho letto un articolo *che riguarda* ...	I read an article concerning (*that concerns*) . . .
I paesi *che appartengono* all'ONU ...	The countries *that belong* to the United Nations . . .

(iii) *Use of the present participle as an adjective*

One of the most frequent uses of the present participle is as an adjective.

acqua *corrente*	*running* water
la lezione *seguente*	the *following* lesson
un bambino *ubbidiente*	an *obedient* child

When it functions as an adjective, the participle must agree with the noun it describes.

una borsa *pesante* — a *heavy* bag

but

delle borse *pesanti* — *heavy* bags

[For agreement of adjectives ending in **-e** ➤22a(i)B.]

(iv) *Present participle as a noun*

There are a number of instances where the present participle has acquired the function of a noun, as shown by the following examples:

il cantante	singer
il conoscente	acquaintance
la corrente	stream, draft / draught
l'insegnante	teacher
il passante	passerby
il rappresentante	agent, representative

Note, however, that many '-ing' nouns in English have equivalents in Italian that do not derive from the present participle, for example:

la caccia	hunting	**la lettura**	reading
la dattilografia	typing	**il nuoto**	swimming
l'equitazione	horseback riding	**la pesca**	fishing
il giardinaggio	gardening	**la scherma**	fencing

10d The Gerund

Formation

The gerund is formed in the same way as the present participle, except that the endings are **-ando** for **-are** verbs and **-endo** for **-ere** and **-ire** verbs. Italian has two forms of the gerund, the present and the past.

arrivare	**arriv*ando***	arriving (present)
arrivare	**ess*endo* arrivato**	having arrived (past)
vedere	**ved*endo***	seeing (present)
vedere	**av*endo* visto**	having seen (past)
finire	**fin*endo***	finishing (present)
finire	**av*endo* finito**	having finished (past)

Unlike the present participle, the gerund never changes.

It is worth noting the irregular forms of the following verbs:

bere	**bevendo**	drinking
dire	**dicendo**	saying
fare	**facendo**	doing, making
porre	**ponendo**	putting
tradurre	**traducendo**	translating
trarre	**traendo**	pulling, drawing

Should the need arise to use the present participle of the above verbs, then replace **-endo** with **-ente**.

10e Main Uses of the Gerund

(i) 'By doing,' 'on doing,' 'while doing,' 'because of doing'

The gerund has a verbal function and is often used to convey the English 'by —ing,' 'on —ing,' 'while —ing,' and 'because of —ing.'

Seguendo **il corso a Firenze, spero di migliorare molto il mio italiano.**	*By taking* the course in Florence, I hope to improve my Italian a lot.
Passando **per la Francia, io e la mia amica coglieremo l'occasione per visitare altri luoghi.**	*While going* through France, my friend and I will take the opportunity to visit other places.
Arrivando **a Firenze, dobbiamo trovare una sistemazione.**	*On arriving* in Florence, we have to find accommodations.
Non avendo **molti soldi, cercheremo di prenotare due posti in un albergo della gioventù.**	*Not having (because we don't have)* much money, we shall try to reserve two places in a youth hostel.

When the meaning being conveyed is 'although —ing,' then the gerund in Italian is preceded by **pur:**

Pur avendo **una conoscenza elementare della lingua italiana, preferiamo iscriverci al corso per principianti.**	*Although having (Although we have)* an elementary knowledge of the language, we prefer to enroll in a beginners' course.

The present form of the gerund can be used to indicate a simultaneous action.

Sfogliando **un giornale italiano ho visto l'annuncio per questo corso a Firenze.**	*While looking through* an Italian newspaper, I saw the advertisement for this course in Florence.

The past gerund tends to be used less frequently. When it is used, the action described occurs prior to the action of the verb in the main sentence.

Avendo visto **l'annuncio, ho deciso di scrivere subito per chiedere informazioni relative al corso.**	*Having seen* the advertisement, I decided to write immediately to ask for information about the course.

Note that the past gerund is formed from the present gerund of the auxiliary **essere** or **avere** and the past participle of the verb.

[For which auxiliary to use ➤11c; for position of pronouns with the gerund ➤23b(iv).]

The gerund nearly always refers to the subject of the main sentence. This is true for all the examples quoted above. When the gerund does not refer to the subject of the main sentence, then it is advisable to use a subordinate clause introduced by the appropriate conjunction.

***Sfogliando* il giornale ho visto l'annuncio.** — *While looking through* the newspaper, I saw the advertisement. (same subject = *I*)

Ho visto la mia amica *che sfogliava* il giornale. — I saw my friend *looking through* the newspaper. (different subject, i.e., *the friend* was looking, not *I*)

(ii) *Progressive tenses*

The gerund is also used after **stare, andare,** and occasionally **venire** to form the *progressive tenses* [➤8k(i) – 8k(ii)].

Perché *stai sfogliando* il giornale italiano? — Why *are you looking through* the Italian newspaper?

La mia amica *andava leggendo* le riviste e i giornali italiani per migliorare la sua comprensione della lingua. — My friend *kept on reading* Italian magazines and newspapers to improve her understanding of the language.

(iii) *Translating the English '-ing'*

In other circumstances, the English verb ending '-ing' is usually rendered by the infinitive in Italian, either dependent upon another verb (with or without a linking preposition [➤8i, 8j]) or used as a verbal noun [➤10a(iii)]. If the subjects of the two verbs are different, a subjunctive clause may be needed.

Smetti di *guardare* la televisione un attimo. Come faccio a parlarti del corso se continui a *fissare* quel televisore? — Stop *watching* television for a moment. How can I speak to you about the course if you continue *staring at* that television set?

***Leggere* mi aiuta a migliorare la comprensione della lingua.**	*Reading* helps me to improve my understanding of the language.
Prima di *andare* a fare il corso in Italia, intendo *leggere* molto in italiano.	Before *going* to take the course in Italy, I intend to read a lot in Italian.

10f The Past Participle

(i) Formation

The past participle of regular verbs is formed as follows:

Infinitive	***Past Participle***
trovare	trov*ato*
vendere	vend*uto*
finire	fin*ito*

[For verbs that have irregular past participles ➤ 18d(i), 19g(ii),19h.]

(ii) The uses of the past participle

(A) In the formation of compound tenses [➤ 11c]:

Ho *mandato* la lettera.	I have *sent* the letter.
Saranno già *partiti.*	They will already have *left.*

[For agreement of the past participle in compound tenses ➤ 11d.]

(**B**) To form the passive with **essere, andare,** and **venire**

La lettera è stata *imbucata.*	The letter has been *mailed/posted.*
Questa lettera va *imbucata* oggi.	This letter must be *mailed/posted* today.
Ulteriori dettagli verranno *mandati* domani.	Further details will be *sent* tomorrow.

Note that the past participle agrees in gender and number with the subject of **essere, andare,** and **venire.** [For full details of the passive ➤ 17.]

(**C**) As an adjective, in which case it agrees with the noun in the usual way ➤ 22a(i):

un'occasione *mancata*	a *missed* opportunity
le finestre *chiuse*	the *closed* windows

- Some past participles have become an adjective in their own right and may be used with **essere** with no hint of a passive:

Nella mia famiglia, siamo tutti *appassionati* dello sport.	In my family, we are all *enthusiastic* about sports.

(**D**) As a noun:

i *sopravvissuti* della tragedia	the *survivors* of the tragedy
la *scomparsa* della ragazza	the *disappearance* of the girl

(**E**) In *participle* clauses, where English may need a relative or other construction:

Il bambino, *investito* dalla macchina, è stato ricoverato all'ospedale.	The child, (who was) *knocked down* by the car, has been admitted to the hospital.

The past participle can also be used in absolute clauses meaning 'something having been done' or 'when something has / had been done.'

***Scritta* la lettera, sono andato ad imbucarla.**	*When I had written the letter (the letter written)*, I went to mail / post it.

When the verb in the absolute clause is transitive, then it must agree in gender and number with the object (**la lettera**) it governs. When the verb in the absolute clause is intransitive and it refers to the subject of the main clause, then the past participle agrees in gender and number with that subject.

***Partiti* di casa, siamo andati subito alla stazione.**	*Having left* the house, we went straight to the station.

The *past* participle is sometimes used in Italian, particularly when describing positions, where in English the *present* participle is used:

appoggiato	leaning
sdraiato	lying (down)
seduto	sitting

Il ragazzo era *sdraiato* per terra.	The boy was *lying* on the ground.

11 The Passage of Time and the Use of Tenses

11a *What Do Tenses Tell Us?*

Tense is not the same thing as *time*, though the same words are often used to refer to both. Time is a fact of life, in which there are only three time zones (past, present, and future). Tenses, on the other hand, are grammatical structures that often reflect a way of looking at an event as well as recording when it happened. Both the number of tenses, the names given to them, and their uses vary greatly from one language to another.

11b *One Word or Two? Simple and Compound Tenses*

Italian verbs have two series of tenses: the *simple* and the *compound.* In the language of grammar, a *simple* tense is a one-word form, while a *compound* tense is a form of two or more words (an auxiliary verb + one or more past participles or a gerund, depending on the tense).

Therefore, the different tenses of **stare, andare,** and occassionaly **venire** + gerund may be referred to as compound tenses. They correspond closely to the *progressive* (or *continous*) tenses in English [➤10e(ii)] and will be referred to as *progressive* tenses throughout this book. In theory, any tense can have a progressive form, though it is most frequently used in the present and imperfect.

Cosa *stai facendo* in cucina?	What *are you doing* in the kitchen?
***Sto lavando* i piatti.**	*I am washing* the dishes.
***Stavo mangiando* quando hai telefonato.**	*I was eating* when you called / rang.

11c *Auxiliary Verbs Used to Form Compound Tenses*

(i) *Avere*

Most verbs in Italian—all transitive verbs and a certain number of intransitive verbs—form their compound tenses using **avere** as the auxiliary.

aver trovato	to have found	perfect infinitive
ho trovato	I have found, I found	present perfect
avevo trovato	I had found	pluperfect
avrò trovato	I shall have found	future perfect
avrei trovato	I would have found	conditional perfect
ebbi trovato	I had found	past anterior
abbia trovato	I have found, I found	perfect subjunctive
avessi trovato	I had found	pluperfect subjunctive

(ii) Essere

A considerable number of Italian verbs form their compound tenses with **essere:**

essere andato	to have gone	perfect infinitive
sono andato	I have gone, I went	present perfect
ero andato	I had gone	pluperfect
sarò andato	I shall have gone	future perfect
sarei andato	I would have gone	conditional perfect
fui andato	I had gone	past anterior
sia andato	I have gone, I went	perfect subjunctive
fossi andato	I had gone	pluperfect subjunctive

Which verbs form their compound tenses with **essere**?
The MAJORITY of intransitive verbs;
MOST impersonal verbs;
ALL reflexive verbs.
[For a definition of transitive and intransitive ➤8a(i).]

(iii) *Intransitive verbs*

It is possible to categorize a number of verbs used intransitively under certain headings:

(**A**) Verbs that indicate movement from place to place (locomotion) and, in some instances, lack of movement (or states of being):

andare	go
arrivare	arrive
cadere	fall
emigrare	emigrate
entrare	enter
essere	be
fuggire	escape
giungere	arrive, reach
partire	leave

passare	go through, drop in
restare	stay, remain
rimanere	stay, remain
salire	go / come up / get in (car) / get on (bus, train)
scappare	run away
scendere	go / come down / get out of / from (car, bus, train)
sorgere	rise
stare	be, stay
tornare	return
uscire	go out
venire	come

Ieri *siamo stati* a casa tutto il giorno.	Yesterday *we were* at home all day.
Sabato sera *sono andato* al cinema. *Sono uscito* verso le sette e *sono tornato* a casa a mezzanotte.	On Saturday evening *I went* to the movies / cinema. *I went out* about seven o'clock and *got back* home at midnight.

(**B**) Verbs that indicate some process of change, often of a physical or psychological nature:

apparire	appear
arrossire	blush
comparire	appear
crescere	grow up
dimagrire	lose weight
divenire	become
diventare	become
fiorire	flower, blossom
guarire	recover
impallidire	turn pale
impazzire	go mad
ingrassare	put on weight
invecchiare	age, grow old
morire	die
nascere	be born
scomparire	disappear
scoppiare	blow up, burst out
sparire	disappear
svanire	vanish, disappear
svenire	faint

***Sono cresciuto* in campagna.**	*I grew up* in the country.
***È nata* nel 1978.**	*She was born* in 1978.
***Sono scoppiati* a ridere.**	*They burst out* laughing.
***Sono ingrassato* di cinque chili.**	*I have put on* eleven pounds / five kilos.

(**C**) Other verbs used intransitively that take **essere** include:

dipendere	depend
durare	last
emergere	emerge, come out
esistere	exist
intervenire	intervene
prevalere	prevail
ricorrere	turn to, resort to
risultare	turn out to be
riuscire	succeed, manage

***Sono riuscito* a capire tutto.**	*I managed* to understand everything.
Lo spettacolo *è durato* due ore e mezza.	The show *lasted* two and a half hours.

(iv) *Impersonal and 'back-to-front' verbs*

(**A**) Verbs referring to the weather [▶ 8g(i)], such as **piovere, nevicare, gelare, grandinare, lampeggiare, tuonare,** traditionally took the auxiliary **essere** but modern usage tends to accept either **essere** or **avere,** for example:

è nevicato or **ha nevicato**	it has snowed / it snowed

(**B**) A number of verbs that are, or can be, used as impersonal or 'back-to-front' verbs take **essere**. They include the following:

accadere	happen
avvenire	happen
bastare	be sufficient
bisognare	be necessary
capitare	happen
convenire	be fitting, be advisable
costare	cost
dispiacere	be sorry
importare	matter

mancare	lack, miss
occorrere	be necessary
parere	seem, appear
piacere	like, be pleasing to
rincrescere	be sorry
sembrare	seem, appear
servire	be of use
spettare	be up to, be the duty of
succedere	happen
toccare	be up to
valere	be worth
volerci	take, require

Cos'*èsuccesso?*	What *has happened?*
Ci *è voluta* più di un'ora per arrivare alla stazione.	*It took* more than an hour to get to the station.
Mi *è piaciuto* molto il libro.	I *liked* the book a lot.
Però, mi *è costato* parecchio.	However, *it cost* me a lot.

Note that **voluta** agrees with the feminine singular subject **un'ora**.

(v) Reflexive verbs

All verbs used reflexively take **essere**:

Mi sono svegliato* alle sette, *mi sono alzato* subito, *mi sono lavato e mi sono vestito.	*I woke up* at seven o'clock, *got up* immediately, *washed*, and *got dressed.*

Many verbs used reflexively also have nonreflexive forms, in which case they take **avere**:

***Ho svegliato* mio fratello.**	*I woke up* my brother.
***Ho alzato* la mano.**	*I raised* my hand.
***Ho lavato* i piatti.**	*I washed* the dishes.
***Ho vestito* il bambino.**	*I dressed* the child.

*(vi) Verbs that can take either **essere** or **avere***

There are some verbs that take **essere** when they are used intransitively and **avere** when they are not. Some of the most common ones include:

aumentare	increase
cambiare	change
cominciare	start
correre	run
diminuire	decrease, go down
finire	finish
guarire	cure, recover
migliorare	improve
passare	pass, spend (time)
peggiorare	worsen
salire	go up, get in, get on
saltare	jump, skip
scendere	go down, get out of, get off
suonare	ring
vivere	live
volare	fly

La mia vita *è cambiata.*	My life *has changed.* (intransitive)
***Ho cambiato* idea.**	*I have changed* my mind. (transitive)
***È saltato* in acqua.**	*He jumped* into the water. (intransitive)
***Ha saltato* il pranzo.**	*He skipped* lunch. (transitive)
***Siamo scesi* dal treno.**	*We got off* the train. (intransitive)
***Abbiamo sceso* le scale.**	*We went down* the stairs. (transitive)
Il mio italiano *è migliorato.*	My Italian *has improved.* (intransitive)
***Ho migliorato* il mio italiano.**	*I have improved* my Italian. (transitive)

Note that some of the verbs mentioned in the above list take either **avere** or **essere** in intransitive expressions. In such cases, there is a difference in meaning according to the auxiliary used.

Correre, saltare, and **volare** take **essere** when they indicate 'movement to a place,' and **avere** in other intransitive expressions.

***Siamo volati* alla stazione.**	*We flew (rushed)* to the station.
Dopo la lezione *sono corso* a casa.	After the lesson, *I ran* home.
***Sono saltato* dalla macchina.**	*I jumped* from the car.

but

***Abbiamo corso* per un'ora.**	*We ran* for an hour.
***Ho saltato* per dieci minuti.**	*I jumped* for ten minutes.
Non *ho* mai *volato* in un elicottero.	*I have* never *flown* in a helicopter.

Note also that **vivere** can take either **avere** or **essere** when used intransitively.

***Sono vissuti (Hanno vissuto)* in quell'appartamento per quasi dieci anni.**	*They lived* in that apartment / flat for almost ten years.

(vii) *The modals **dovere, potere,** and **volere*** *[➤ 9a, 9b, 9d]*

Although it was considered more correct to use **essere** with the above modals when their accompanying infinitive required **essere**, modern usage accepts either **essere** or **avere**. In fact, the tendency is to use **avere** relatively frequently these days when one wishes to emphasize the value of the modal verb.

Non *siamo potuti* venire al matrimonio.	*We could* not come to the wedding.
***Sono voluto* partire di buon'ora.**	*I wanted* to leave early.
La mia amica *è dovuta* rimanere a casa.	My friend *had to* stay at home.

These three modals take **avere** when the infinitive that follows would use **avere** to form its compound tense.

Non *abbiamo voluto* prendere il treno delle sette.	*We did* not *want* to catch the seven o'clock train.
Alla fine *ho dovuto* mandare un telegramma.	In the end, *I had* to send a telegram(me).
Non *ha potuto* prestarmi il libro.	*She could* not lend me the book.

If **dovere, volere,** or **potere** is used with a reflexive verb, then there are two possible constructions. The auxiliary is **essere** when the reflexive pronoun precedes the modal, and **avere** when the reflexive pronoun remains attached to the infinitive.

***Mi sono* dovuto alzare presto.** but ***Ho dovuto alzarmi* presto.**	I had to get up early.

(viii) *The passive [➤17]*

Essere is used to form all tenses of the passive.

La macchina *è riparata.*	The car *is repaired.*
Non *saranno* tutti *invitati.*	*They will* not all *be invited.*
Molte case *sono state danneggiate.*	Many houses *have been damaged.*

[For verbs other than **essere** to express the passive ➤17d.]

11d Past Participle Agreement in Compound Tenses

The following rules for agreement of past participles apply across all compound tenses.

(i) *Compound tenses formed with* ***avere***

The past participle of a verb conjugated with **avere** *never* agrees:

- with the subject:

***Maria* ha *comprato* la gonna.**	*Maria* has *bought* the skirt.

- nor with a preceding indirect object pronoun [➤23b(iii)]:

***Le* ho *dato* il giornale.**	I *gave her (= to her)* the newspaper.

Agreement is *optional:*

- when the direct object precedes the verb:

***La gonna che* Maria ha *comprata* è molto cara.** or ***La gonna che* Maria ha *comprato* è molto cara.**	*The skirt that* Maria has *bought* is very expensive.

The direct object is the relative pronoun [▶ 23m(ii)] **che**, which stands for **la gonna,** thus the agreement. In this type of relative construction it is much more common to leave the past participle unchanged, i.e., **la gonna che Maria ha *comprato.***

- when the direct object pronouns are **mi, ti, ci, vi** [▶ 23b(ii)]:

Maria, *ti* ho *vista* (*ti* ho *visto*) in città.	Mary, I *saw you* in town.

- when the pronoun **ne** [▶ 23f] refers to a specific quantity. In this case, the **ne** can agree with the noun it refers to or the quantity:

Quanto vino hai bevuto?—Ne ho *bevuto/bevuti* due bicchieri.	How much wine did you drink? —I drank two glasses.
Quante sigarette hai comprato? —Ne ho *comprate/comprati* tre pacchetti.	How many cigarettes did you buy? —I bought three packs.
Quanti cioccolatini hai mangiato? —Ne ho *mangiati/mangiato* parecchi.	How many chocolates did you eat? —I ate a lot.

The past participle *must* agree:

- when it is preceded by the direct object pronouns **lo, la, li, le** [▶ 23b(ii)]:

Maria *l'(la)* ha *comprata* stamattina.	Maria *bought it* this morning.

- when the pronoun is **ne** and the meaning being conveyed is 'some' or 'part of' something:

Hai bevuto del vino?—Sì, *ne* ho *bevuto.*	Have you drunk some wine? —Yes, I have *drunk some (of it).*
Hai comprato delle sigarette? —Sì, *ne* ho *comprate.*	Have you bought some cigarettes?—Yes, I have *bought some (of them).*
Hai mangiato dei cioccolatini? —Sì, *ne* ho *mangiati.*	Have you eaten some chocolates? —Yes, I have *eaten some.*

*(ii) Compound tenses formed with **essere***

The past participles of compound tenses formed with **essere** agree in number and gender with the subject of the verb:

Ieri sera sono *andato* al concerto con mio fratello. *I miei genitori sono rimasti* a casa, e *mia sorella* è *uscita* con il suo ragazzo.	Last night *I went* to the concert with my brother. *My parents stayed* at home, and *my sister went out* with her boyfriend.

In the case of reflexive verbs, the past participle can agree either with the subject:

***La ragazza* si è *lavata* i capelli.**	*The girl washed* her hair.

or the direct object:

La ragazza si è *lavati i capelli.*	The girl *washed her hair.*

12 The Present Tenses

The *indicative* tenses explained in chapters 12 to 14 (as opposed to *subjunctive* tenses explained in chapter 16) are used to assert that something is true or certain.

12a The Simple Present [➤ 18c(i)]

This has a variety of functions. It can describe the following:

(i) What the situation is now

Cosa *fai?*— *Leggo* il giornale.	What *are you doing?* — *I'm reading* the newspaper.

[See also the present progressive ➤12b.]

(ii) What happens sometimes or usually

***Leggo* il giornale ogni sera.**	*I read* the newspaper every evening.
Di solito *guardo* il telegiornale prima di cenare.	*I* usually *watch* the TV news before having dinner.

(iii) What is going to happen soon or in the future

In such expressions the future is specified by a *time expression.*

Marco, apparecchia per favore, fra poco *mangiamo.*	Marco, set / lay the table please; *we shall be eating* shortly.

Note: In Italian it is fairly common to express immediate future tense ideas using the present tense.

***Ci vediamo* l'anno prossimo.**	*We shall see each other* next year.

La settimana prossima *andiamo* in vacanza.	Next week *we are going* on vacation / holiday.

(iv) *What has been happening up to now and may be going to continue*

***Abito* in questa casa da parecchi anni, cioè dal 1994.**	*I have been living* in this house for several years, that is, since 1994.

This is an occasion where different tenses are used in Italian and English. Note also that the English words 'since' or 'for' are conveyed in Italian by ***da.***

The above construction can also be expressed in the following ways:

È da parecchi anni che abito in questa casa. or **Sono parecchi anni che abito in questa casa.**	I have been living in this house for several years

Note that in the first example the verb **è** is *always* singular, whereas in the second type of construction the verb has to agree in number with the noun that follows, for example, **è un anno** but **sono parecchi anni**.

To ask 'how long someone / something has been —ing,' it is possible to use either **da quanto tempo** or **quanto tempo è che?**

***Da quanto tempo* abiti in questa casa? — Da parecchi anni.**	*How long* have you been living in this house? — For several years.
***Quanto tempo è che* piove? — Da tre ore.**	*How long* has it been raining? — For three hours.

(v) *Narrative present*

The present tense in Italian can be used in both speech and writing to describe recent or distant past events. This is called the *historic* or *narrative* present, and it has the effect of bringing to life or of dramatizing the action or event. Its use is more widespread in Italian than in English, where it tends to be limited to newspaper headlines of the type 'Tennis star signs new contract.'

Ti *chiedo* di darmi una mano a spostare i mobili, *dici* che *vieni* subito e mezz'ora dopo *stai* ancora *seduto* davanti al televisore.

I ask(ed) you to give me a hand to move the furniture; *you say (said) you will come (would come)* right away, and half an hour later *you are (were)* still *sitting* in front of the television set.

Un anno dopo, il regista di questo film *muore* in un incidente stradale.

A year later, the director of this movie / film *died* in a road accident.

12b *The Present Progressive*

The present progressive is formed with the present tense of **stare** + the gerund [➤10e(ii)]. In some circumstances it may also be formed using **andare** or **venire** as the auxiliary. It is used as an alternative to the simple present [➤12a(i)], but the action *must* be in progress at the time referred to.

Cosa *stai facendo*? — *Sto leggendo* il giornale.

What *are you doing*? — *I am reading* the newspaper.

You cannot use this tense to say what *is happening shortly,* as in 12a(iii).

The Past Tenses

Italian has the following past tenses: the present perfect (**passato prossimo**), the imperfect (**imperfetto**), the past definite (**passato remoto**), the pluperfect (**trapassato prossimo**), and the past anterior (**trapassato remoto**).

13a The Present Perfect

This is a compound tense formed with the present tense of **avere** or **essere** and the past participle [➤11c(i), 11c(ii)]. [For complete conjugation of the present perfect tense ➤19; for past participle agreements ➤11d.]

In Italian the present perfect tense has two uses. One corresponds almost exactly to the English present perfect tense 'I have written.' The other replaces the simple past or past definite tense [➤18c(vi)] 'I wrote.'

The present perfect tense can be used:

(i) To convey the idea of something that started in the past but is still connected to the here and now:

***Mi è sempre piaciuto* l'italiano.**	*I've always liked* Italian. (and I *still* like it)
Ma *non sono mai andato* in Italia.	But *I've never been* to Italy. (up to *now)*

(ii) To talk about a series of repeated actions that have happened up to the present:

***Ho spesso pensato* di andare in Italia con una mia amica.**	*I've often thought* of going to Italy with a friend of mine.

(iii) To talk about a past action or event that is completely finished but whose effects are still felt now:

Purtroppo, questa mia amica *ha perso* il suo lavoro.	Unfortunately, this friend of mine *has lost* her job. (and *now* she cannot afford to come to Italy with me even if she wanted to)

(iv) To talk about a recent event:

Hai visto* la tua amica? — Sì, l'*ho vista stamattina.	*Have you seen* your friend? — Yes, *I saw (have seen) her this morning.*

Note: In the North and some parts of Central Italy, it is common to use the present perfect tense, rather than the past definite, to talk about completed past actions and events, even though they happened some time ago.

Due anni fa *ho pensato* di andare in Italia, ma alla fine *ho deciso* di andare in Francia.	Two years ago *I thought* of going to Italy, but then *I decided* to go to France.

13b The Imperfect [➤ 18c(v)]

One of the most frequent uses of the imperfect tense is to convey the English 'was / were + — ing,' 'used to'. The tense often denotes an unfinished or repeated action in the past. It is used in the following situations:

(i) *To indicate something that was unfinished or continuing, often interrupted by another event:*

***Guardavo* un film alla televisione quando la mia amica mi ha telefonato.**	*I was watching* a movie / film on television when my friend called / rang me.

Note: There is also a progressive form of the imperfect that may be used in examples such as the one above [➤ 8k(i)].

***Stavo guardando* un film alla televisione quando la mia amica ha telefonato.**	*I was watching* a movie / film on television when my friend called / rang.

(ii) *To indicate something repeated or habitual in the past:*

Quando la mia amica *lavorava*, *uscivamo* insieme almeno due volte alla settimana.	When my friend *was working, we went out (we would go out / we used to go out)* together at least twice a week.

As the above examples show, the imperfect is expressed in English in a number of forms. When the English is 'was / were doing' or 'used to do,' the decision to use the imperfect is straightforward. Care is needed, however, on the many occasions where the English form suggests another tense, as in 'went out / would go out' above. Note also that a repeated past action, which is not a habit, is conveyed by the present perfect tense [➤13a] and *not* the imperfect:

La mia amica mi *ha telefonato* due volte.	My friend *called / rang* me twice. (i.e., on *two separate occasions*, each one *complete* in itself)

(iii) *To indicate two simultaneous actions:*

Mentre *guardavo* la televisione, *sbrigavo* le faccende domestiche.	While *I was watching* television, *I did* the housework.

(iv) *To give a descriptive background in the past:*

La mia amica *lavorava* in un'agenzia di viaggi. Le *piaceva* molto il suo lavoro anche se la paga non *era* molto buona. Siccome l'agenzia *si trovava* a un chilometro da casa sua, *andava* sempre a piedi. Quando *pioveva, prendeva* l'autobus.	My friend *worked* in a travel agency. She *liked* her work a lot even if the pay *was*n't very good. As the agency *was situated* a kilometer / kilometre from her home, she always *went* on foot. When it *rained*, she *took* the bus.

(v) To express an intention or wish that remains unfulfilled or unrealized. In spoken Italian, the imperfect is often used instead of the conditional perfect [➤14e], and especially with **dovere, potere,** and **volere:**

La mia amica *poteva (avrebbe potuto)* trasferirsi a un'altra agenzia e allora non *perdeva* (*avrebbe perduto*) il lavoro, ma ha respinto l'offerta.	My friend *could have* transferred to another agency and then *she would*n't *have lost* her job, but she rejected the offer.

(vi) Instead of the present tense or present conditional to express polite requests:

***Vuoi (Volevi)* uscire stasera?**	*Did you want (Were you wanting)* to go out this evening?
Ti ho telefonato perché *vorrei* (*volevo*) chiederti un piacere.	I called / rang you because *I would like (was wanting)* to ask you a favor / favour.

(vii) Instead of the pluperfect subjunctive and conditional perfect in constructions introduced by **si** [▶ 16j(iii)], but only in informal spoken Italian:

Se *ti trasferivi (ti fossi trasferita)* a quell'altra agenzia, non *perdevi (avresti perduto)* il lavoro.	If *you had transferred* to that other agency, *you would*n't *have lost* the job.

(viii) In expressions of time, introduced by **da,** to indicate that something had been going on a certain time, and might well have continued:

***Lavoravo* da tre anni presso quell'agenzia di viaggi quando mi hanno chiesto di trasferirmi.**	*I had been working* at that travel agency for three years when they asked me to transfer.

Note: The same construction can also be expressed as follows:

Erano tre anni che lavoravo presso quell'agenzia... or **Era da tre anni che lavoravo presso quell'agenzia...**	I had been working at that agency for three years. . . .

13c The Past Definite [▶ 18c(vi)]

The past definite is used to describe past events that have completely finished. It tells you what *happened* on a particular occasion.

La mia amica *lasciò la scuola* all'età di sedici anni e *trovò* subito un lavoro presso un'agenzia di viaggi.	My friend *left* school at the age of sixteen and immediately *found* a job with a travel agency.

The past definite can refer to short, quickly finished actions or to events that ended after a longer period of time, which could be weeks, months, years, or even centuries.

***Lavorò* presso quest'agenzia per tre anni.**	*She worked* at this agency for three years.

The use of the past definite is now mainly limited to the written language. However, this tense is used in spoken Italian in some parts of Central Italy and particularly in the South, even when the actions or events referred to are *recent*.

Ieri sera io e la mia amica *andammo* al cinema.	Yesterday evening my friend and I *went* to the movies / cinema.

In Northern Italy, the tendency would be to use the present perfect instead of the past definite in all of the above examples, both in speech and informal writing.

13d The Pluperfect

This is a compound tense formed with the imperfect of the auxiliary **avere** or **essere** [▶ 11c(i), 11c(ii)] and the past participle. It corresponds in most cases to the English pluperfect, indicating what *had happened before* a subsequent event in the past. Its name means 'more than perfect, further back in the past.'

***Ero* appena *arrivato* a casa quando *squillò* il telefono.**	*I had* just *arrived* home when the phone *rang*.

Voleva dirmi che *aveva deciso* di lasciare il suo posto presso l'agenzia di viaggi.	She wanted to tell me that *she had decided* to leave her job at the travel agency.
***Aveva lavorato* lì per tre anni.**	*She had worked* there for three years.

When you want to say that something had been going on for a certain time, and was likely to continue, you use the imperfect with **da** + time expression [▶ 13b(viii)], *not* the pluperfect.

13e *The Past Anterior [▶ 19]*

This is a compound tense formed with the past definite of **avere** or **essere** and the past participle. This tense is not used in spoken Italian. It can be found in literary and other printed texts. It has the same meaning as the pluperfect [▶ 13d] and is used after conjunctions of time (**dopo che** 'after,' **quando** 'when,' **appena** 'as soon as') when the past definite is used in the main clause:

Appena la mia amica *ebbe lasciato* la scuola, trovò un lavoro.	As soon as my friend *had left* school, she found a job.

In speech, and often in writing, the past anterior would be replaced by the pluperfect.

Appena la mia amica *aveva lasciato* la scuola...	As soon as my friend *had left* school. . . .

14 The Future and Conditional Tenses

14a *The Simple Future [▶ 18c(iii)]*

The simple future (**il futuro semplice**) is the literal equivalent of the English future tense, i.e., it tells you what will happen at a point in the future, although it is not the only, or even necessarily the most common way of expressing this concept [▶ 12a(iii)]. It is used for the following:

(i) *To state simply what will happen*

Prima di uscire *mi laverò* i capelli.	Before going out, *I shall wash* my hair.

(ii) *To express definite convictions and plans*

Domani sera *resterò* a casa e non *farò* niente.	Tomorrow evening *I shall stay* at home and *do* nothing.

(iii) *To give emphatic, often rather condescending, instructions, as in English*

Non *starai seduto* tutta la sera a fare niente, *risponderai* a quella lettera.	*You will* not *sit down* all evening doing nothing; *you will answer* that letter.

(iv) *To express supposition or approximation. In English such expressions are often conveyed by 'must,' 'may be,' 'could.'*

***Saranno* le undici passate e non è ancora tornato a casa. Dove *sarà?*—*Sarà* con il suo amico Roberto.**	*It must be* after eleven o'clock, and he hasn't come home yet. Where *could he be?*—*He may be* with his friend Roberto.

(v) *In sentences introduced by **se***

Se non *tornerà* fra poco, *telefonerò* al suo amico.	If *he is* not *back* soon, *I shall call/ ring* his friend.

Note that English uses the present tense after 'if' whereas Italian has a future tense. However, it is also possible and fairly common to use the present tense in Italian after **se**.

Se non *torna* fra poco, *telefonerò* al suo amico.	If *he is* not *back* soon, *I shall call/ ring* his friend.

(vi) *After conjunctions of time*

The future is normally required after a range of time words such as **quando** 'when,' **appena** 'as soon as,' and **finché** 'as long as,' when the verb in the main sentence is also future. After the conjunction of time, a present tense would be used in English.

Quando *arriverà* a casa, *sarà* stanco morto. Finché *vivrò*, non *capirò* mai perché deve sempre tornare a casa tardi.	When *he arrives* home, *he will be* dead tired. As long as *I live, I shall* never *understand* why he always comes home late.

14b *The Future Perfect*

The future perfect (**il futuro anteriore**) is a compound tense using the auxiliary **essere** or **avere** in the future tense [➤11c(i), 11c(ii)] + the past participle. It tells you what *will have happened* and is used:

(i) *To say what will have happened, often by the time something else happens*

Saranno preoccupati i tuoi genitori? — No, *saranno andati* a letto.	Will your parents be worried? — No, *they will have gone* to bed.

(ii) To indicate supposition and approximation, similarly to paragraph 14a(iv), where the English verb would usually be in the present perfect.

Ma dove *sarà andato? Avrà perduto* l'ultima corriera.	But where *can he have gone? He must have missed* the last bus.

(iii) *After conjunctions of time*

The rule governing the use of the future perfect after the conjunctions of time **quando** 'when,' **appena** 'as soon as,' and **dopo che** 'after' is the same as for the use of the simple future tense referred to in 14a(vi) above.

Quando *avremo finito* di guardare questo programma, andremo a letto.	When *we have finished* watching this program(me), we shall go to bed.

Notice that such sentences do not use a future or future perfect in English after the conjunction of time, but a present perfect tense. Particular care is therefore needed when expressing this idea in Italian.

14c Alternatives to the Future

The simple future tense is not the most frequent way of expressing future time in Italian, especially in everyday speech. Other forms are often used and these include:

(i) *The present tense [➤ 12a(iii)]*

The present tense is frequently used, as in English, to refer to the immediate future, especially for prearranged events.

A che ora *ci vediamo* domani sera? — Alle otto in piazza. — E cosa *facciamo?* — Prima, *facciamo* una bella passeggiata lungo il fiume, poi *andiamo* a mangiare una pizza. — E dopo? — Dopo, *torniamo* a casa.	At what time *are we seeing (shall we see) each other* tomorrow evening? — At eight o'clock in the square. — And what *are we doing?* — First, *we are going* for a nice walk along the river, then *we are going* to have a pizza. — And then? — Then, *we are going* home.

Italian uses the simple present here, *never* the present progressive.

(ii) *Pensare di* and so forth

Future plans and intentions are also conveyed by **pensare di, avere intenzione di, avere in mente di,** and **avere in programma**.

Cosa *pensi di* fare quest'estate? — *Ho in mente di* andare negli Stati Uniti.	What *are you thinking of* doing this summer? — *I intend* to go to the United States.
***Hai* qualcosa *in programma* per questo fine settimana? — No, *ho intenzione di* rimanere a casa.**	*Have you* something *planned* for this weekend? — No, *I intend* to stay at home.

Care must be taken with English expressions such as 'Will you close the door?' where the English auxiliary 'will' does not express futurity but willingness [➤9d(ii)].

***Vuoi* chiudere la porta, per favore?**	*Will you* close the door, please?

14d The Present Conditional [➤ 18c(iv)]

The present conditional (**il condizionale presente**) has a number of uses, including:

(i) Polite requests and preference

***Vorrei* un chilo di pomodori.**	*I would like* a kilo of tomatoes.
***Potrei* assaggiare un po' di questo formaggio?**	*Could I* try a bit of this cheese?
***Preferirei* pagare con un assegno.**	*I would rather* pay by check / cheque.

(ii) Making suggestions and giving advice

***Dovrebbero* prendere il treno delle nove e quindici.**	*They should* take the 9:15 train.
Io non *prenderei* quello che parte mezz'ora prima perché è sempre affollato.	*I would*n't *take* the one that leaves half an hour before because it's always crowded.

(iii) *In indirect speech*

To report what someone else is saying:

Anche gli altri dicono che *sarebbe* meglio partire più tardi.	Even the others say that *it would be* better to leave later.

Great care has to be taken over the use of the conditional in indirect speech. When the verb of reporting is in the past tense, then the conditional perfect must be used in the dependent clause [➤14e(iv)].

(iv) *To say what would happen under certain conditions, often after a clause with* ***se*** *[➤16j]*

Che cosa *faresti* tu Maria?	What *would you do*, Maria?
Se io fossi in te, *accetterei* il consiglio degli altri.	If I were you, *I would accept* the advice of the others.

(v) *To express a doubt*

È meglio partire più tardi? —Non *saprei.*	Is it better to leave later? — *I don't know* (*I wouldn't know*).

The use of the conditional tense conveys a mood of *uncertainty,* which would not be the case if the present indicative tense were used.

(vi) *To quote someone else's opinion or to report unconfirmed news*

Secondo un mio amico, i macchinisti *farebbero* sciopero domani.	According to a friend of mine, the train engineers *are going on* strike tomorrow.

14e *The Conditional Perfect*

The conditional perfect tense (**il condizionale passato**) is a compound tense formed with the conditional of the auxiliary **avere** or **essere** [➤11c(i), 11c(ii)] and the past participle. It tells you what *could have happened.* The uses are much the same as those explained under paragraph 14d, only now the actions and events referred to are in the *past.* It is used in the following situations:

(i) *To express an unfulfilled wish or preference*

Avrei voluto **un chilo di pomodori.**	*I would have liked* a kilo of tomatoes.
Avrei preferito **pagare con un assegno.**	*I would have preferred* to pay by check / cheque.

(ii) *To make suggestions and give advice*

Avresti dovuto **prendere il treno delle nove e quindici come avevo detto io.**	*You should have* caught the 9:15 train as I told you.

(iii) *When used negatively, to convey a sense of surprise or disbelief*

Io non *avrei* mai *preso* il treno che parte mezz'ora prima perché è sempre affollato.	*I would* never *have taken* the train that leaves half an hour before because it's always crowded.

(iv) *In indirect speech*

Gli altri hanno detto che *sarebbe stato* meglio partire più tardi.	The others said that *it would be* better to leave later.

In indirect (reported) speech, when the verb in the main sentence is in the *past tense,* the *conditional perfect* must be used in the subordinate clause introduced by ***che,*** unlike in English where the present conditional is used. This rule applies to similar constructions when the main sentence contains the past tense of verbs such as **pensare, credere, sperare, immaginare, promettere.**

Sapevo che *avresti preso* il treno delle nove e quindici.	I knew that *you would take* the 9:15 train.

However, the present conditional may be used when the action is to be realized at some point in the future.

Speravo che *partiresti* domani mattina.	I was hoping that *you would leave* tomorrow morning.

(v) *To say what would have happened under certain conditions, after a clause with* ***se*** *[➤16j]*

Che cosa *avresti fatto* tu Maria?	What *would you have done,* Maria?
Se fossi stata in te, *avrei accettato* il consiglio degli altri.	If I had been you, *I would have accepted* the advice of the others.

Note: Past hypotheses after **se** can be expressed in informal, spoken Italian by using an imperfect tense in both sentences [➤16j(iii)]:

Se *ero* in te, *accettavo* il consiglio degli altri.	If *I had been* you, *I would have accepted* the advice of the others.

(vi) *To express a personal opinion about a past action*

Penso che *avresti dovuto* accettare il loro consiglio.	I think *you should have* accepted their advice.

Note: To express 'should' or 'ought to' use **dovere**. To express 'could' or 'might' use **potere**.

***Avresti potuto* prendere il pullman.**	*You could have* taken the bus / coach.

'Would' in English does not necessarily imply condition and may denote willingness [➤9d(ii)], in which case the imperfect or past definite of **volere** is used.

Non *voleva/volle* dare retta a nessuno. He *would*n't listen to anyone.

It may also describe an habitual action in the past, when the imperfect of the verb is used [➤13b(ii)].

Ogni mattina *si alzavano* alla stessa ora. Every morning *they would get up* at the same time.

It is possible to convey the same meaning by using **solere** 'be accustomed/used to' + the infinitive.

Ogni mattina *solevano alzarsi* alla stessa ora. Every morning *they would (used to) get up* at the same time.

15 Requests and Commands: The Imperative

15a What Does the Imperative Express?

The *imperative* is used for a variety of purposes, including requests, commands, warnings, instructions, invitations, and advice.

15b Formation of the Imperative

In Italian, because there are four ways of saying 'you'—informal singular and plural, formal singular and plural [➤ 23b(i)]—there are four imperative forms, both positive and negative. They all say DO something or DON'T do it. The informal **tu** and **voi** forms are the same as those of the present indicative [➤ 18c(i)], with the exception of the **tu** form of regular **-are** verbs. The formal **Lei** and **Loro** take the corresponding forms of the *present subjunctive* [➤ 18c(ii)]. The first person plural **noi** 'let's' is also expressed by the corresponding form of the subjunctive, which is identical to that of the present indicative. The imperative forms of regular verbs are as follows:

	Parlare	*Prendere*	*Aprire*	*Finire*
(tu)	**parla**	**prendi**	**apri**	**finisci**
(Lei)	**parli**	**prenda**	**apra**	**finisca**
(noi)	**parliamo**	**prendiamo**	**apriamo**	**finiamo**
(voi)	**parlate**	**prendete**	**aprite**	**finite**
(Loro)	**parlino**	**prendano**	**aprano**	**finiscano**

Parla **più piano per favore.** — *Speak* more slowly, please.
Prendiamo **il treno delle sei.** — *Let's take* the six o'clock train.
Apra **la finestra per cortesia.** — *Open* the window, please.
Finite **di parlare delle vacanze.** — *Stop* talking about the vacation / holidays.

Note also the following verbs that have some irregular **tu** and occasionally **voi** forms (marked with an asterisk):

	Essere	*Avere*	*Andare*	*Dare*
(tu)	**sii***	**abbi***	**va'* (vai)**	**da'* (dai)**
(Lei)	**sia**	**abbia**	**vada**	**dia**
(noi)	**siamo**	**abbiamo**	**andiamo**	**diamo**
(voi)	**siate***	**abbiate***	**andate**	**date**
(Loro)	**siano**	**abbiano**	**vadano**	**diano**

	Dire	*Fare*	*Stare*
(tu)	**di'***	**fa'* (fai)**	**sta'* (stai)**
(Lei)	**dica**	**faccia**	**stia**
(noi)	**diciamo**	**facciamo**	**stiamo**
(voi)	**dite**	**fate**	**state**
(Loro)	**dicano**	**facciano**	**stiano**

(i) *Negative imperatives*

Negative imperatives are formed by putting **non** before the verb form. The exception to the rule is the second person singular **tu** where **non** is followed by the infinitive:

Apri la porta. Open the door.
but
***Non aprire* la porta.** *Don't open* the door.

otherwise

Andiamo. Non andiamo. Let's go. Let's not go.
Guardi. Non guardi. Look. Don't look.

(ii) *Position of pronouns with the imperative*

Pronouns are attached to the **tu, noi,** and **voi** forms of the imperative so that they form one word:

Guarda*lo*. Look at *him*.
Andiamo*ci*. Let's go *there*.
Vendete*la*. Sell *it*.
Comprate*ne* due. Buy two *of them*.

However, they are placed in front of the **Lei** and **Loro** forms:

Le **dica di aspettare.**	Tell *her* to wait.
Lo **vendano.**	Sell *it.*

The one exception to this rule is **loro** 'to them,' which always comes after an imperative form and can never be attached to it.

Di' ***loro*** di aspettare.	Tell *them* (= to them) to wait.

When **va'**, **da'**, **di'**, **fa'**, and **sta'** are followed by an object pronoun — with the exception of **gli** — the initial consonant of the pronoun is doubled.

Di*mmi* tutto.	Tell *me* everything.
Va*cci* subito.	Go *there* straightaway.
Di*lle* la verità.	Tell *her* the truth.
Fa*llo* per domani.	Do *it* by tomorrow.
but	
Di*gli* di telefonarmi.	Tell *him* to call / ring me.
Da*gli* qualcosa da bere.	Give *him* something to drink.

(iii) Position of pronouns with the negative imperative

With the **tu** form the pronoun can precede the infinitive or be attached to it:

Non *lo* fare or **Non far*lo.***	Don't do *it.*

Although this option is open to the **noi** and **voi** forms, common practice is to attach the object pronouns to the imperative.

Non compriamo*lo* adesso.	Let's not buy *it* now.
Non guardate*mi.*	Don't look at *me.*

With **Lei** and **Loro** the pronouns *remain* in front of the imperative:

Non *la* mangi.	Don't eat *it.*
Non *ci* vadano.	Don't go *there.*

Note: These same rules, as well as those described under ➤15(ii) above, apply to the position of the reflexive pronouns [➤23c] of reflexive verbs.

Non *ti* preoccupare or **Non preoccupar*ti*.**	Don't worry.
Non preoccupate*vi*.	Don't worry.
Non *si* alzi.	Don't get up.
Sbriga*ti*.	Hurry up.
Sediamo*ci*.	Let's sit down.
Svegliate*vi*.	Wake up.

[For more detailed information on the uses and position of pronouns ➤23b(ii–v).]

15c Some Common Uses of the Imperative

The imperative may indicate:

- A request

***Telefonami* quando hai più informazioni.**	*Call/ ring* me when you have more information.

- A command or order

***Vai* a lavarti le mani prima di mangiare.**	*Go* and wash your hands before eating.

- A warning

***Non toccare* la frutta.**	*Don't touch* the fruit.

- An instruction

***Rispondete* alle seguenti domande.**	*Answer* the following questions.

- An invitation

Se non ti piace la birra, *prendi* qualcos'altro.	If you don't like beer, *have* something else.

- A piece of advice

***Ripassate* l'imperativo prima dell'esame.**	*Review/Revise* the imperative before the exam.

15d Other Ways of Expressing Imperatives

(i) Infinitive

The infinitive [➤10a] is frequently used as an imperative in *written* notices, instructions, recipes, and so forth, for reasons of clarity and brevity.

Non *sporgersi* dal finestrino.	*Do*n't *lean out* of the window.
***Leggere* attentamente il testo.**	*Read* the text carefully.

(ii) ***divieto di*** *+ noun,* ***è vietato*** *+ infinitive*

Divieto di accesso.	No access / No entry.
È vietato fumare.	No smoking.

(iii) Present indicative

In colloquial speech, the present indicative with question intonation is sometimes used to soften the command into a request. The same effect can be created by a modal verb [➤9] + infinitive, similar to the English device.

Mi *porta/può portare* un'altra bottiglia di acqua minerale, per favore?	*Can* you *bring* me another bottle of mineral water, please?
Mi *spiega/vuole spiegare* la differenza?	*Will* you *explain* the difference to me?

16 Areas of Uncertainty: The Subjunctive

16a What Does the Subjunctive Do?

The subjunctive (**il congiuntivo**) is widely used in Italian both in speech and in writing. It tends to refer to events or actions that are *not* certain to happen. The expressions used to convey such actions or events reflect uncertainty, wish, preference, fear, doubt, vagueness, unreality, and so forth. This is in direct contrast with the *indicative*, which describes with a greater degree of *certainty* what has happened, is happening, or will happen. Compare the following sentences:

Sono sicuro che *vengono*.	I am sure that *they are coming*. (indicative, states certainty)
È possibile che *vengano*.	It's possible that *they are coming*. (subjunctive, expresses uncertainty)

As in the above example, the subjunctive is mainly used in subordinate clauses, in many cases introduced by **che,** but it can occur in main clauses in certain forms of the imperative [▶ 15 and 16h(i)] and in a few other cases [▶ 16h(ii)]. The subjunctive is an *important* part of the Italian language and one that requires close study.

The following paragraphs aim to set out general principles and guidelines relating to the use of the subjunctive in Italian. It would be unwise to think that *all* the following rules are strictly applied, particulary in the spoken language, where you will come across variations in its use. Reference will be made to such variations whenever possible.

As a *general rule* the subjunctive is not used unless there is a change of subject in the sentence. If the subject remains the same, other constructions such as the infinitive are usually preferred:

Stasera *voglio uscire*.	This evening *I want to go out*.
Non *voglio che tu esca* stasera.	*I don't want you to go out* this evening.

In the first example there is no change of subject and therefore the infinitive has to be used after **voglio**. In the second example the subjunctive must be used because there is a change of subject.

16b *The Tenses of the Subjunctive*

[For the formation of the present and imperfect subjunctive ➤18c(ii), 18c(vii); for present perfect and pluperfect subjunctive ➤16b, 19; for auxiliary **avere** or **essere** to form compound tenses ➤11c.]

The subjunctive has four tenses: present, imperfect, present perfect, and pluperfect. All four tenses are used in Italian and the tense of the subjunctive will be determined by the tense of the verb in the clause on which the subjunctive depends. [For sequence of tenses ➤16i.]

Penso che *capiscano* tutto.	I think *they understand* everything. (present)
Penso che *abbiano capito* tutto.	I think *they have understood* everything. (present perfect)
Pensavo che *capissero* tutto.	I thought *they understood* everything. (imperfect)
Pensavo che *avessero capito* tutto.	I thought *they had understood* everything. (pluperfect)

16c *The Subjunctive after Certain Verbs*

The subjunctive is used with the following categories of verbs, of which the most common examples are listed:

(i) Verbs of wishing, wanting, liking, preferring, ordering, permitting, forbidding, insisting, and expecting when followed by ***che****:*

aspettare che ...	await . . .
aspettarsi che ...	expect . . .

attendere che ...	await . . .
augurarsi che ...	wish, hope . . .
desiderare che ...	want . . .
impedire che ...	prevent . . .
insistere che ...	insist . . .
lasciare che ...	let . . .
ordinare che ...	order . . .
permettere che ...	permit, allow . . .
piacere che (mi piace etc.) ...	like . . .
preferire che ...	prefer . . .
proibire che ...	forbid, prohibit . . .
sperare che ...	hope . . .
suggerire che ...	suggest . . .
volere che ...	wish, want . . .

Ai miei genitori *non piace che* io *esca* ogni sera. *Preferiscono che stia* a casa almeno due o tre sere alla settimana. *Insistono* sempre *che io studi di* più perché, naturalmente, *vogliono che superi* a pieni voti gli esami di fine anno. *Si aspettano che vada* all'università.

My parents do not *like me going out* every evening. *They prefer me to stay* at home at least two or three evenings a week. *They* always *insist on my studying* more because, naturally, *they want me to pass* my final exams with flying colors / colours. *They are expecting me to go* to college.

• Of the verbs listed above, **impedire, ordinare, permettere, proibire, suggerire,** and **lasciare** may be used with the infinitive [➤8i(ii)C, 9e(ii)], even when the subject of the main verb and the infinitive would be different. In fact, this construction is *preferable* particularly when the object of the main verb is a pronoun.

I miei genitori non *proibiscono che io esca*.
but the preferred way of saying is
I miei genitori non *mi proibiscono di uscire*.

My parents *don't forbid me to go out.*

After **aspettarsi, augurarsi, desiderare, piacere, preferire, sperare,** and **volere,** the infinitive construction should be used only if the subject is the same in both halves of the sentence.

Mi piace *uscire*. Non voglio *stare* sempre a casa a studiare. Spero di *passare* gli esami ma non mi aspetto di *passar*li a pieni voti.	I like *to go out*. I don't want always *to be* at home studying. I hope *to pass* the exams, but I don't expect *to pass* them with flying colors / colours.

[For verbs that require a preposition before a following infinitive ➤8j.]

(ii) *Verb constructions expressing emotions such as pleasure, surprise, disbelief, disappointment, regret, anger, and fear, when followed by* ***che****:*

avere paura che ...	be afraid that . . .
dispiacere (mi dispiace, etc.) che ...	be sorry, regret that . . .
essere arrabbiato che ...	be annoyed that . . .
essere contento / felice che ...	be pleased / happy that . . .
essere deluso che ...	be disappointed that . . .
essere infelice / scontento che ...	be unhappy / displeased that . . .
essere sorpreso / stupito che ...	be surprised that . . .
essere spiacente che ...	be sorry that . . .
essere triste che ...	be sad that . . .
meravigliarsi che ...	be amazed that . . .
rincrescere che ...	regret that . . .
stupirsi che ...	be surprised that . . .
temere che ...	fear that . . .

***Sono contento che* i tuoi esami *siano andati* bene. *Mi meraviglio*, però, *che tu sia riuscito* a superarli con dei voti così alti dato che uscivi quasi ogni sera.**	*I am happy that* your exams *went* well. *I am amazed*, however, *that you managed* to pass them with such high marks given that you went out almost every evening.

As with many of the verbs in these lists, if the subject is the same in both halves of the sentence, an infinitive construction is preferred to the subjunctive:

Sono molto contento *di aver superato* tutti i miei esami.	I am very pleased *that I have passed* all my exams.

Siamo spiacenti *di non poter* venire al ristorante per festeggiare la buona notizia.	We are sorry *(that) we are unable* to come to the restaurant to celebrate the good news.

(iii) *Impersonal constructions expressing necessity, possibility, probability, importance, and urgency, when followed by **che**:*

accade che ...	it happens that . . .
basta che ...	it is enough that . . .
è bene che ...	it is a good thing that . . .
bisogna che ...	it is necessary that . . .
capita che ...	it happens that . . .
conviene che ...	it is better / advisable that . . .
è difficile che ...	it is difficult for / unlikely that . . .
è facile che ...	it is easy / likely that . . .
importa che ...	it matters / is important that . . .
è impossibile che ...	it is impossible that . . .
è improbabile che ...	it is unlikely that . . .
è inutile che ...	it's no use / pointless . . .
è male che ...	it is a bad thing that . . .
è meglio che ...	it is better that . . .
è naturale che ...	it is natural that . . .
è necessario che ...	it is necessary that . . .
occorre che ...	it is necessary that . . .
pare che ...	it seems that . . .
è peggio che ...	it is worse that . . .
è un peccato che ...	it is a pity that . . .
è possibile che ...	it is possible that . . .
è preferibile che ...	it is preferable that . . .
è probabile che ...	it is probable / likely that . . .
può darsi che ...	it may be that . . .
sembra che ...	it seems that . . .
è strano che...	it is strange / odd that . . .
succede che ...	it happens that . . .
è utile che ...	it is useful that . . .
vale (la pena) che ...	it is worth (the trouble) that . . .

***È meglio che* si *faccia* qualcosa al più presto possibile.**	*It is better that* we *do* something as quickly as possible.

***Bisogna che* il governo *prenda* questi provvedimenti per ridurre il tasso di inflazione.**	*It is necessary that* the government *take* these steps to reduce the rate of inflation.
***Sembra che* le cose *vadano* di male in peggio.**	*It seems that* things *are going* from bad to worse.

Many of these impersonal constructions will be followed by the infinitive in Italian if they are followed immediately by the infinitive in English.

Bisogna *prendere* questi provvedimenti.	It is necessary *to take* these steps.
È meglio *fare* qualcosa al più presto possibile.	It is better *to do* something as quickly as possible.
Mi sembra *di aver letto* un articolo sul giornale di ieri riguardo agli ultimi provvedimenti presi dal governo.	I seem *to have read* an article in yesterday's newspaper regarding the latest measures taken by the government.

(iv) *Verb constructions expressing personal opinion, doubt, uncertainty, denial:*

credere che ...	believe that . . .
(non) dire che ...	(not) say that . . .
dubitare che ...	doubt that/whether . . .
negare che ...	deny that . . .
pensare che ...	think that . . .
(non) sapere che ...	(not) know that . . .
ritenere che ...	consider, think that . . .

***Dubito che* questi provvedimenti *possano* risolvere l'attuale crisi economica.**	*I doubt whether* these measures *can* solve the present economic crisis.
Non *credo che* il governo *abbia fatto* abbastanza per rimediare alla situazione.	*I don't believe that* the government *has done* enough to remedy the situation.

Note that some of the above expressions are used negatively and that this contributes to the idea of doubt and uncertainty.

Positive statements of certainty take the indicative.

***So che* il governo non *ha fatto* abbastanza.**	*I know that* the government *has*n't *done* enough.

This also applies where plain statements of fact are made, such as **è vero/certo che ...** 'it's true/certain that . . .,' **sono sicuro che ...** 'I am sure that . . .,' without an emotional reaction or value judgment.

***È vero che* il governo non *ha fatto* abbastanza.**	*It is true that* the government *has*n't *done* enough.

(v) *The subjunctive is used in indirect questions introduced by* ***se, come, quando, quanto, perché****, and* ***dove****.*

Mi domando *perché* il governo non *abbia fatto* di più.	I wonder *why* the government *has*n't *done* more.
Non capisci forse *quanto sia* delicata l'attuale situazione.	Perhaps you don't understand *how* delicate the present situation *is.*

While it is more correct to use the subjunctive in indirect questions, there is a growing tendency to use the indicative in the spoken language.

Non capisco *perché* non *hanno fatto* qualcosa.	I don't understand *why* they *have*n't *done* something.

(vi) The subjunctive is used after **il fatto che** ... 'the fact that . . .' when its clause begins a sentence in which the main verb represents an emotional reaction or value judgment. Sometimes **il fatto** is omitted but the subjunctive is still used.

***Il fatto che ci sia* tanta disoccupazione è inaccettabile.** ***Che ci sia* tanta disoccupazione è inaccettabile.**	(*The fact*) *that there is* so much unemployment is unacceptable.

È un fatto che ... ('it is a fact that . . .') would not take a subjunctive because it is stating a *reality.*

È un fatto che *c'è* troppa disoccupazione.	It's a fact that *there is* too much unemployment.

16d The Subjunctive in Adverbial Clauses

The subjunctive is used in subordinate adverbial clauses when the action *was not a reality* at the time of the action of the main verb. Some subordinating conjunctions [▶5a(ii)] will always take the subjunctive; others do sometimes, depending on the 'reality' of the action they refer to.

(i) Clauses of time

The subjunctive is required after **prima che** 'before' and **finché non** 'until.'

Devo preparare la loro camera *prima che arrivino.* Però, non voglio buttare giù la pasta *finché non siano arrivati.*	I have to prepare their room *before they arrive.* However, I don't want to put the pasta on to cook *until they have arrived.*

The indicative is used after **finché** 'as long as' and also with other conjunctions and adverbial expressions of time [▶14a(vi)], such as:

appena	as soon as
dopo che	after
mentre	while
quando	when
una volta che	once

***Appena saranno arrivati,* preparerò da mangiare.**	*As soon as they have arrived,* I shall prepare the meal.

(ii) Clauses of purpose

The following conjunctions and phrases, all containing the basic idea 'in order that something shall happen,' need the subjunctive since the action is clearly not yet a reality, i.e., it has not yet happened.

affinché ...	so that, in order that . . .
in maniera che ...	so that . . .
in/di modo che ...	so that . . .
perché ...	so that, in order that . . .

Vi faccio tutti questi esempi *perché impariate* a usare correttamente il congiuntivo. — I am giving you all these examples *so that you learn* to use the subjunctive correctly.

Cerco di spiegare un po' alla volta *in modo che* tutto *sia* chiaro. — I am trying to explain a little at a time *so that* everything *is* clear.

When **in/di modo che** ... and **in maniera che** ... mean 'with the result that . . . ' (i.e., when the action has or had clearly happened), then they take the indicative and not the subjunctive.

Il professore ha spiegato un po' alla volta il congiuntivo *in modo che* la maggior parte degli studenti lo *sa* usare correttamente. — The teacher explained the subjunctive a bit at a time *with the result that (so that)* the majority of the students *can* use it correctly.

Note also that **perché** takes the indicative when it means 'because.'

La maggior parte degli studenti usa correttamente il congiuntivo *perché* il professore l'*ha spiegato* un po' alla volta. — The majority of the students use the subjunctive correctly *because* the teacher *explained* it a little at a time.

(iii) Clauses of concession

The subjunctive is used after the following conjunctions:

benché ...	although, even though, even if . . .
malgrado (che) ...	in spite of the fact that . . .
nonostante (che) ...	in spite of the fact that . . .
sebbene ...	although, even though, even if . . .
seppure ...	even if, even though . . .

These conjunctions normally refer to a hypothesis rather than an actual fact, hence the need for the subjunctive.

Che is usually omitted after **malgrado** and **nonostante.**

Benché sia **difficile, farò del mio meglio per spiegare l'uso del congiuntivo.**	*Although it is* difficult, I shall do my best to explain the use of the subjunctive.

The following expressions are always followed by the subjunctive because they always introduce a hypothesis:

ammettiamo che ...	let's assume that . . .
mettiamo che ...	let's suppose that . . .
poniamo che ...	let's suppose that . . .
supponiamo che ...	let's suppose that . . .

Ammettiamo che **il professore non** ***riesca*** **a spiegare tutto in una volta.**	*Let's assume that* the teacher *does*n't *manage* to explain everything in one try.

(iv) *Clauses of condition*

The subjunctive is always used after the following conjunctions:

a condizione che ...	on condition that, provided that . . .
a meno che (non) ...	unless . . .
a patto che ...	on condition that . . .
purché ...	provided that, on condition that . . .
salvo che (non) ...	unless, provided that . . .

A meno che non piova **preferisco partire di buon'ora.**	*Unless it is raining* I prefer to leave early.
Sono disposto ad andare con la mia macchina ***a condizione che paghiate*** **la benzina.**	I am willing to go in my car *on condition that you pay* for the gasoline / petrol.

(v) *Other conjunctions requiring the subjunctive*

caso mai ...	should, in the event that . . .
nel caso che ...	in the event that . . .
per paura che (non) ...	for fear that . . .
qualora ...	in case, if . . .
senza che ...	without . . .

***Caso mai faccia* brutto tempo domani, possiamo sempre fare qualcos'altro.**	*Should* the weather *be* bad tomorrow, we can always do something else.
Ho deciso di prendere la macchina *senza che* i miei genitori lo *sapessero.*	I decided to take the car *without* my parents *knowing.*

(vi) *Uses of the infinitive when the subjects are the same*

When the subjects of the main and subordinate verbs are the same, the following prepositional forms are used with the infinitive [➤10a(iv)]:

per	in order to	**prima di**	before + —ing
per paura di	for fear of + —ing	**senza**	without + —ing

***Prima di partire,* ascolterò il bollettino meteorologico alla radio.**	*Before leaving,* I shall listen to the weather report on the radio.
Ho deciso di prendere la macchina *senza dire* niente ai miei genitori.	I have decided to take the car *without saying* anything to my parents.

'I' is the subject of both 'leave' and 'listen' in the first example and 'decide' and 'say' in the second. It is natural in such cases to avoid the use of the subjunctive.

16e *The Subjunctive after Indefinite Pronouns and Adjectives*

The subjunctive is used in clauses introduced by the following indefinite pronouns and adjectives:

chiunque	whoever
comunque	however, no matter how
dovunque	wherever
qualunque	whichever
qualunque cosa	whatever
qualsiasi cosa	whatever

***Chiunque venga* con noi deve contribuire al costo della benzina.**	*Whoever comes* with us must contribute to the cost of the gasoline / petrol.

***Dovunque vogliate* andare sono disposto a guidare.**	*Wherever you want* to go, I am willing to drive.
***Qualunque* decisione *prendiate* sull'itinerario, fatemela sapere entro stasera.**	*Whatever* decision *you make* about the route, let me know it by this evening.
***Comunque decidano* i miei amici, io andrò lo stesso.**	*However* my friends *decide*, I shall go all the same.

None of the statements made after **chiunque, dovunque, qualunque,** and **comunque** is a reality and that is the reason for using the subjunctive.
Note that another way of expressing 'however' is **per quanto** followed by an adjective + verb:

***Per quanto brutto sia* il tempo domani, preferisco fare qualcosa che stare a casa.**	*However bad* the weather *may be* tomorrow, I prefer to do something than to stay at home.

Whether . . . or not

This type of construction also requires a subjunctive.

***Che piova o che faccia bello*, non mi importa.**	*Whether it's raining or nice* doesn't matter to me.

16f The Subjunctive in Relative Clauses [➤23m]

(i) The subjunctive after the indefinite antecedent

The subjunctive is used in relative clauses that imply 'anyone who . . . ,' 'anything that . . . '—i.e., when the antecedent [➤23m(i)] is not exactly defined. Compare the following examples:

La ditta vuole assumere *una segretaria che abbia* un'ottima conoscenza dell'inglese e dello spagnolo.	The firm wants to employ *a secretary who has* a very good knowledge of English and Spanish.

i.e., any secretary who meets that requirement, therefore the subordinate verb is in the subjunctive.

L'amministratore delegato della ditta ha già *una segretaria che parla* perfettamente queste due lingue.	The general manager of the firm already has *a secretary who speaks* these two languages perfectly.

This secretary is already employed by the firm and it is a known fact that she speaks these languages, therefore the verb is in the indicative.

Quando l'amministratore delegato va a Torino per motivi di affari, la sua segretaria gli deve sempre trovare *un albergo che sia* proprio in centro città.	When the general manager goes to Turin on business, his secretary always has to find him *a hotel that is* right in center / centre of the city.

i.e., any hotel that is centrally located: subjunctive.

Non gli piace *quell'albergo che si trova* a tre chilometri dall'aeroporto perché è troppo lontano dallo stabilimento che deve visitare.	He doesn't like *the hotel that is* three kilometers / kilometres from the airport because it's too far from the factory that he has to visit.

i.e., the (known) hotel that he stayed in before: indicative.

• Sometimes, especially when used with **cercare, volere,** and similar verbs, this construction also carries the idea of purpose [➤16d(ii)], and translates the English 'somebody to do something.'

Cerco *qualcuno che faccia* da interprete quando vengono i rappresentanti da Madrid.	I am looking for *someone to act* as interpreter when the representatives from Madrid come.

(ii) *The subjunctive after a negative antecedent*

The subjunctive is used in relative clauses that depend on a negative, such as **niente / nulla** 'nothing' or **nessuno** 'no one' / 'no.'

Non c'è *nessuno* in ufficio *che sappia* parlare spagnolo.	There is *no one* in the office *who can* speak Spanish.
Non c'è *nessuna probabilità che si possa* trovare un interprete prima di domani.	There is *no likelihood of being able* to find an interpreter before tomorrow.

(iii) The subjunctive after a superlative

The subjunctive is used in a relative clause following a superlative:

Questa è una delle mansioni segretariali *più esigenti che io abbia* mai *dovuto* compiere.	This is one of the *most demanding* secretarial tasks that *I have* ever *had to* carry out.

Note that the words **primo** 'first,' **ultimo** 'last,' **unico,** and **solo** 'only' are treated as superlatives for this purpose:

È *l'unica* persona in ufficio *che sia* in grado di compiere questa mansione.	She's *the only* person in the office *who is* able to carry out this task.

The use of the subjunctive after a superlative is not always strictly adhered to in contemporary *spoken* Italian.

The subjunctive is not required after 'the only . . . to . . . ' / 'the first . . . to.' In constructions of this type use **a** + the infinitive.

Era la *prima* segretaria *ad essere* assunta da questa ditta.	She was the *first* secretary to *be* hired by this firm.

Note the optional but often preferable use of **ad** before an infinitive that begins with a vowel.

16g The Subjunctive after a Comparative

The subjunctive is used in clauses following a comparative:

Questa segretaria è *più dotata di quanto pensassimo.*	This secretary is *more talented than we thought.*
È *più dotata che non sembri.*	She is *more talented than she seems.*

In the second type of construction **non** must precede the verb. It is also possible to express this type of comparison with **di quel che** + the indicative.

È *più dotata di quel che sembra.*	She is *more talented than she seems.*

16h The Subjunctive in Main Clauses

(i) As an imperative [➤15]

The subjunctive is used to convey the **Lei / Loro** forms of the imperative, i.e., the polite forms.

Si accomodino.	*Please take a seat.*
***Parli* più piano per cortesia.**	*Speak* more slowly, please.

(ii) To express a wish

***Che tu sia* sempre felice!**	*May you* always *be* happy!

A strong wish that something should or should not happen can be expressed in Italian by **magari** + the imperfect or pluperfect subjunctive — the imperfect perhaps suggesting that the likelihood of the wish being granted is very remote, and the pluperfect a regret that the wish hasn't been fulfilled.

***Magari fosse* possibile!**	*If only it were* possible!
***Magari fosse stato* possibile!**	*If only it had been* possible!

Note: **Magari** can also stand by itself to endorse a previous statement or question.

Sarebbe bello avere più tempo libero. *Magari!*	It would be nice to have more free time. *I should say so! / If only! / Of course!*
Ti piacerebbe avere più tempo libero? *Magari!*	Would you like to have more free time? *I should say so!*

16i The Sequence of Tenses with the Subjunctive

The most usual combinations of tenses are as follows:

(i) *Main clause* in present, imperative, future, or present perfect indicative — *subordinate clause* in present or present perfect subjunctive [➤18c].

***Spero* che tutto *vada* bene.**	*I hope* that everything *goes* well.
***Sono contento* che *abbiano deciso* di venire a trovarci.**	*I am pleased* that *they have decided* to come and see us.
***Spolvera* i mobili *prima che arrivino* gli ospiti!**	*Dust* the furniture *before* the guests *arrive*!
Non *penso* che *arrivino* oggi.	*I don't think* that *they are arriving* today.

It is possible to have a present tense in the main clause and the imperfect subjunctive in the subordinate clause if the sense requires it.

***Mi dispiace* che non *potessero* venire tutti quanti.**	*I am sorry* that everyone *could*n't come.

(ii) *Main clause* in imperfect, present perfect, past definite, pluperfect, present conditional, conditional perfect indicative — *subordinate clause* in imperfect or pluperfect subjunctive [➤18c].

***Pensavo* che *venissero* alla fine del mese.**	*I thought* that *they were coming* at the end of the month.
***Sarebbe* difficile che *cambiassero* i loro progetti.**	*It would be* difficult for them *to change* (= *that they change*) their plans.
Mi *sembrò* che *si fossero riferiti* alla data del loro arrivo nell'ultima lettera.	*It seemed* to me that *they had referred* to the date of their arrival in their last letter.

It is important to bear in mind that where the future or conditional is used in the subordinate clause in English, then the appropriate future or conditional tense can be used after many constructions in Italian, i.e., there is no need to use the subjunctive.

Spero che *arriveranno* fra poco.	I hope that *they will arrive* soon. (future indicative)
or	
Spero che *arrivino* fra poco.	I hope that *they will arrive* soon. (present subjunctive).
Speravo che *sarebbero venuti* alla fine del mese.	I was hoping that *they would come* at the end of the month. (conditional perfect)
or	
Speravo che *venissero* alla fine del mese.	I was hoping that *they would come* at the end of the month. (imperfect subjunctive)

Note that the past conditional is used in Italian when the verb in the main clause is a past tense [➤14e(iv)].

16j 'If' Clauses

[See also paragraph 14d on the present conditional and 14e on the conditional perfect.]

Whether the subjunctive is used or not in the 'if' clause after **se** depends on the type of condition: is it open, remote, fulfilled, or unfulfilled? The following are the most common structures.

(i) Open condition

The condition is entirely open, it may or may not be fulfilled: **se** is followed by the present or future *indicative* [➤18c] (*never* the present subjunctive); and the main verb will usually be in the present, imperative, or future [➤18c], just as in English.

Se non *arrivano/arriveranno* fra poco, *dovrò* uscire.	If *they don't arrive* soon, *I shall have* to go out.
Se non *vengono* prima dell'una, *possiamo* mangiare.	If *they don't come* before one o'clock, *we can* eat.

It is also possible to use the present perfect tense after **se** to convey this idea of an open condition.

Se non *sono arrivati* prima dell'una, possiamo mangiare.	If *they have* not *arrived* before one o'clock, we can eat. (i.e., they may or may not have arrived before one o'clock)

(ii) *Remote condition*

The condition is remote or *contrary to fact*: **se** is followed by the imperfect subjunctive [➤18c(vii)], and the main clause is in the present conditional [➤18c(iv)].

Se *arrivassero* prima dell'una, *potremmo* mangiare tutti insieme.	If *they arrived (were to arrive)* before one o'clock, *we could* eat all together. (i.e., they are unlikely to arrive before one)

(iii) *Unfulfilled condition*

The condition is unfulfilled, *contrary to fact*: **se** is followed by the pluperfect subjunctive [➤16b, 19], and the main clause is in the conditional perfect [➤14e].

Se *fossero arrivati* prima dell'una, *avremmo potuto* mangiare tutti insieme.	If *they had arrived* before one o'clock, *we could have* eaten all together. (but they didn't arrive before one, so we couldn't all eat together — *condition unfulfilled*)

It is possibile to have a present conditional in the main clause if the situation requires it.

Se *fossero arrivati* in orario, non *sarei* così preoccupato ora.	If *they had arrived* on time. *I would* not *be* so worried now.

Note: It is fairly common, particularly in spoken Italian, to replace the pluperfect subjunctive after **se** and the conditional perfect in the main clause with the imperfect indicative in both clauses.

Se *arrivavano* prima dell'una, *potevamo* mangiare tutti insieme.	If *they had arrived* before one o'clock, *we could* all *have* eaten together.

(iv) *Fulfilled condition*

The condition can be considered as fulfilled if the action / event has taken place. In these cases, the most suitable tense of the indicative is used after **se.**

Se non *sono arrivati*, è perché c'è molto traffico sull'autostrada.	If *they have*n't *arrived*, it's because there is a lot of traffic on the highway / motorway.

(v) *What if . . . ?*

'What if . . . ?' is expressed by **e se ...** + present *indicative*, imperfect or pluperfect *subjunctive* as in the following examples:

E se* non *vengono?	*What if they do*n't *come*?
E se* non *venissero?	*What if they were*n't to *come*?
***E se* non *fossero venuti*?**	*What if they had*n't *come*?

(vi) *As if . . .*

'As if . . . ' is expressed by **come se ...** with the imperfect or pluperfect subjunctive.

Parli *come se* non *venissero.*	You are talking *as if they were*n't *coming.*
Parli *come se fosse successo* qualcosa.	You are talking *as if* something *had happened.*

17 Things Done to You: The Passive

17a What Does the Passive Express?

Receivers and doers of action

In the passive, the subject of the verb is the receiver of the action of the verb, rather than the doer. Compare these two examples:

Il meccanico *ha riparato* la macchina.	The mechanic *has repaired* the car. (active)
but	
La macchina *è stata riparata* dal meccanico.	The car *has been repaired* by the mechanic. (passive)

In the passive, the *direct object* (**la macchina**) of the transitive verb becomes the subject. That is why it is only transitive verbs that can be used in the passive [▶8a(i), 8d]. All the same, the passive is not just another way of saying the same thing as the active form. It emphasizes different things, especially what happens to the subject. The passive construction also enables us to omit the doer of the action because it is not necessarily important to know who (or what) did it.

La macchina è stata riparata.	The car has been repaired.

17b Formation of the Passive

The passive is formed with the appropriate tense of **essere** + the past participle. The past participle must agree with the subject. This rule applies also when two past participles are used.

La portiera della macchina è *stata ammaccata*, ma *sarà riparata* fra un paio di settimane.	The car door *has been dented*, but *it will be repaired* within a couple of weeks.

17c Expressing the Agent or Instrument

The person or thing the action is done *by* is called the *agent* or *instrument*, respectively. These would have been the subject of the transitive verb. In Italian both the agent and the instrument are preceded by **da**, meaning 'by.'

La portiera della macchina sarà riparata *da un meccanico.*	The car door will be repaired *by a mechanic.*
La portiera è stata ammaccata *da una motocicletta.*	The car door has been dented *by a motorcycle.*

17d Verbs Other than Essere to Express the Passive

(i) Venire

Venire can be used in place of **essere** but *only* in simple tenses [▶11b]. Although **venire** underlines the *carrying out* of the action whereas **essere** puts emphasis on the *state*, the difference in meaning is often minimal.

La macchina *viene* riparata.	The car *is being* repaired.

(ii) Andare

Andare can replace **essere** with verbs such as **perdere** 'lose,' **disperdere** 'lose,' 'waste,' **sprecare** 'waste.'

La mia polizza d'assicurazione *è andata persa.*	My insurance policy *has been lost.*

Andare can also be used, in the simple tenses only, to convey the meaning of *obligation.*

La riparazione *va fatta* entro la fine di questa settimana.	The repair *must be done* by the end of this week.
La fattura *andrà inviata* alla compagnia di assicurazioni.	The bill *will have to be sent* to the insurance company.

In this type of structure **andare** is taking the place of the relevant tense of **dovere** + **essere**.

La riparazione *deve essere* fatta ...	The repair must be done. . . .
La fattura *dovrà essere* inviata ...	The bill will have to be sent. . . .

(iii) *Restare* and *rimanere*

Restare and **rimanere** can replace **essere** when the following past participle describes a state, such as **sconvolto** 'upset,' **deluso** 'disappointed,' **stupito** 'amazed,' **chiuso** 'closed,' **aperto** 'open.'

In seguito all'incidente stradale *sono rimasto* molto depresso.	Following the road accident, *I was* very depressed.
Questa officina *resterà* chiusa per le prime due settimane di agosto.	This garage / auto repair shop *will remain* closed for the first two weeks of August.

As in English, the modal verbs [>9] do *not* have a passive form. The accompanying infinitive must therefore be put into the passive.

La compagnia di assicurazioni *deve* pagare la fattura.	The insurance company *must* pay the bill. (active)
La fattura deve *essere pagata* dalla compagnia di assicurazioni.	The bill must *be paid* by the insurance company. (passive)

17e Alternatives to Passive Constructions

The passive is used far more widely in Italian in the written language—newspaper reporting, for example—than it is in the spoken language, where the constructions outlined below tend to be preferred.

(i) The *si passivante*

A widely used construction in Italian is the pronoun **si**—known as the **si passivante**—with the third person singular or plural of the verb. The verb after **si** will be in the *active* form. In this type of construction **da** cannot be used to introduce an agent or instrument, i.e., you cannot express who or what the action is done by.

Dove *si faranno* le riparazioni?	Where *will* the repairs *be done*?
Non *si fa* la carrozzeria in questa autorimessa.	The bodywork *is* not *done* in this garage / auto repair shop.

(ii) *The impersonal* ***si***

The impersonal **si,** with the third person singular of the verb, performs the same general function in Italian as the English 'one' and can, therefore, be expressed in a variety of ways, such as 'we,' 'you,' 'they,' 'people.'

Non *si* sa mai quello che succederà.	*You* never know what will happen.
Cosa *si* fa adesso senza la macchina?	What do *we* do now without the car?

- **Si** is used in a range of impersonal expressions [▶8g]. It is an extremely useful way of avoiding an English passive construction.

si crede	it is believed
si dice	it is said
si pensa	it is thought
si prega	it is requested, you are asked
si prevede	it is envisaged
si può	one may
si sa	it is known
si spera	it is hoped

***Si prevede* che finiranno il più del lavoro entro la fine di questa settimana.**	*It is envisaged* that they will finish most of the work by the end of this week.

Great care has to be taken when the verb following **si** has a *plural direct object*. In this case, the **si passivante** [▶17e(i) above] must be used, and the verb agrees with the following plural.

Dove *si comprano i pezzi di ricambio?*	Where *do you buy spare parts?*

17f Passive Constructions: Limitations of Use in Italian

Passive constructions can be used in Italian *only* where the verb in the active form would take a *direct object*. In the passive, the direct object of the transitive verb becomes the subject [➤17a above].

It is important to remember, therefore, that English constructions such as 'I was given . . . ,' 'I was taught . . . ,' 'I was told . . . ,' cannot be translated literally into Italian, since each of the corresponding verbs in Italian — **dare, insegnare,** and **dire** — takes an *indirect* object [➤8e(i)]. It is possible therefore to translate a sentence such as 'I was given a book' in the following ways:

Mi è stato dato un libro.	A book has been given to me.
or	
Mi hanno dato un libro.	They gave me a book.

The second type of construction is the one that Italians are more likely to use.

Types of Italian Verb

18a Predictability: Conjugating a Verb

The whole set of a verb's stems and endings is known as its *conjugation.* The various parts of this set are predictable at several levels.

(i) *Regular verbs*

Regular verbs are verbs for which you can predict any part of any tense from the spelling of the infinitive [➤ 10a] plus of course a knowledge of the rules! In Italian, there are three conjugations of regular verbs, each with a distinct infinitive ending:

parlare	speak	(first conjugation)
vendere	sell	(second conjugation)
dormire	sleep	(third conjugation)

By far the majority of Italian verbs are of the **-are** type. Moreover, virtually all newly coined verbs are automatically **-are** verbs; for example, **fotocopiare** 'photocopy.'

(ii) *Irregular verbs*

Verbs in which some parts cannot be predicted in this way are known as *irregular.* Some of the most frequently used verbs in Italian are irregular. [For tables of irregular verbs ➤ 19g, 19h; for a more extensive treatment ➤ Berlitz *Italian Verb Handbook.*] Some irregular verbs form groups; so if you know one, you can predict the forms of any of the others. For example, **togliere** 'remove,' **cogliere** 'pick,' 'gather,' and **sciogliere** 'dissolve' all behave in the same way [➤ 19h].

(iii) *Compound verbs*

A compound verb is a verb where a prefix is added to the *base* verb. With very few exceptions, compound verbs [➤ 18e] conjugate in the same way as their base verb. So, for example, **contenere** 'contain,' **mantenere** 'maintains,' and **sostenere** 'support' all follow the model of **tenere** 'hold.'

18b Major Groups of Verbs: How Are They Conjugated?

The three major conjugations

In the formation of tenses in Italian, there are many features that are common to all conjugations, and to both regular and irregular verbs. These will be evident from the descriptions of the rules for the formation of each tense. Frequent reference will be made to the *stem* of the infinitive. For the three regular conjugations, this is obtained by removing the **-are, -ere,** or **-ire** ending from the infinitive:

Infinitive	*Stem*
parlare	**parl-**
vendere	**vend-**
dormire	**dorm-**

There are two types of verbs that belong to the second conjugation; verbs like **leggere,** where the stress falls on the third-to-last syllable, and verbs like **vedere,** where the stress falls on the penultimate syllable. Verbs belonging to the third conjugation also fall into two categories; those that follow the **dormire** model, and a substantial number of others that insert **-isc-** between the stem and the ending in the **io, tu, lui / lei**, and **loro** forms of the present indicative and present subjunctive and the **tu, Lei,** and **Loro** forms of the imperative. An example of this type of verb is **capire** [➤19f].

18c Formation of Tenses

In all verbs there are some tenses whose stems and endings can be predicted if you know one of the other parts of the verb. Parts that cannot be predicted in this way have to be learned; but once these principal parts are known, it is usually possible to predict other parts.

It is helpful to know how to get the stem onto which the endings for each tense are added, and any spelling adjustments that may need to be made. The following sections give a breakdown of the stem endings for each tense and any pitfalls to watch out for.

The term *indicative* is used to describe the 'ordinary' tenses, as opposed to the *subjunctive* forms [➤16].

The model regular verbs used in chapters 18 and 19 are **parlare** 'speak,' **vendere** 'sell,' and **dormire** 'sleep.'

(i) Present indicative [➤12a]

Regular forms of the present indicative are produced by adding the following endings to the stem of the infinitive:

parl(are)	**-o**	**-i**	**-a**	**-iamo**	**-ate**	**-ano**
vend(ere)	**-o**	**-i**	**-e**	**-iamo**	**-ete**	**-ono**
dorm(ire)	**-o**	**-i**	**-e**	**-iamo**	**-ite**	**-ono**

[For subject pronouns **io** 'I,' **tu** 'you,' and so forth ➤ 23b(i).]

Remember that verbs like **capire** insert **-isc-** between the stem and the endings for the first three persons of the singular and the third person plural. The endings are the same as for **dormire**.

It is worth noting that the endings for the first and second person singular and the first person plural are identical for the three conjugations. The second person plural retains the characteristic vowel of the infinitive ending; **-a, -e, -i**.

Attention needs to be paid to the following groups of verbs that undergo modifications or spelling changes, usually in order to maintain the same pronunciation.

(A) First conjugation verbs

- Verbs whose stem ends in **-g** or **-c**—for example, **pagare** 'pay' and **cercare** 'look for'—have an **h** before the vowel **i**: **paghi, paghiamo, cerchi, cerchiamo**. (This same rule is applied when the following vowel is **e** [➤ 18c(iii) below].)

- Verbs in **-iare** have only one **-i** in the second person singular if the **-i** of **-iare** is unstressed for—example, **studi** (**studiare** 'study'), because the stress falls on the first syllable.

- Verbs in **-iare** have a double **i** in the second person singular if the **-i-** of the stem is stressed, for example **scii** (**sciare** 'ski').

(B) Second conjugation verbs

- Although verbs in **-gliere**—for example, **scegliere** 'to choose'—will be listed under irregular verbs, they do not have that many irregular forms. In the present tense, the consonants **-gl-** are reversed in the first person singular and third person plural, **scelgo** and **scelgono,** but the endings are those for regular second conjugation verbs. As the stress does not fall on the final **-i** of the stem, the second person singular of this verb, and others like it, has only one **-i**: **scegli**.

- Verbs ending in **-durre**—such as **produrre** 'produce,' **tradurre** 'translate,' **ridurre** 'reduce,' are straightforward once the first person singular is known. For example, **produrre** changes to **produco**, and the endings are then the same as those of any other regular second conjugation verb.

- Similarly, verbs like **trarre** 'pull,' 'draw,' have a pattern that once acquired, can be applied to other verbs based on it. To form the stem remove **-rre**. The endings are those for regular second conjugation verbs. The first person singular and third person plural have a **-gg-** between the stem and the ending, i.e., **traggo, traggono**.

(ii) *Present subjunctive [➤16]*

The present subjunctive of regular verbs is formed by adding the following endings to the stem of the infinitive:

parl(are)	**-i**	**-i**	**-i**	**-iamo**	**-iate**	**-ino**
vend(ere)	**-a**	**-a**	**-a**	**-iamo**	**-iate**	**-ano**
dorm(ire)	**-a**	**-a**	**-a**	**-iamo**	**-iate**	**-ano**

Verbs of the **capire** type have the same endings as **dormire,** and the formation is the same as for the present indicative.

As you can see, the endings of the singular are the same, **-i** for the first conjugation and **-a** for the second and third conjugations. The endings of the first and second persons plural are identical for all three conjugations. The third person plural retains the characteristic vowel of the singular form.

As the first three persons of the present subjunctive are the same, the subject pronouns— **io, tu,** and so forth—are often used to avoid any ambiguity.

Refer to the explanations in 18c(i) above for rules governing the following:

- Verbs whose stem ends in **-c** or **-g**
- Verbs in **-iare** with unstressed **i**
- Verbs ending in **-iare** with stressed **i**
- Verbs ending in **-durre**
- Verbs based on **trarre**

(iii) *Future [➤14a]*

The stem of the future tense of regular verbs is obtained by removing the final **-e** of the infinitive. The characteristic vowel **-a-** of first conjugation verbs changes to **-e-**. Therefore, the stems, are:

parler- **vender-** **dormir-**

The future endings are the same for both regular and irregular verbs.

Note the grave accent on the first and third person singular, indicating that the ending is stressed.

-ò	-ai	-à	-emo	-ete	-anno

Attention needs to be paid to the following groups of verbs that undergo modifications or spelling changes:

(A) Verbs ending in **-care** and **-gare** will have an **h** after the **c** or **g** throughout the future tense to retain the hard sound, for example:

cercare 'look for' → **cerc*h*erò, cerc*h*erai,** etc.
pagare 'pay for' → **pag*h*erò, pag*h*erai,** etc.

(B) Verbs ending in **-ciare, -giare,** and **-sciare** drop the **i** throughout the future tense:

cominciare 'begin' → **comincerò, comincerai,** etc.
viaggiare 'travel' → **viaggerò, viaggerai,** etc.
lasciare 'leave, let' → **lascerò, lascerai,** etc.

(C) Some verbs, and also their compounds [➤18e], have contracted stems—i.e., they lose the characteristic vowel of the infinitive ending.

andare	**andrò**	go
avere	**avrò**	have
cadere	**cadrò**	fall
dovere	**dovrò**	have to, must
potere	**potrò**	be able
sapere	**saprò**	know
vedere	**vedrò**	see
vivere	**vivrò**	live

(D) Some verbs, and also their compounds, modify their spelling, so that the stem has a double **r**:

bere	**berrò**	drink
parere	**parrò**	seem
rimanere	**rimarrò**	remain
tenere	**terrò**	hold, keep
valere	**varrò**	be worth
venire	**verrò**	come
volere	**vorrò**	want

(E) A few two-syllable verbs in **-are** retain the vowel of the infinitive ending:

dare	**darò**	give
fare	**farò**	do, make
stare	**starò**	be, stay, remain

(iv) *Conditional [▶ 14d]*

The stem of the conditional is formed in exactly the same way as the future [▶ 18c(iii)]. The present conditional endings are:

-ei **-esti** **-ebbe** **-emmo** **-este** **-ebbero**

Note: Any modifications to the future stem referred to in 18c(iii) above will also apply to the conditional.

⚠ Do not confuse the first person plural ending of the future tense **-emo** with that of the conditional **-emmo.**

(v) *Imperfect indicative [▶ 13b]*

To obtain the stem remove the infinitive ending. The imperfect indicative endings are as follows:

-are verbs
-avo **-avi** **-ava** **-avamo** **-avate** **-avano**

-ere verbs
-evo **-evi** **-eva** **-evamo** **-evate** **-evano**

-ire verbs
-ivo **-ivi** **-iva** **-ivamo** **-ivate** **-ivano**

Thus the first person singular of each of the model verbs is: **parlavo, vendevo, dormivo**.

⚠ **Essere** is the only verb in this tense that has a completely irregular form:

ero **eri** **era** **eravamo** **eravate** **erano**

Note also the following:

bere	**bevevo**	drink
dire	**dicevo**	say, tell
fare	**facevo**	do, make

Verbs ending in **-durre**:

produrre	**producevo**	produce
tradurre	**traducevo**	translate

Verbs ending in **-arre**:

attrarre	**attraevo**	attract
distrarre	**distraevo**	distract

(vi) Past definite [>13c]

To obtain the stem remove the infinitive ending. The past definite endings are as follows:

-are verbs

-ai	**-asti**	**-ò**	**-ammo**	**-aste**	**-arono**

-ere verbs

-ei	**-esti**	**-é**	**-emmo**	**-este**	**-erono**
(-etti)		**(-ette)**			**(-ettero)**

-ire verbs

-ii	**-isti**	**-ì**	**-immo**	**-iste**	**-irono**

Note: • **-ere** verbs have an alternative form for the first and third person singular and the third person plural. It is acceptable to use either form.

As a general rule, verbs whose stem ends in **t** — for example, **battere** (**batt-**) 'beat' — do not have this alternative form.

• With the exception of the third person singular of **-are** verbs, which have **-o** instead of **-a**, the past definite endings are identical but for the characteristic vowel of the infinitive.

• The endings of the third person singular are stressed: **-ò, -é, -ì.**

• Although there are a considerable number of irregular verbs, it is worth noting that *they all follow a pattern*, for example:

accendere 'switch,' 'turn on,' 'light'

accesi	**accendesti**	**accese**
accendemmo	**accendeste**	**accesero**

The first and third person singular and the third person plural are the irregular forms. However, once you know the first person, then you can form the other two by replacing **-i** with **-e** or **-ero**, respectively. The second person singular and the first and second person plural are formed from the stem of the verb. This guideline can be applied to most irregular verbs. For common irregular verbs that do not conform to this pattern, consult the Verb Tables [>19g, 19h].

Unlike the regular conjugations, irregular verbs are not stressed on the third person singular.

(vii) Imperfect subjunctive [>16]

To obtain the stem remove the ending of the infinitive. The only difference in the endings of the imperfect subjunctive is that each conjugation retains the characteristic vowel of the infinitive. The endings are:

-are verbs

-assi	**-assi**	**-asse**	**-assimo**	**-aste**	**-assero**

-ere verbs

-essi	**-essi**	**-esse**	**-essimo**	**-este**	**-essero**

-ire verbs

-issi	**-issi**	**-isse**	**-issimo**	**-iste**	**-issero**

Note the following group of verbs. Some have stem changes, others use **-ere** endings when you might expect those of the **-are** group.

bere	**bevessi**	drink
dare	**dessi**	give
dire	**dicessi**	say, tell
fare	**facessi**	do, make
stare	**stessi**	be, stay, remain

Note also verbs ending in **-durre** and **-arre**

produrre	**producessi**	produce
trarre	**traessi**	pull, draw

(viii) *Formation of compound tenses*

The following compound tenses are formed with the auxiliary verb **avere** 'have' or **essere** 'be' + the past participle [➤10f(i)]:

Indicative
- present perfect [➤13a]
- pluperfect [➤13d]
- past anterior [➤13e]
- future perfect [➤14b]
- conditional perfect [➤14e]

Subjunctive
- present perfect and pluperfect [➤16]

[For information on which verbs take **avere** or **essere** ➤ 11c(i) – 11c(ii).]

18d *Formation of Nonfinite Parts*

Formation of the imperative ➤15b.
Formation of the gerund ➤10d(i).

Past participle [➤10f(i)]

To form the past participle remove the infinitive ending and replace it with **-ato** (**-are** verbs), **-uto** (**-ere** verbs), or **-ito** (**-ire** verbs).

parlato	**venduto**	**dormito**

Many past participles are irregular. The following are a few of the most common:

assistere	**assistito**	attend, be present at
chiudere	**chiuso**	close
correggere	**corretto**	correct
discutere	**discusso**	discuss
distruggere	**distrutto**	destroy
dividere	**diviso**	divide
muovere	**mosso**	move
offrire	**offerto**	offer
prendere	**preso**	take
ridere	**riso**	laugh
risolvere	**risolto**	solve
rispondere	**risposto**	reply
scendere	**sceso**	go down, get out of
sciogliere	**sciolto**	dissolve
spendere	**speso**	spend
succedere	**successo**	happen
tradurre	**tradotto**	translate
uccidere	**ucciso**	kill

[For other irregular past participles ➤19h.]

Any compound forms of the above examples will form their past participles in the same way.

18e Compound Verbs

(i) Prefixes: ***s-, ri-, mal-***

A prefix can be added to any base verb as long as it makes sense.

s- often serves to create the opposite meaning:

coprire	cover	**scoprire**	uncover, discover
gelare	freeze	**sgelare**	thaw

ri- can be used like the English 're-,' i.e., to indicate repetition:

cominciare	begin	**ricominciare**	begin again
fare	do	**rifare**	redo
leggere	read	**rileggere**	reread

mal- gives the meaning of *bad, badly,* or *evil.*

intendere	understand	**malintendere**	misunderstand
trattare	treat	**maltrattare**	treat badly

(ii) -porre, -tenere, -venire

A large number of verbs are derived from these three base verbs.

Porre 'put' has derivatives that often correspond to English verbs ending in '-pose.'

comporre	compose	**posporre**	postpone
decomporre	decompose	**presupporre**	presuppose
disporre	dispose, arrange	**proporre**	propose
imporre	impose	**supporre**	suppose
opporre	oppose		

Tenere 'hold' has derivatives that correspond to English verbs ending in '-tain':

contenere	contain	**ritenere**	retain
detenere	detain, stop	**sostenere**	sustain
mantenere	maintain	**trattenere**	hold back; hold up; detain

Venire 'come' has a number of derivatives:

avvenire	happen	**provenire**	come from, originate from
convenire	agree, suit	**sopravvenire**	arrive, happen (suddenly, unexpectedly)
divenire	become	**svenire**	faint
intervenire	intervene		

(iii) -durre

Sometimes the base verb does not exist. For example, there is no verb **durre** yet there are several verbs based on this ending, corresponding to the English verbs ending in '-duce' or '-duct.'

condurre	conduct, lead, drive	**produrre**	produce
dedurre	deduce	**ridurre**	reduce
indurre	induce, induct	**riprodurre**	reproduce
introdurre	introduce, insert	**sedurre**	seduce

Verb Tables

19a Regular Verbs

The three conjugations (or groups) of Italian verbs that follow a regular pattern have infinitives ending in **-are, -ere,** and **-ire**. The model verbs we shall use for each group are:

parlare	speak
vendere	sell
dormire	sleep

Unless otherwise stated, the *stem* (i.e., the part of the verb you add the endings to) is what you are left with when you remove the **-are, -ere,** or **-ire** of the infinitive.

19b Conjugation of Regular -are Verbs

Present	*Present perfect*
parlo	ho parlato
parli	hai parlato
parla	ha parlato
parliamo	abbiamo parlato
parlate	avete parlato
parlano	hanno parlato

Imperfect	*Pluperfect*
parlavo	avevo parlato
parlavi	avevi parlato
parlava	aveva parlato
parlavamo	avevamo parlato
parlavate	avevate parlato
parlavano	avevano parlato

Future	*Future perfect*
parlerò	avrò parlato
parlerai	avrai parlato
parlerà	avrà parlato
parleremo	avremo parlato
parlerete	avrete parlato
parleranno	avranno parlato

Present conditional
parlerei
parleresti
parlerebbe
parleremmo
parlereste
parlerebbero

Conditional perfect
avrei parlato
avresti parlato
avrebbe parlato
avremmo parlato
avreste parlato
avrebbero parlato

Past definite
parlai
parlasti
parlò
parlammo
parlaste
parlarono

Past anterior
ebbi parlato
avesti parlato
ebbe parlato
avemmo parlato
aveste parlato
ebbero parlato

Present subjunctive
parli
parli
parli
parliamo
parliate
parlino

Perfect subjunctive
abbia parlato
abbia parlato
abbia parlato
abbiamo parlato
abbiate parlato
abbiano parlato

Imperfect subjunctive
parlassi
parlassi
parlasse
parlassimo
parlaste
parlassero

Pluperfect subjunctive
avessi parlato
avessi parlato
avesse parlato
avessimo parlato
aveste parlato
avessero parlato

Imperative
—
parla
parli
parliamo
parlate
parlino

Present participle
parlante

Past participle
parlato

Present gerund
parlando

Past gerund
avendo parlato

19c *Verbs Ending in* -are *with Minor Changes*

(i) Verbs with infinitives in ***-care*** *and* ***-gare***

Whenever the **c** or **g** of the stem of verbs of this type is followed by **i** or **e**, an **h** must be put in to retain the hard sound. Examples of this type are **cercare** 'look for' and **pagare** 'pay for.'

Present
cerco
cerc**h**i
cerca
cerc**h**iamo
cercate
cercano

Future
cerc**h**erò, etc.

Present Conditional
cerc**h**erei, etc.

The **h** will be retained throughout the future and conditional.

Present subjunctive
cerc**h**i
cerc**h**i
cerc**h**i
cerc**h**iamo
cerc**h**iate
cerc**h**ino

Imperative
—
cerca
cerc**h**i
cerc**h**iamo
cercate
cerc**h**ino

Pagare and other verbs ending in **-gare** follow *exactly* the same pattern as **cercare**.

(ii) Verbs with infinitives in ***-iare***

Verbs ending in **-iare** that have an unstressed **i** — for example, **studiare** 'study' — have only *one* **i** in the forms referred to below, not the double **i** you might expect.

studi (second person singular, present tense)
studi, studi, studi (first three persons, present subjunctive)
studi (singular, polite form, imperative)

Verbs ending in **-iare** that have a stressed **i**—for example, **sciare** 'ski'—have a double **i** in all the above forms, i.e., ***scii.***

(iii) *Verbs in **-ciare, -giare,** and **-sciare***

Examples of verbs in this category are **cominciare** 'begin,' **viaggiare** 'travel,' and **lasciare** 'leave.'
These verbs will also have just one **i** in all the forms mentioned in 19c(ii) above. However, these same verbs drop the **i** of the stem throughout the future and present conditional.

Future
cominцerò, comincerai, etc.
viaggerò, viaggerai, etc.
lascerò, lascerai, etc.

Present conditional
comincerei, cominceresti, etc.
viaggerei, viaggeresti, etc.
lascerei, lasceresti, etc.

19d Conjugation of Regular **-ere** *Verbs*

Present
vendo
vendi
vende
vendiamo
vendete
vendono

Present perfect
ho venduto
hai venduto
ha venduto
abbiamo venduto
avete venduto
hanno venduto

Imperfect
vendevo
vendevi
vendeva
vendevamo
vendevate
vendevano

Pluperfect
avevo venduto
avevi venduto
aveva venduto
avevamo venduto
avevate venduto
avevano venduto

Future
venderò
venderai
venderà
venderemo
venderete
venderanno

Future perfect
avrò venduto
avrai venduto
avrà venduto
avremo venduto
avrete venduto
avranno venduto

Present conditional
venderei
venderesti
venderebbe
venderemmo
vendereste
venderebbero

Conditional perfect
avrei venduto
avresti venduto
avrebbe venduto
avremmo venduto
avreste venduto
avrebbero venduto

Past definite
vendei (vendetti)
vendesti
vendé (vendette)
vendemmo
vendeste
venderono (vendettero)

Past anterior
ebbi venduto
avesti venduto
ebbe venduto
avemmo venduto
aveste venduto
ebbero venduto

Present subjunctive
venda
venda
venda
vendiamo
vendiate
vendano

Perfect subjunctive
abbia venduto
abbia venduto
abbia venduto
abbiamo venduto
abbiate venduto
abbiano venduto

Imperfect subjunctive
vendessi
vendessi
vendesse
vendessimo
vendeste
vendessero

Pluperfect subjunctive
avessi venduto
avessi venduto
avesse venduto
avessimo venduto
aveste venduto
avessero venduto

Imperative

—
vendi
venda
vendiamo
vendete
vendano

Present participle
vendente

Past participle
venduto

Present gerund
vendendo

Past gerund
avendo venduto

19e Conjugation of regular -ire *verbs*

Present
dormo
dormi
dorme
dormiamo
dormite
dormono

Present perfect
ho dormito
hai dormito
ha dormito
abbiamo dormito
avete dormito
hanno dormito

Imperfect
dormivo
dormivi
dormiva
dormivamo
dormivate
dormivano

Pluperfect
avevo dormito
avevi dormito
aveva dormito
avevamo dormito
avevate dormito
avevano dormito

Future
dormirò
dormirai
dormirà
dormiremo
dormirete
dormiranno

Future perfect
avrò dormito
avrai dormito
avrà dormito
avremo dormito
avrete dormito
avranno dormito

Present conditional
dormirei
dormiresti
dormirebbe
dormiremmo
dormireste
dormirebbero

Conditional perfect
avrei dormito
avresti dormito
avrebbe dormito
avremmo dormito
avreste dormito
avrebbero dormito

Past definite
dormii
dormisti
dormì
dormimmo
dormiste
dormirono

Past anterior
ebbi dormito
avesti dormito
ebbe dormito
avemmo dormito
aveste dormito
ebbero dormito

Present subjunctive
dorma
dorma
dorma
dormiamo
dormiate
dormano

Perfect subjunctive
abbia dormito
abbia dormito
abbia dormito
abbiamo dormito
abbiate dormito
abbiano dormito

Imperfect subjunctive
dormissi
dormissi
dormisse
dormissimo
dormiste
dormissero

Pluperfect subjunctive
avessi dormito
avessi dormito
avesse dormito
avessimo dormito
aveste dormito
avessero dormito

Imperative
—
dormi
dorma
dormiamo
dormite
dormano

Present participle
dormiente (dormente)

Past participle
dormito

Present gerund
dormendo

Past gerund
avendo dormito

19f *Verbs That Have* -isc- *between the Stem and the Ending*

There are a considerable number of verbs that belong to the third conjugation—i.e., that end in **-ire**—that insert **-isc-** between the stem and the ending. This happens in the present indicative, the present subjunctive, and the imperative; and these will be written out completely, using **capire** 'understand' as the model. The other parts of the verb will not be listed since they are formed as in 19e above.

Present	*Present subjunctive*	*Imperative*
cap**isc**o	cap**isc**a	—
cap**isc**i	cap**isc**a	cap**isc**i
cap**isc**e	cap**isc**a	cap**isc**a
capiamo	capiamo	capiamo
capite	capiate	capite
cap**isc**ono	cap**isc**ano	cap**isc**ano

- Other verbs of this type are:

abolire	abolish
agire	act, behave
approfondire	deepen, examine closely
arricchire	enrich
arrossire	blush
chiarire	clarify
colorire	color/colour
colpire	hit, strike
condire	season (a dish)
contribuire	contribute
costruire	build
custodire	look after, guard
definire	define, make clear
demolire	demolish
digerire	digest
diminuire	decrease, reduce
distribuire	distribute
esaurire	exhaust, use up
esibire	exhibit, display
esordire	begin (one's career)
fallire	fail, go bankrupt
favorire	favor/favour, encourage
ferire	hurt, injure
finire	finish
fiorire	flower, blossom, flourish

garantire	guarantee
gradire	welcome, accept, like
guaire	whine, yelp
guarire	heal, cure
impadronirsi	take hold of, seize
impallidire	turn pale
impazzire	go mad
impedire	prevent, hinder
infastidire	annoy, bother
ingerire	swallow
inserire	insert, put, introduce (into)
istituire	found, set up
istruire	teach, instruct
marcire	go bad, rot, decay
munire	provide, equip
obbedire (ubbidire)	obey
patire	suffer, endure
preferire	prefer
proibire	prohibit
pulire	clean
punire	punish
rapire	kidnap
reagire	react
restituire	return, give back
riunire	assemble, get / put together
sbalordire	astonish, amaze
seppellire	bury
smarrire	lose, mislay
smentire	deny, prove wrong
sostituire	substitute, replace
sparire	disappear
spedire	send
stabilire	establish, fix
starnutire	sneeze
stupire	amaze, astonish
suggerire	suggest
svanire	disappear
tradire	betray
trasferire	transfer
trasgredire	transgress, violate, disobey
unire	unite, join, bring together
usufruire	benefit, profit

Note: Some **-ire** verbs can take either pattern with or without **-isc-**. The most common of these are:

applaudire	applaud
assorbire	absorb
inghiottire	swallow
mentire	lie
nutrire	nourish
tossire	cough

Scomparire 'disappear,' and **comparire** and **apparire** 'appear' can also follow the **capire** pattern, although the forms more commonly used are listed under the Irregular Verbs section [➤19h].

19g The Irregular Verbs Avere *and* Essere

(i) ***Avere*** *'have'*

Present	***Present perfect***
ho	ho avuto
hai	hai avuto
ha	ha avuto
abbiamo	abbiamo avuto
avete	avete avuto
hanno	hanno avuto

Imperfect	***Pluperfect***
avevo	avevo avuto
avevi	avevi avuto
aveva	aveva avuto
avevamo	avevamo avuto
avevate	avevate avuto
avevano	avevano avuto

Future	***Future perfect***
avrò	avrò avuto
avrai	avrai avuto
avrà	avrà avuto
avremo	avremo avuto
avrete	avrete avuto
avranno	avranno avuto

Present conditional	***Conditional perfect***
avrei	avrei avuto
avresti	avresti avuto
avrebbe	avrebbe avuto
avremmo	avremmo avuto
avreste	avreste avuto
avrebbero	avrebbero avuto

Past definite	***Past anterior***
ebbi	ebbi avuto
avesti	avesti avuto
ebbe	ebbe avuto
avemmo	avemmo avuto
aveste	aveste avuto
ebbero	ebbero avuto

Present subjunctive	***Perfect subjunctive***
abbia	abbia avuto
abbia	abbia avuto
abbia	abbia avuto
abbiamo	abbiamo avuto
abbiate	abbiate avuto
abbiano	abbiano avuto

Imperfect subjunctive	***Pluperfect subjunctive***
avessi	avessi avuto
avessi	avessi avuto
avesse	avesse avuto
avessimo	avessimo avuto
aveste	aveste avuto
avessero	avessero avuto

Imperative

—
abbi
abbia
abbiamo
abbiate
abbiano

Present participle	***Past participle***
avente	avuto

Present gerund	***Past gerund***
avendo	avendo avuto

(ii) **Essere** *'be'*

Present	***Present perfect***
sono	sono stato / a
sei	sei stato / a
è	è stato / a
siamo	siamo stati / e
siete	siete stati / e
sono	sono stati / e

Imperfect	***Pluperfect***
ero	ero stato / a
eri	eri stato / a
era	era stato / a
eravamo	eravamo stati / e
eravate	eravate stati / e
erano	erano stati / e

Future	***Future perfect***
sarò	sarò stato / a
sarai	sarai stato / a
sarà	sarà stato / a
saremo	saremo stati / e
sarete	sarete stati / e
saranno	saranno stati / e

Present conditional	***Conditional perfect***
sarei	sarei stato / a
saresti	saresti stato / a
sarebbe	sarebbe stato / a
saremmo	saremmo stati / e
sareste	sareste stati / e
sarebbero	sarebbero stati / e

Past definite	***Past anterior***
fui	fui stato / a
fosti	fosti stato / a
fu	fu stato / a
fummo	fummo stati / e
foste	foste stati / e
furono	furono stati / e

Present subjunctive	***Perfect subjunctive***
sia	sia stato / a
sia	sia stato / a
sia	sia stato / a
siamo	siamo stati / e
siate	siate stati / e
siano	siano stati / e

Imperfect subjunctive	***Pluperfect subjunctive***
fossi	fossi stato / a
fossi	fossi stato / a
fosse	fosse stato / a
fossimo	fossimo stati / e
foste	foste stati / e
fossero	fossero stati / e

Imperative

—
sii
sia
siamo
siate
siano

Present participle	***Past participle***
essente	stato / a / i / e

Present gerund	***Past gerund***
essendo	essendo stato / a / i / e

19h Other Irregular Verbs

The following are the most common irregular verbs in Italian. Only irregularly formed tenses are mentioned. In the future and present conditional, only the stem can be irregular — the same endings are always used. Any irregularity in the future will therefore apply to the conditional, so it is not listed separately. For the formation of the imperative and any commonly used irregular forms ➤15b.

accendere *switch, turn on, light*

Past definite
accesi, accendesti, accese, accendemmo, accendeste, accesero

Past participle
acceso

Also all verbs ending in **-endere**, such as:

apprendere	learn	**rendere**	give back, make
comprendere	understand, include	**scendere**	descend, get out of
difendere	defend	**sorprendere**	surprise
intendere	intend	**sospendere**	suspend, put off
offendere	offend	**spendere**	spend

accorgersi *notice, realize, become aware of*

Past definite
mi accorsi, ti accorgesti, si accorse, ci accorgemmo, vi accorgeste, si accorsero

Past participle
accorto

Also

porgere	hand, hold out	**sporgersi**	lean out

andare *go*

Present indicative
vado, vai, va, andiamo, andate, vanno

Present subjunctive
vada, vada, vada, andiamo, andiate, vadano

Future
andrò

apparire *appear*

Present indicative
appaio, appari, appare, appariamo, apparite, appaiono

Present subjunctive
appaia, appaia, appaia, appariamo, appariate, appaiano

Past definite
apparvi, apparisti, apparve, apparimmo, appariste, apparirono

Past participle
apparso

Also

comparire	appear	**scomparire**	disappear

---

aprire *open*

Past participle
aperto

Also

coprire	cover	**scoprire**	discover
offrire	offer	**soffrire**	suffer

---

assumere *employ, hire, assume*

Past definite
assunsi, assumesti, assunse, assumemmo, assumeste, assunsero

Past participle
assunto

Also
riassumere reemploy, rehire, reassume, summarize

---

bere *drink*

Present indicative
bevo, bevi, beve, beviamo, bevete, bevono

Present subjunctive
beva, beva, beva, beviamo, beviate, bevano

Future
berrò

Past definite
bevvi, bevesti, bevve, bevemmo, beveste, bevvero

Imperfect indicative
bevevo

Imperfect subjunctive
bevessi

Present participle
bevente

Past participle
bevuto

Gerund
bevendo

cadere *fall*

Future
cadrò

Past definite
caddi, cadesti, cadde, cademmo, cadeste, caddero

Also
accadere happen

chiedere *ask*

Past definite
chiesi, chiedesti, chiese, chiedemmo, chiedeste, chiesero

Past participle
chiesto

Also
richiedere request

cogliere *pick, gather*

Present indicative
colgo, cogli, coglie, cogliamo, cogliete, colgono

Present subjunctive
colga, colga, colga, cogliamo, cogliate, colgano

Past definite
colsi, cogliesti, colse, cogliemmo, coglieste, colsero

Past participle
colto

Also

accogliere	welcome	**sciogliere**	dissolve
raccogliere	gather, pick	**togliere**	remove

condurre *take, lead, conduct*

Present indicative
conduco, conduci, conduce, conduciamo, conducete, conducono

Present subjunctive
conduca, conduca, conduca, conduciamo, conduciate, conducano

Imperfect indicative
conducevo

Imperfect subjunctive
conducessi

Past definite
condussi, conducesti, condusse, conducemmo, conduceste, condussero

Present participle
conducente

Past participle
condotto

Gerund
conducendo

Also all verbs ending in **-durre**

---

conoscere *know, meet*

Past definite
conobbi, conoscesti, conobbe, conoscemmo, conosceste, conobbero

Past participle
conosciuto

Also
riconoscere recognize

---

correre *run*

Past definite
corsi, corresti, corse, corremmo, correste, corsero

Past participle
corso

Also any derivatives, such as

accorrere	run, rush	**ricorrere**	resort, turn to
percorrere	go through, travel	**soccorrere**	aid, assist
		trascorrere	spend (time)

---

dare *give*

Present indicative
do, dai, dà, diamo, date, dano

Present subjunctive
dia, dia, dia, diamo, diate, diano

Future
darò

Past definite
diedi, desti, diede, demmo, deste, diedero

Imperfect subjunctive
dessi, dessi, desse, dessimo, deste, dessero

---

decidere *decide*

Past definite
decisi, decidesti, decise, decidemmo, decideste, decisero

Past participle
deciso

Also

dividere	divide	**sorridere**	smile
ridere	laugh	**uccidere**	kill

---

dire *say, tell*

Present indicative
dico, dici, dice, diciamo, dite, dicono

Present subjunctive
dica, dica, dica, diciamo, diciate, dicano

Imperfect indicative
dicevo

Imperfect subjunctive
dicessi

Past definite
dissi, dicesti, disse, dicemmo, diceste, dissero

Present participle
dicente

Past participle
detto

Gerund
dicendo

Also

contraddire	contradict	**disdire**	cancel

dovere *have to, must, owe*

Present indicative
devo (debbo), devi, deve, dobbiamo, dovete, devono (debbono)

Present subjunctive
deva (debba), deva (debba), deva (debba), dobbiamo, dobbiate, devano (debbano)

Future
dovrò

---

fare *do, make*

Present indicative
faccio, fai, fa, facciamo, fate, fanno

Present subjunctive
faccia, faccia, faccia, facciamo, facciate, facciano

Future
farò

Imperfect indicative
facevo

Imperfect subjunctive
facessi

Past definite
feci, facesti, fece, facemmo, faceste, fecero

Present participle
facente

Past participle
fatto

Gerund
facendo

Also
soddisfare satisfy

---

giungere *arrive at, reach*

Past definite
giunsi, giungesti, giunse, giungemmo, giungeste, giunsero

Past participle
giunto

Also

aggiungere	add	**raggiungere**	reach, attain

---

leggere *read*

Past definite
lessi, leggesti, lesse, leggemmo, leggeste, lessero

Past participle
letto

Also
proteggere protect

---

mettere *put*

Past definite
misi, mettesti, mise, mettemmo, metteste, misero

Past participle
messo

Also any derivatives, such as

ammettere	admit	**promettere**	promise
commettere	commit	**smettere**	stop, cease
permettere	permit		

---

morire *die*

Present indicative
muoio, muori, muore, moriamo, morite, muoiono

Present subjunctive
muoia, muoia, muoia, moriamo, moriate, muoiano

Future
morirò (morrò)

Present participle
morente

Past participle
morto

Gerund
morendo

nascere *be born*

Past definite
nacqui, nascesti, nacque, nascemmo, nasceste, nacquero

Past participle
nato

nascondere *hide*

Past definite
nascosi, nascondesti, nascose, nascondemmo, nascondeste, nascosero

Past participle
nascosto

Also
rispondere reply

parere *seem*

Present indicative
paio, pari, pare, paiamo, parete, paiono

Present subjunctive
paia, paia, paia, paiamo, paiate, paiano

Future
parrò

Past definite
parvi, paresti, parve, paremmo, pareste, parvero

Present participle
parvente

Past participle
parso

Gerund
parendo

perdere *lose*

Past definite
persi, perdesti, perse, perdemmo, perdeste, persero

Past participle
perso (perduto)

persuadere *persuade*

Past definite
persuasi, persuadesti, persuase, persuademmo, persuadeste, persuasero

Past participle
persuaso

Also

evadere	escape	**invadere**	invade

piacere *please*

Present indicative
piaccio, piaci, piace, piacciamo, piacete, piacciono

Present subjunctive
piaccia, piaccia, piaccia, piacciamo, piacciate, piacciano

Past definite
piacqui, piacesti, piacque, piacemmo, piaceste, piacquero

Past participle
piaciuto

Also

dispiacere	be sorry	**tacere**	be silent
giacere	be situated, lie		

piangere *cry*

Past definite
piansi, piangesti, pianse, piangemmo, piangeste, piansero

Past participle
pianto

Also

rimpiangere	regret

porre *put*

Present indicative
pongo, poni, pone, poniamo, ponete, pongono

Present subjunctive
ponga, ponga, ponga, poniamo, poniate, pongano

Future
porrò

Imperfect indicative
ponevo

Imperfect subjunctive
ponessi

Past definite
posi, ponesti, pose, ponemmo, poneste, posero

Present participle
ponente

Past partciple
posto

Gerund
ponendo

Also all compounds [➤18e(ii)]

---

potere *be able to, can*

Present indicative
posso, puoi, può, possiamo, potete, possono

Present subjunctive
possa, possa, possa, possiamo, possiate, possano

Future
potrò

---

rimanere *remain, stay*

Present indicative
rimango, rimani, rimane, rimaniamo, rimanete, rimangono

Present subjunctive
rimanga, rimanga, rimanga, rimaniamo, rimaniate, rimangano

Future
rimarrò

Past definite
rimasi, rimanesti, rimase, rimanemmo, rimaneste, rimasero

Past participle
rimasto

rompere *break*

Past definite
ruppi, rompesti, ruppe, rompemmo, rompeste, ruppero

Past participle
rotto

---

salire *go up, get on board, get in (a vehicle)*

Present indicative
salgo, sali, sale, saliamo, salite, salgono

Present subjunctive
salga, salga, salga, saliamo, saliate, salgano

---

sapere *know, know how to*

Present indicative
so, sai, sa, sappiamo, sapete, sanno

Present subjunctive
sappia, sappia, sappia, sappiamo, sappiate, sappiano

Future
saprò

Past definite
seppi, sapesti, seppe, sapemmo, sapeste, seppero

Present participle
sapiente

---

scegliere *choose*

Present indicative
scelgo, scegli, sceglie, scegliamo, scegliete, scelgono

Present subjunctive
scelga, scelga, scelga, scegliamo, scegliate, scelgano

Past definite
scelsi, scegliesti, scelse, scegliemmo, sceglieste, scelsero

Past participle
scelto

scrivere *write*

Past definite
scrissi, scrivesti, scrisse, scrivemmo, scriveste, scrissero

Past participle
scritto

Also

descrivere	describe	**iscrivere**	enroll
friggere	fry	**sconfiggere**	defeat

scuotere *shake*

Past definite
scossi, scuotesti, scosse, scuotemmo, scuoteste, scossero

Past participle
scosso

Also

commuovere	move, affect (emotion)		
muovere	move	**promuovere**	promote

sedere *sit*

Present indicative
siedo, siedi, siede, sediamo, sedete, siedono

Present subjunctive
sieda, sieda, sieda, sediamo, sediate, siedano

Also
possedere possess

spingere *push*

Past definite
spinsi, spingesti, spinse, spingemmo, spingeste, spinsero

Past participle
spinto

Also

dipingere	paint	**fingere**	pretend
distinguere	distinguish	**tingere**	dye

stare *be, stay*

Present indicative
sto, stai, sta, stiamo, state, stanno

Present subjunctive
stia, stia, stia, stiamo, stiate, stiano

Future
starò

Past definite
stetti, stesti, stette, stemmo, steste, stettero

Imperfect subjunctive
stessi, stessi, stesse, stessimo, steste, stessero

---

stringere *clasp, grip, hold tight*

Past definite
strinsi, stringesti, strinse, stringemmo, stringeste, strinsero

Past participle
stretto

Also
costringere force, compel

---

tenere *hold*

Present indicative
tengo, tieni, tiene, teniamo, tenete, tengono

Present subjunctive
tenga, tenga, tenga, teniamo, teniate, tengano

Future
terrò

Past definite
tenni, tenesti, tenne, tenemmo, teneste, tennero

Also any compounds [➤18e(ii)]

trarre *draw, pull*

Present indicative
traggo, trai, trae, traiamo, traete, traggono

Present subjunctive
tragga, tragga, tragga, traiamo, traiate, traggano

Imperfect indicative
traevo

Imperfect subjunctive
traessi

Past definite
trassi, traesti, trasse, traemmo, traeste, trassero

Present participle
traente

Past participle
tratto

Gerund
traendo

Also any compounds

---

uscire *go out*

Present indicative
esco, esci, esce, usciamo, uscite, escono

Present subjunctive
esca, esca, esca, usciamo, usciate, escano

Also
riuscire manage, succeed

---

valere *be worth*

Present indicative
valgo, vali, vale, valiamo, valete, valgono

Present subjunctive
valga, valga, valga, valiamo, valiate, valgano

Future
varrò

Past definite
valsi, valesti, valse, valemmo, valeste, valsero

Past participle
valso

Also
prevalere prevail

---

vedere *see*

Future
vedrò

Past definite
vidi, vedesti, vide, vedemmo, vedeste, videro

Past participle
visto

Also
prevedere foresee, arrange

---

venire *come*

Present indicative
vengo, vieni, viene, veniamo, venite, vengono

Present subjunctive
venga, venga, venga, veniamo, veniate, vengano

Future
verrò

Past definite
venni, venisti, venne, venimmo, veniste, vennero

Past participle
venuto

Also
avvenire happen
pervenire reach, arrive
svenire faint

vincere *win*

Past definite
vinsi, vincesti, vinse, vincemmo, vinceste, vinsero

Past participle
vinto

Also
convincere convince

---

vivere *live*

Future
vivrò

Past definite
vissi, vivesti, visse, vivemmo, viveste, vissero

Past participle
vissuto

Also
sopravvivere survive, outlive

---

volere *want, wish*

Present indicative
voglio, vuoi, vuole, vogliamo, volete, vogliono

Present subjunctive
voglia, voglia, voglia, vogliamo, vogliate, vogliano

Future
vorrò

Past definite
volli, volesti, volle, volemmo, voleste, vollero

D

PEOPLE, THINGS, AND IDEAS: NOUNS & NOUN PHRASES

20 Labeling the World: Nouns

20a What Does a Noun Do?

Nouns answer the questions **Chi è?** 'Who is it?' and **Cos' è?** 'What is it?' They are the labels we attach to everything in the world around us or in our own minds: people, animals, things, events, processes, ideas.

Oggi è il mio *compleanno.* Per festeggiarlo vado al *ristorante* italiano con i miei *genitori* e alcuni miei *amici.*	Today is my *birthday.* To celebrate it I am going to the Italian *restaurant* with my *parents* and some of my *friends.*

20b Adding Detail: The Noun Phrase

More often than not, nouns have other words or groups of words (phrases or clauses) attached to them, making what is known as a noun phrase. The additional items may take the form of:

- determiners [➤21];
- adjectives and adjectival phrases [➤22];
- relative clauses [➤5b, 23m];
- prepositional phrases [➤25b(i) – 25b(ii)].

To avoid repetition, nouns (and therefore noun phrases) are often replaced by pronouns [➤23].

20c Proper, Common, and Collective Nouns

(i) Proper nouns

A *proper noun* is the name of a particular person, animal, place or thing. For example:

Michelangelo	**il Monte Bianco**
Federico Fellini	**il Chianti**
il Papa	**il Portogallo**
il Colosseo	**la Toscana**
gli Appennini	**il Giro d'Italia**

(ii) *Common nouns*

A *common noun* refers to a member of a group or species, such as:

un fiore	a flower	**una sedia**	a chair
un fiume	a river	**un uomo**	a man
una mosca	a fly		

(iii) *Collective nouns*

Nouns that refer to groups of individuals (people or animals) are called *collective nouns.*

il bestiame	cattle	**la gente**	people
la clientela	clientele	**la polizia**	police
la famiglia	family	**il pubblico**	public
la folla	crowd	**lo stormo**	swarm, flock

Although these nouns have a plural meaning, they take a singular verb.

C'*era* troppa gente alla festa.	There *were* too many people at the party.

(iv) *Use of capital letters*

There are a number of instances in Italian where capital letters are not used with proper nouns (days of the week, months of the year, names of languages, titles) [➤2a(ii)].

Note: It is worth remembering also that while some names are always proper nouns, such as **Roma, Maria, Fiat,** others may be used as common nouns in different contexts. Much depends on the emphasis that the writer wishes to place on a particular word, for example:

Quel *palazzo* è molto bello.	That *building* is very beautiful.

but

Quello è *il Palazzo* Pitti.	That is *the* Pitti *Palace.*

20d Gender of Nouns in Italian

The word *gender* means 'kind' or 'type.' There are only two genders in Italian — *masculine* and *feminine*. Since there is no neuter gender, this means that all Italian nouns are categorized as masculine or feminine, whether they are living creatures or not. The gender of a noun may often be established by meaning or by ending. However, because there are many illogicalities and exceptions, the most advisable thing to do is to learn the noun *with the definite article* [▶21c] — for example, **il libro** 'book,' **la rivista** 'magazine,' not just **libro, rivista**. The majority of nouns in the following examples are shown with the definite article. Sometimes it is more appropriate to learn the noun with the indefinite article [▶21e].

20e Gender by Meaning

(A) In the case of human beings, common domestic animals and a few others, male beings are normally masculine and female ones feminine:

Masculine	
l'uomo	man
il marito	husband
il ragazzo	boy
il nonno	grandfather
il fratello	brother
il gatto	cat
il cane	dog

Feminine	
la donna	woman
la moglie	wife
la ragazza	girl
la nonna	grandmother
la sorella	sister
la gatta	she-cat
la cagna	bitch

However, there are some nouns whose gender does not necessarily indicate the sex of the person or animal being referred to, and the following examples illustrate this point:

la giraffa	giraffe	**la persona**	person
la guida	guide	**il topo**	mouse
l'orso	bear	**la vittima**	victim

Despite the masculine or feminine article, each of the above nouns can refer to a male or a female person or animal.

(B) The names of trees tend to be masculine:

l'abete	fir tree	**il pino**	pine tree
il frassino	ash	**il pioppo**	poplar
il larice	larch	**il salice**	willow

There are quite a number, however, that are feminine, such as:

la betulla	birch	**la palma**	palm tree
la magnolia	magnolia	**la quercia**	oak tree

(C) Many fruit trees are masculine and their fruit feminine:

il ciliegio	cherry tree	**la ciliegia**	cherry
il melo	apple tree	**la mela**	apple
il pero	pear tree	**la pera**	pear
il pesco	peach tree	**la pesca**	peach

Some exceptions to this general rule include:

il fico	fig tree / fig
il lampone	raspberry bush / raspberry
il limone	lemon tree / lemon
il pompelmo	grapefruit tree / grapefruit

Note also that exotic fruits are mainly masculine:

l'ananas	pineapple	**il mango**	mango
il kiwi	kiwi		

(D) Names of cities, regions, islands, countries, and continents are mostly feminine:

l'Africa	Africa	**la Norvegia**	Norway
l'America	America	**(la) Roma**	Rome
la Calabria	Calabria	**la Sardegna**	Sardinia
l'Europa	Europe	**la Sicilia**	Sicily
la Lombardia	Lombardy	**la Spagna**	Spain

Note: The definite article is not normally used before the names of cities [➤21c(viii)D].

Some exceptions to the above are the following Italian regions:

l'Abruzzo (gli Abruzzi)
il Friuli
il Lazio
il Molise
il Piemonte
il Trentino-Alto Adige
il Veneto

Note also the following countries that are masculine:

il Belgio	Belgium	**l'Egitto**	Egypt
il Brasile	Brazil	**il Messico**	Mexico
il Canada	Canada	**il Portogallo**	Portugal
il Giappone	Japan	**gli Stati Uniti**	United States

(E) Names of rivers, lakes, seas, oceans, and mountains are mostly masculine:

il Po	the Po
il Tevere	the Tiber
il (lago di) Garda	Lake Garda
il Mediterraneo	the Mediterranean
l'Atlantico	the Atlantic
il Monte Bianco	Mont-Blanc
gli Appennini	the Apennines

Some exceptions:

le Alpi	the Alps	**la Loira**	the Loire
le Dolomiti	the Dolomites	**la Senna**	the Seine

(F) Languages are always masculine:

l'inglese	English
il portoghese	Portuguese
il tedesco	German

(G) The days of the week and months of the year [➤ 30a, 30b] are masculine with the exception of **domenica** 'Sunday.'

(H) The names of metals and chemical elements tend to be masculine:

l'alluminio	aluminum / aluminium	**l'ossigeno**	oxygen
l'argento	silver	**il piombo**	lead
il bronzo	bronze	**il rame**	copper
il mercurio	mercury	**lo zinco**	zinc
l'oro	gold		

(I) The names of the cardinal points are masculine:

il nord (il settentrione)	the north
il sud (il meridione / il mezzogiorno)	the south
l'est (l'oriente / il levante)	the east
l'ovest (l'occidente / il ponente)	the west

Any compounds of the above would also be masculine, for example, **il nordovest**, 'the northwest,' **il sudest** 'the southeast.'

Note that it is possible to use capital letters if reference is being made to a geographical area, for example, **il Mezzogiorno** 'the South (of Italy),' **il Medio Oriente** 'the Middle East.'

(J) Subjects of study, areas of knowledge, and arts are mostly feminine:

l'architettura	architecture	**la grammatica**	grammar
la filosofia	philosophy	**la matematica**	mathematics
la fisica	physics	**la pittura**	painting
la geografia	geography	**la storia**	history

(K) Metric weights, measures and fractions are mostly masculine:

un etto	100 gram(me)s	**un chilo**	a kilo
un metro	a meter / metre	**un quarto**	a quarter, quart
un litro	a liter / litre	**un quinto**	a fifth

(L) Foreign words introduced into the language, particularly if they end in a consonant, are mostly masculine:

il bar
il jazz
lo sport
il tram
il walkman®

(M) Many abstract nouns are feminine:

l'allegria	cheerfulness	**la miseria**	poverty
la bellezza	beauty	**la pace**	peace
la delusione	disappointment	**la tristezza**	sadness
la giustizia	justice	**la vergogna**	shame
l'intelligenza	intelligence		

However, in this category there are also a number of masculine words:

l'amore	love	**il diritto**	law, right
il buonumore	good mood	**il disaccordo**	disagreement
il coraggio	courage	**il dolore**	pain

20f Gender by Ending

(i) -o, -a: *masculine, feminine*

In many of the above examples you will have noticed that the nouns ending in **-o** are masculine, and those ending in **-a** are feminine. This is indeed the case with most Italian nouns ending in **-o** and **-a**.

il lago	lake	**la cartolina**	postcard
il negozio	shop	**la finestra**	window

With some nouns, the **-o** / **-a** ending not only changes the gender but also the meaning.

il pero	pear tree
la pera	pear [▶20e(i)C]
il porto	port
la porta	door
il tappo	plug, stopper
la tappa	stop, stage (of journey)

(ii) *Exceptions*

There are some exceptions to the general rule.

(A) Nouns ending in **-o** that are feminine include:

l'auto	car	**la moto**	motorbike
la foto	photo	**la radio**	radio
la mano	hand		

Note that four of the above are abbreviations of nouns that are feminine by origin: **l'automobile, la fotografia, la motocicletta,** and **la radiotrasmettitrice**.

(B) Masculine nouns ending in **-a** include many that end in **-ma**. (A great number of these words are of Greek origin.)

il clima	climate	**il dramma**	drama
il diagramma	diagram	**il fantasma**	ghost

il panorama	panorama	**il sistema**	system
il problema	problem	**il telegramma**	telegram(me)
il programma	program(me)	**il tema**	theme, topic
lo schema	plan	**il teorema**	theorem

(C) There are nouns ending in **-a, -ista,** and **-cida,** that can be both masculine and feminine:

l'atleta (m. & f.)	athlete	**il / la collega**	colleague
il / la dentista	dentist	**lo / la specialista**	specialist
il / la tennista	tennis player	**il / la turista**	tourist
l'omicida (m. & f.)	murderer	**il / la suicida**	suicide

(iii) -e *ending*

Nouns ending in **-e** can be either masculine or feminine.

la fine	end	**la salute**	health
il mestiere	trade, profession	**il sole**	sun
il pettine	comb	**la voce**	voice

(iv) Other endings

Other endings can also indicate gender.

(A) Feminine

- Most nouns ending in **-ione, -udine, -ite** (includes many medical terms that end in '-itis' in English), **-igine**, and **-ice** (often used to refer to female professionals):

la decisione	decision	**la lezione**	lesson
la nazione	nation	**la televisione**	television
l'abitudine	habit	**la solitudine**	solitude
l'appendicite	appendicitis	**la meningite**	meningitis
la tonsillite	tonsilitis	**l'origine**	origin
l'attrice	actress	**la pittrice**	painter (female)

- Nouns that end in **-tà** or **-tù:**

la bontà	goodness	**la città**	city
la felicità	happiness	**l'università**	university
la volontà	will	**la gioventù**	youth
la virtù	virtue		

- Most nouns ending in **-i** (many of which correspond to the English ending '-sis'):

l'analisi	analysis	**la diagnosi**	diagnosis
la crisi	crisis	**l'enfasi**	emphasis

la sintesi	synthesis	**la tesi**	thesis

A commonly used word that is masculine is **il brindisi** 'toast' (drink to).

- Nouns ending in **-ie:**

la serie	series
la specie	sort, kind
la superficie	surface

(B) Masculine

- Nouns ending in **-ore:**

il colore	color / colour	**l'odore**	smell
il fattore	factor	**il settore**	sector
il fiore	flower	**il valore**	value
il motore	motor		

- Most nouns ending in **-ame, -ale, -ile,** and **-ere:**

il catrame	tar	**il bestiame**	cattle
il rame	copper	**il rottame**	scrap (iron)
il canale	canal	**il giornale**	newspaper
lo schienale	back (of chair)	**il temporale**	storm
il tribunale	(law-)court	**il barile**	barrel
il canile	kennel	**il fienile**	haystack
il benessere	well-being, welfare	**il carcere**	prison
il malessere	malaise, discomfort	**il potere**	power

The gender of **il carcere** 'prison' changes to feminine in the plural: ***le* carceri.**

20g Formation of Feminines

You have already seen in 20e(i) and 20f(ii)C how to form the feminine equivalent of some masculine nouns. In some instances, the noun remains the same and the gender is indicated by the article:

il / la nipote	nephew / niece, grandson / granddaughter
il / la tennista	male / female tennis player

In some cases, the feminine form is obtained by changing **-o** to **-a:**

il ragazzo / la ragazza	boy / girl
il figlio / la figlia	son / daughter

In others, a completely different word is required:

l'uomo	man
la donna	woman
il marito	husband
la moglie	wife

Other general guidelines

• A great many masculine nouns ending in **-e** have a feminine form in **-a**:

il cameriere	waiter
la cameriera	waitress
l'infermiere	male nurse
l'infermiera	female nurse
il padrone	male owner / boss
la padrona	female owner / boss
il parrucchiere	male hairdresser
la parrucchiera	female hairdresser

• Some masculine nouns ending in **-o, -a,** and **-e** have a feminine form in **-essa**:

l'avvocato	male lawyer
l'avvocatessa	woman lawyer
il dottore	male doctor
la dottoressa	female doctor
il duca	duke
la duchessa	duchess
il poeta	male poet
la poetessa	female poet
il conte	count
la contessa	countess
il professore	male teacher / professor
la professoressa	female teacher / professor

• There are a number of nouns ending in **-tore,** many of which refer to professions, that have a feminine equivalent form in **-trice**:

l'attore	actor	**l'attrice**	actress
il conoscitore	connoisseur	**la conoscitrice**	connoisseuse
il redattore	male editor	**la redattrice**	female editor
lo scrittore	male writer	**la scrittrice**	female writer
lo scultore	sculptor	**la scultrice**	sculptress

il vincitore	male winner	**la vincitrice**	female winner

Note that where there is no feminine equivalent, then either the masculine noun is used for both genders or the distinction can be made by placing **una donna** in front of the masculine noun—for example, **una donna poliziotto** 'a police woman,' **una donna controllore** 'a female ticket inspector.'

A similar rule applies to animals where a single noun form exists, of which the gender cannot be changed:

il pavone	peacock	**la giraffa**	giraffe

To express the idea of a female peacock, one has to say **il pavone femmina** or **la femmina del pavone**.
A male giraffe would be **la giraffa maschio** or **il maschio della giraffa**.

- There are a few masculine nouns whose feminine equivalent does not conform to a regular pattern.

l'eroe	hero	**l'eroina**	heroine
il gallo	rooster	**la gallina**	hen
il re	king	**la regina**	queen

20h One or More? Plural of Nouns

(i) -i, -e

The rules for making most nouns plural in Italian are as follows:

- Masculine nouns ending in **-o** or **-a** change to **-i**:

il ragazz*o*	**i ragazz*i***	boy(s)
il problem*a*	**i problem*i***	problem(s)

- Feminine nouns ending in **-a** change to **-e**:

la finestr*a*	**le finestr*e***	window(s)

- Masculine and feminine nouns ending in **-e** change to **-i**:

il costum*e*	**i costum*i***	custom(s), habit(s)
la luc*e*	**le luc*i***	light(s)

(ii) Exceptions

- There is a small number of feminine nouns ending in **-o** that do not change in the plural, for example:

la moto	**le moto**	motorcycle(s)
la radio	**le radio**	radio(s)

[See also ➤20h(iv).]

One commonly used feminine noun ending in **-o** has a plural form in **-i**:

la mano	**le mani**	hand(s)

• The following feminine nouns ending in **-a** change to **-i** in the plural:

l'ala	**le ali**	wing(s)
l'arma	**le armi**	weapon(s)

• Some masculine nouns ending in **-o** in the singular form their plural in **-a**. Except for **mille / mila**, which has no gender agreement, in the plural these nouns change their gender to feminine:

un centinaio	about a hundred	**delle centinaia**	hundreds
mille	thousand	**mila**	thousands
un migliaio	about a thousand	**delle migliaia**	thousands
il miglio	mile	**le miglia**	miles
il paio	pair	**le paia**	pairs
l'uovo	egg	**le uova**	eggs

• Some masculine nouns form their plurals according to the rules explained under 20h(i), but their plural form has a stem change:

il bue	**i buoi**	ox / oxen
il dio	**gli dei**	god(s)
l'uomo	**gli uomini**	man / men

(iii) *Other plurals*

• Nouns ending in **-ca** and **-ga** in the singular form their plural in **-che** and **-ghe** if they are feminine and **-chi** and **-ghi** if they are masculine. This preserves the hard sound of the **c** and **g**.

l'amica	**le amiche**	friend(s)
la collega	**le colleghe**	colleague(s)
il monarca	**i monarchi**	monarch(s)
il collega	**i colleghi**	colleague(s)

but

il belga	**i belgi**	Belgian(s)

- Nouns ending in **-cia** and **-gia** retain the **i** in the plural if it is stressed and omit it if it is unstressed:

la bugia	**le bugie**	lie(s) (stressed **i**)
la faccia	**le facce**	face(s) (unstressed **i**)
la farmacia	**le farmacie**	drugstore(s) / chemist's / chemists' (stressed **i**)
la spiaggia	**le spiagge**	beach(es) (unstressed **i**)

However, the unstressed **i** is sometimes retained in the plural to avoid ambiguity between words that would otherwise have the same spelling, for example:

la camicia	**le camic*i*e**	shirt(s)

(to avoid confusion with **il camice** 'surplice')

l'audacia	**le audac*i*e**	courage / daring deeds

(to avoid confusion with the adjective **audace** 'daring')

It is normal to retain the **i** whenever the **-cia** or **-gia** is preceded by a vowel, as in **la valigia / le valigie** 'suitcase(s)' and omit it when these endings are preceded by a consonant, as in **la goccia / le gocce** 'drop(s).'

- Nouns ending in **-io** have a double **i** in the plural when the **i** of **-io** is stressed and just one **i** if unstressed:

lo zio	**gli zii**	uncle(s)
il negozio	**i negozi**	shop(s)

There are occasions where the plurals of words ending in **-io** are identical to those of other nouns or adjectives. In the written form, an accent or a double **i** is used to avoid confusion:

il conservatorio	**i conservat*ò*ri**	conservatory
conservatore	**conservat*ó*ri**	conservative
il principe	**i pr*ì*ncipi**	prince
il principio	**i princ*ì*pi**	principle

In the spoken language, the distinction between these words is made by sound — the open **o** of **conservatorio** and the closed **o** of **conservatore,** the stress on the first **i** of **principe** and the second **i** of **principio**.

il tempio	**i tempii** (more commonly **i templi**)	temple

Double **i** in the plural to avoid confusion with:

il tempo	**i tempi**	time
l'omicidio	**gli omicidii**	murder

Double **i** in the plural to avoid confusion with the adjective / noun:

omicida	**omicidi**	murderous, murderer

Without the doubling of the **i,** spelling of the plural forms would be identical.

- Nouns ending in **-co** and **-go** form their plurals in **-chi** or **-ci** and **-ghi** or **-gi**. Because there are a number of exceptions, it is not easy to provide clearcut rules. When you come across unfamiliar words with these endings, it would be advisable to check their plural form in a dictionary. However, the following general guidelines should be of some help:

(A) Many nouns that have the stress on the penultimate syllable form their plurals in **-chi** and **-ghi**. These nouns preserve the hard **c / g** sound.

il fuoco	**i fuochi**	fire(s)
il parco	**i parchi**	park(s)
l'albergo	**gli alberghi**	hotel(s)
il lago	**i laghi**	lake(s)
il luogo	**i luoghi**	place(s)

but

l'amico	**gli amici**	friend(s)
il greco	**i greci**	Greek(s)
il nemico	**i nemici**	enemy (enemies)
il porco	**i porci**	pig(s)

The above nouns undergo a sound change in the plural. The **i** after the **c** softens the sound. The same applies when the **g** is followed by **i,** as in the examples below. The **-ci** and **-gi** are pronounced in the same way as the **C** and **G** of the Italian alphabet [▶ 2a(i)].

(B) If the stress falls before the penultimate syllable, the general tendency for these nouns is to form their plurals in **-ci** or **-gi**:

il medico	**i medici**	doctor(s)
il portico	**i portici**	portico(s) / porch(es)
l'asparago	**gli asparagi**	asparagus
il teologo	**i teologi**	theologian(s)

but

l'obbligo	**gli obblighi**	obligation(s)
il profugo	**i profughi**	refugee(s)

Note that there are some nouns that have two possible plural forms:

il chirurgo	**i chirurgi / chirurghi**	surgeon(s)

il farmaco	**i farmaci / i farmachi**	drug(s) (*medicine*)
lo stomaco	**gli stomaci / stomachi**	stomach(s)

- Nouns in **-logo** tend to change to **-logi** when they refer to *people* and **-loghi** when they refer to *things.*

l'archeologo	**gli archeologi**	archaeologist(s)
il catalogo	**i cataloghi**	catalogue(s) / catalog(s)
il dialogo	**i dialoghi**	dialogue(s) / dialog(s)
lo psicologo	**gli psicologi**	psychologist(s)

(iv) *Nouns that do not change in the plural*

- Abbreviated noun forms:

l'auto	**le auto**	car(s)
la bici	**le bici**	bicycle(s) / bike(s)
il cinema	**i cinema**	movie theater(s) / cinema(s)
la foto	**le foto**	photo(s)

[See also ➤20h(ii).]

The complete forms of these nouns change from singular to plural in the normal way [➤20h(i)]:

l'automobile	**le automobili**
la fotografia	**le fotgrafie**

- Nouns ending in a consonant:

l'autobus	**gli autobus**	bus(es)
il bar	**i bar**	coffee shop(s) / coffee bars / bar(s)
lo sport	**gli sport**	sport(s)

- Monosyllabic nouns:

la gru	**le gru**	crane(s)
il re	**i re**	king(s)
lo sci	**gli sci**	ski(s)

- Nouns ending in an accented vowel:

la città	**le città**	city (cities) / town(s)
il falò	**i falò**	bonfire(s)
il lunedì	**i lunedì**	Monday(s)
il tè	**i tè**	tea(s)
la virtù	**le virtù**	virtue(s)

⚠ The article is not normally used with days of the week in the singular. **Lunedì** without the article conveys both 'Monday' and 'on Monday.' **Il lunedì** is used to express 'on Mondays' [➤30a].

- Nouns ending in **-i:**

l'analisi	**le analisi**	analysis (analyses)
la crisi	**le crisi**	crisis (crises)
l'ipotesi	**le ipotesi**	hypothesis (hypotheses)

- Nouns ending in **-ie:**

la serie	**le serie**	series

but

la moglie	**le mogli**	wife (wives)
la superficie	**le superfici**	surface(s)

- Others:

il paria	**i paria**	outcast(s)
il sosia	**i sosia**	double(s) (a look alike)
il vaglia	**i vaglia**	money order(s)

(v) *Nouns used only in the plural*

Some nouns are generally used only in the plural. They include:

- Nouns denoting pairs of things:

le forbici	scissors
le manette	handcuffs
gli occhiali	eyeglasses / spectacles
i pantaloni / i calzoni	pants / trousers

- Nouns referring to things or events that have a plural sense:

i dintorni	surroundings
le ferie	vacation / holidays
le macerie	ruins *(rubble)*
le posate	cutlery
le stoviglie	dishes
i viveri	provisions

Note also:

le nozze	wedding

(vi) *Nouns used only in the singular*

Some nouns are generally used only in the singular. They include:

- Many nouns referring to food products, because they are noncountable:

l'aceto	vinegar	**il pane**	bread
il sale	salt	**lo zucchero**	sugar

- Names of the months:

gennaio, febbraio	January, February

- Metals and chemical elements:

l'oro	gold	**l'ossigeno**	oxygen

- Abstract nouns:

il coraggio	courage	**l'orgoglio**	pride

(vii) *Nouns with two plural forms*

- There is a small number of nouns that have two plural forms, one masculine and one feminine. The difference in gender also carries a difference in meaning.

il braccio	**i bracci**	arms (of cross, etc.), wings (of building)
	le braccia	arms (of body)
il ciglio	**i cigli**	edges (of ditch, road)
	le ciglia	eyelashes
il corno	**i corni**	horns (instrument)
	le corna	horns (of animal)
il dito	**i diti**	fingers (considered individually)
	le dita	fingers (considered collectively)
il filo	**i fili**	threads, wires
	le fila	threads (of plot)
il fondamento	**i fondamenti**	basic principles
	le fondamenta	foundations (of building)
il frutto	**i frutti**	fruits (different individual fruits or fruits of labor)
	le frutta (la frutta)	fruit (in a collective sense)
il grido	**i gridi**	cries (of animal)
	le grida	cries (of human)
il labbro	**i labbri**	lips (of a wound)
	le labbra	lips (of mouth)
il lenzuolo	**i lenzuoli**	sheets (two or more, i.e., considered separately)

	le lenzuola	pair of sheets (to make the bed)
il membro	**i membri**	members (of group, etc.)
	le membra	limbs (of body)
il muro	**i muri**	walls (of house)
	le mura	walls (of city)
l'osso	**gli ossi**	bones (considered individually or bones for a dog, etc.)
	le ossa	bones (of a human skeleton)

Note that you use the feminine plural of these nouns (**le ciglia, le dita, le lenzuola**) in a collective sense but that you use the masculine plural (**uno dei cigli, uno dei diti, uno dei lenzuoli**) in a partitive sense (i.e., '*one of* the eyelashes,' '*one of* the fingers,' '*one of* the sheets').

• The following nouns have two singular and two plural forms, with no difference in meaning.

l'arancio	**l'arancia**	orange
gli aranci	**le arance**	oranges
l'orecchio	**l'orecchia**	ear
gli orecchi	**le orecchie**	ears

(viii) Plural of compound nouns [➤3a(i)]

Compound nouns are nouns formed by combining words together. The formation of the plural depends on the components that make up the compound word. Since there are various inconsistencies, it is only possible to give the following general guidelines.

• Compound nouns comprising *adjective + noun* or *adjective + adjective* form their plural by changing the ending of the *second* part:

l'altoparlante	**gli altoparlant*i***	loudspeaker(s)
il francobollo	**i francoboll*i***	stamp(s)
il pianoforte	**i pianofort*i***	piano(s)
il sordomuto	**i sordomut*i***	deaf and dumb person, deaf mute

• Compound nouns made up of *noun + adjective* form their plural by changing the ending of *both* parts:

il caposaldo	**i cap*i*sald*i***	stronghold(s)
la cassaforte	**le cass*e*fort*i***	safe(s)

• Compounds comprising *two nouns of the same gender* normally make the *second* noun plural:

l'arcobaleno	**gli arcobalen*i***	rainbow(s) (both nouns are masculine)
la madreperla	**le madreperl*e***	mother-of-pearl (both nouns are feminine)

However, if the compound comprises *two nouns of different genders* then you normally make the *first* noun plural:

il capostazione	**i cap*i*stazione**	stationmaster(s)
il pescespada	**i pesc*i*spada**	swordfish

but

la banconota	**le banconot*e***	banknote(s)
la ferrovia	**le ferrovi*e***	railway(s) / railroad(s)

The reason for the second noun changing to plural and not the first is that **banco** and **ferro** are used adjectivally, and therefore you have the *adjective + noun* combination previously explained.

- Compounds comprising *verb + plural noun* do not change in the plural:

il cavatappi	**i cavatappi**	corkscrew(s)
la lavastoviglie	**le lavastoviglie**	dishwasher(s)

- Compounds comprising *verb + singular feminine noun* remain unchanged in the plural:

il cacciavite	**i cacciavite**	screwdriver(s)
il salvagente	**i salvagente**	lifebelt(s)

but

l'asciugamano	**gli asciugamani**	towel(s)

- Compounds comprising *verb + singular masculine noun* make the *noun* plural:

il passaporto	**i passaport*i***	passport(s)
il portafoglio	**i portafogl*i***	wallet(s)

- Compounds comprising *two verbs* remain *unchanged* in the plural:

l'andirivieni	**gli andirivieni**	coming(s) and going(s)
il fuggifuggi	**i fuggifuggi**	rush, scramble

- Nouns comprising either *preposition + noun* or *adverb + noun* form their plurals in a variety of ways. It would be advisable, therefore, to check the plural form in a dictionary.

il dopopranzo	**i dopopranzi**	afternoon(s)
il senzatetto	**i senzatetto**	homeless person(s)
il soprannome	**i soprannomi**	nickname(s)
il sottopassaggio	**i sottopassaggi**	underpass(es) / subway(s)

20i Adjectives Used as Nouns

Adjectives are frequently used as nouns in Italian.

(i) Implied noun

Sometimes the noun is strongly implied:

Molti *giovani* hanno lasciato il paese in cerca di lavoro. Per loro, l'*importante* è di guadagnarsi la vita. Adesso la maggior parte degli abitanti del paese è composta da *anziani*.	Many *young people* have left the village in search of work. For them, the *important thing* is to earn a living. Now the majority of the inhabitants of the village is made up of *elderly people*.

(ii) Abstract nouns

Adjectives can also stand alone to represent abstract nouns. In this case they are masculine:

A dire *il vero,* i giovani hanno perfettamente ragione di andare altrove in cerca di lavoro.	To tell *the truth*, young people are perfectly right to go elsewhere in search of work.

(iii) Colors / Colours

When a color / colour is used as a noun it is masculine.

***Il rosso* e *il verde* sono i miei colori preferiti.**	*Red* and *green* are my favorite colors / favourite colours.

Note: An adjective can be used to agree with a noun that has been omitted but is understood.

Quale camicia ti piace? — *La bianca.*	Which shirt do you like? — *The white one.*

20j Nouns Formed from Other Parts of Speech

Prepositions are occasionally used as nouns in Italian:

Bisogna considerare *il pro* e *il contro.*	We must consider *the pros* and *cons* (of the argument).

[For infinitives used as nouns ➤ 10a(iii).]

20k Suffixes and Prefixes

(i) Suffixes

Italian uses a range of suffixes. Suffixes are endings that are added to nouns to modify their meaning. It is not possible to modify the meaning of *all* nouns in this way, and it is advisable to use only those formations that you have seen or heard.

Some of the suffixes are:

-ino / -ina, -etto / -etta, -ello / -ella, which are generally used as *diminutives:*

mio fratello	my brother
il mio fratell*ino*	my *little* brother
un libro	a book
un libr*etto*	a *small* book, a book*let*
una casa	a house
una cas*etta*	a *small* house, a cottage
un paese	a country, a village
un paes*ello*	a *small* village, hamlet

Note that the gender of the suffix is normally that of the original noun.

- **-one / -ona,** which is an *augmentative* denoting size:

una barca	a small boat	**un barc*one***	a *big* boat
una donna	a woman	**un donn*one***	a *huge* woman

Care has to be taken when adding the suffix **-one**, since even feminine words tend to become masculine.

- **-astro / -astra, -accio / -accia,** which tend to create a *negative* meaning:

un poeta	a poet	**un poet*astro***	a *worthless* poet
una sorella	a sister	**una sorell*astra***	a *half-/step*sister
una parola	a word	**una parol*accia***	a *swear*word

- **-ista**, which is frequently used to denote a profession or a sport.

il bar	bar	**il bar*ista***	bar*man*
il tennis	tennis	**il tenn*ista***	tennis *player*

A number of words ending in the above suffixes can have a completely different meaning.

la carta	paper	**il cartone**	cardboard
il cavallo	horse	**il cavalletto**	trestle (horse), easel
il padre	father	**il padrino**	godfather

(ii) *Prefixes*

Italian also uses a large number of prefixes. These are placed before nouns; and like suffixes, they serve to modify their meaning.

- **s-, in-,** and **dis-** are often used to give the opposite meaning:

la fortuna	fortune, luck	**la *s*fortuna**	*mis*fortune
il vantaggio	advantage	**lo *s*vantaggio**	*dis*advantage
la disciplina	discipline	**l'*in*disciplina**	*in*discipline
la felicità	happiness	**l'*in*felicità**	*un*happiness
l'ubbidienza	obedience	**la *dis*ubbidienza**	*dis*obedience
il piacere	pleasure	**il *dis*piacere**	*dis*pleasure

- **sovra-, sopra-,** denote excess:

l'affollamento	crowding
il *sovra*ffollamento	*over*crowding
la popolazione	population
la *sovra*ppopolazione	*over*population
il nome	name
il *sopra*nnome	*nick*name
il peso	weight
il *sopra*ppeso	*excess* weight, *over*weight

Note the doubling of the initial consonant after **sovra-** and **sopra-**.

- **sotto-** conveys 'under':

lo sviluppo	development
il *sotto*sviluppo	*under*development
la valutazione	estimation
la *sotto*valutazione	*under*estimation

[For suffixes and prefixes with adjectives ➤22g; for suffixes with adverbs ➤26c.]

21 Specifying Nouns: Determiners

21a What Are Determiners?

You will not find the word *determiner* in older grammars, but it is a very useful term, that takes in some of the most common words in any language. Determiners are used with nouns to place them in a context, to say whether they are assumed to be known or not, to whom they belong, how many there are, and so on. So, for example, a noun such as **casa** 'house' can be introduced by different determiners according to the context:

***La* casa è troppo piccola.**	*The* house is too small. (not just any house, but a particular one)
Cerchiamo *una* casa più grande.	We are looking for *a* bigger house. (not specified — could be any bigger house)
***Questa* casa ha una vista sul mare.**	*This* house has a view of the sea. (emphatic reference to a particular house)
***La nostra* casa si trova in periferia.**	*Our* house is on the outskirts. (belongs to us)
I miei amici hanno *due* case.	My friends have *two* houses. (number specified)
***Quali* amici?**	*Which* friends? (asking for specification)

These examples serve to remind us of an important difference between Italian and English in the use of determiners. Most determiners in Italian have to *agree with* the noun they modify in gender and number — that is, they may vary according to whether the noun is masculine or feminine, singular or plural.

21b The Interrogative Determiner: Which? What?

- *singular* (masculine and feminine) **quale?**
- *plural* (masculine and feminine) **quali?**

***Quale* film vuoi vedere?**	*Which* movie / film do you want to see?
***Quali* film ti piacciono?**	*Which* movies / films do you like?

Quale can be separated from its noun by a form of the verb **essere:**

***Qual* è l'ultimo film che hai visto?**	*What* is the last movie / film you saw?

Note that it is normal to drop the **-e** of the singular **quale** before the verb **essere**. An apostrophe is *not* used to indicate this omission.

- **Che** 'What?' is another commonly used interrogative determiner and, in most cases, fulfills the same function as **quale**. It is invariable.

***Che* film vuoi vedere?**	*What* movie / film do you want to see?

Note: **Quale? / Quali?** imply a selection (which movie / movies [of, the ones currently playing in town] would you like to see?). **Che?** does not.

21c Already Known: The Definite Article 'The'

The definite article is used most frequently in English to introduce nouns that refer to specific items, either because they have already been mentioned, or because it is obvious from the context that one is referring to a particular item. In Italian, the definite article is used on many occasions with nouns where in English no article would be required. This is described later in this chapter [➤21c(viii)].

(i) Forms

Singular	***Plural***
masculine	
il	**i**
lo, l'	**gli**
feminine	
la, l'	**le**

(ii) il/i

Il and **i** are used before masculine nouns beginning with a consonant:

il giardino	**i giardini**	garden(s)

These articles are also used before foreign words beginning with **j-** and **w-**, for example **il jazz, il judo, il walkman®, il windsurf**.

(iii) lo/gli

Lo and **gli** are used before masculine nouns beginning with an **s-** followed by another consonant or with a **z-**:

lo studente	**gli studenti**	student(s)
lo sbaglio	**gli sbagli**	mistake(s)
lo spazio	**gli spazi**	space(s)
lo zio	**gli zii**	uncle(s)
lo zaino	**gli zaini**	backpack(s), rucksack(s)

These articles are also used before the few nouns that begin with **gn-, ps-, pn-, x-,** or with **y-/i-** + a vowel:

lo gnocco	**gli gnocchi**	dumplings
lo psicologo	**gli psicologi**	psychologist(s)
lo pneumatico	**gli pneumatici**	tire(s)/tyre(s)
lo xenofobo	**gli xenofobi**	xenophobe(s)
lo yacht	**gli yacht**	yacht(s)
lo Ionio	(no plural)	Ionian sea

(iv) l', gli

L' and **gli** are used before masculine nouns beginning with a vowel:

l'adulto	**gli adulti**	adult(s)
l'indirizzo	**gli indirizzi**	address(es)

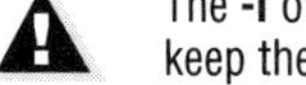

The **-i** of **gli** is hardly ever elided (**gl'**) nowadays, and it is better to keep the complete form.

***gli* Italiani**	*not* ***gl'* Italiani**	Italians

(v) la, le

La and **le** are used before feminine nouns beginning with a consonant:

la ragazza	**le ragazze**	girl(s)

(vi) l', le

L' and **le** are used before feminine nouns beginning with a vowel:

l'amica	**le amiche**	friend(s)
l'uscita	**le uscite**	exit(s)

If the definite article is separated from its noun by an adjective, for example, then the choice of article depends on the adjective, according to the rules 21c(i) to 21c(vi):

***il* giorno** — day

but

***l'*altro giorno** — the other day

***lo* spettacolo** — show

but

***il* primo spettacolo** — the first show

***l'*amica** — friend

but

***la* mia amica** — my friend

(vii) a, da, di, in, su + definite article

When the prepositions **a, da, di, in,** and **su** [➤25c(i) – 25c(vi)] are used in front of the definite articles [➤21c], they combine to produce the compound forms below.

	il	*lo*	*la*	*l'*	*i*	*gli*	*le*
a	al	allo	alla	all'	ai	agli	alle
da	dal	dallo	dalla	dall'	dai	dagli	dalle
di	del	dello	della	dell'	dei	degli	delle
in	nel	nello	nella	nell'	nei	negli	nelle
su	sul	sullo	sulla	sull'	sui	sugli	sulle

Stamattina, per andare in città, sono uscita di casa *alle* nove. Sono salita *sull'* autobus *alla* fermata di fronte a casa mia.

This morning, to go to town, I left the house *at* nine o'clock. I got *on the* bus *at the* stop opposite my house.

Arrivata in città, sono andata subito *dal* fioraio perché volevo comprare *dei* fiori per la Festa *della* Mamma. Poi sono andata *nel* supermercato accanto per comprare *del* pane e *dello* zucchero. Dopo, sono corsa *all'*agenzia di viaggi per chiedere informazioni *sui* voli charter per Boston.	Having arrived in town, I went straight *to the* florist's because I wanted to buy *some* flowers for Mother's Day. Then I went *into* the supermarket next door to buy *some* bread and *some* sugar. After that, I rushed *to the* travel agent's to ask for information *on the* charter flights to Boston.

(viii) Use of the definite article

The definite article is used:

(A) As in English, to make it clear that a particular item is being referred to:

Questo non è *il* libro che ti ho prestato.	This isn't *the* book that I lent you.
Hai imbucato *le* lettere?	Have you mailed / posted *the* letters?

(B) When generalizing or using abstract nouns:

***Lo sport* non mi piace per niente.**	I don't like *sports* at all.
Non mangiamo mai *la carne.*	We never eat *meat.*
***La disoccupazione* è un grosso problema.**	*Unemployment* is a big problem.
***Il denaro* è la fonte di tutti i mali.**	*Money* is the root of all evil.

You will see from the above examples, and the ones that follow, that in English the article is often omitted altogether when generalizing or using abstract terms. Remember that this is not possible in Italian.

(C) With titles when referring to the person in question, but not when addressing them directly:

—Mi dispiace, ma *il dottor* Zambetti sta appena arrivando.	—I'm sorry, but *Doctor* Zambetti is just arriving.
—Buon giorno, dottor Zambetti.	—Good morning, Doctor Zambetti.

Note also that titles such as **dottore** 'doctor,' **professore** 'teacher,' **signore** 'mister,' **ingegnere** 'engineer,' and **ragioniere** 'accountant' drop the final **-e** in front of a person's name.

(D) With names of continents, countries, and other named geographical features — regions, lakes, *large* islands, rivers, mountain ranges:

***L'Italia* è un bellissimo paese.**	*Italy* is a very beautiful country.
***La Toscana* è la regione che conosco meglio.**	*Tuscany* is the region that I know best.

Names of towns and cities are not accompanied by the definite article unless they are an integral part of the name as in **L'Aquila, La Spezia,** and a few others.

If the name of the town or city is qualified or emphasized in some way, however, then the article is used:

***La Roma* della mia gioventù.**	*The Rome* of my youth.

When you wish to say 'to go to' (**andare in**) a country, the article is omitted if the country is singular and not qualified by an adjective.

Quest'anno vogliamo andare *in Danimarca.*	This year we want to go *to Denmark.*
but	
L'anno scorso siamo andati *negli Stati Uniti.*	Last year we went *to the United States.* (plural)
L'Emilia Romagna si trova *nell'Italia centrale.*	Emilia Romagna is *in Central Italy.* (qualified by an adjective)

Note also:

***nell'*Africa del Nord**	*in* North Africa

(E) With possessive adjectives and pronouns:

Io pago *il mio* caffè, e tu paghi *il tuo.*	I'll pay for *my* coffee, and you pay for *yours.*

[For the use of article with possessive adjectives when referring to members of the family ➤21h(v).]

(F) With expressions of time and age:

È *l'una.*	It is *one o'clock.*
Sono *le undici.*	It is *eleven o'clock.*
but	
È mezzogiorno.	It is noon / midday.
È mezzanotte.	It is midnight.

Per me, *il 1995* (millenovecento novantacinque) è stato un anno significativo.	For me *1995* was a significant year.
***La settimana scorsa* ho visto il mio ex professore di matematica.**	*Last week* I saw my former math / maths teacher.
Questo ristorante è sempre chiuso *la domenica.*	This restaurant is always closed *on Sundays.* (*every* Sunday)
but	
Sono partiti *venerdì.*	They left *on Friday.* (article omitted when referring to a *particular* day)
Quella signora dimostra tra *i cinquanta* e *i sessant'anni.*	That lady looks between *fifty* and *sixty years old.*
but	
Mia sorella ha *trent'anni.*	My sister is *thirty.* (article omitted after **avere** when expressing *age*)

(G) With names of languages:

Quale lingua preferisci, *il francese* o *l'italiano*?	Which language do you prefer, *French* or *Italian*?

No article is required after **parlare** 'speak' unless it is separated from the language by another part of speech:

Parli *tedesco*?	Do you speak *German*?
but	
Parli molto bene *l'inglese.*	You speak *English* very well.

(H) With parts of the body, particularly when they are the object of a verb or when the person whom they belong to is the indirect object of a reflexive verb [➤ 8e(iv), 21h(vi)]:

Metti giù *i piedi!*	Put *your feet* down!
Dammi *la mano.*	Give me *your hand.*
Gli fa male *la schiena.*	*His back* hurts.
Mi* sono lavato *i capelli.	I washed *my hair.*
Mi* sono rotto *il braccio.	I have broken *my arm.*

(I) When expressing speeds and prices per quantity (in English the indefinite article 'a' or 'an' is used here) and also percentages:

La sua auto fa 180 (centottanta) chilometri *all'ora/l'ora.*	His car does 180 kilometers/kilometres *an hour.*
Quanto vengono *al chilo*?	How much do they cost *a kilo*?
***L'ottanta percento* degli studenti nella mia classe d'italiano sono ragazze.**	*Eighty percent* of the students in my Italian class are girls.

(J) Before nouns preceded by expressions such as **entrambi/tutti e due** 'both':

Abbiamo già visto *tutti e due i film.*	We have already seen *both movies/films.*

(ix) *Omission of the definite article*

You have already seen a number of examples in the preceding section [➤21c(viii)] where the definite article is omitted in Italian. The article is also omitted:

(A) In a number of adverbial expressions:

L'ho guardato *per curiosità.*	I watched it *out of curiosity.*
Ha salito le scale *di corsa.*	She ran up the stairs. (She went up the stairs *running.*
Hanno reagito *con calma.*	They reacted *calmly.*

Note also the omission of the article in constructions such as *verb + adverbial expression of place*. This is particularly the case when the adverbial expression is introduced by **in:**

Vado *in banca.*	I am going *to the bank.*

Andiamo *in chiesa.*	We are going *to church.*
Abitano *in campagna.*	They live *in the country.*
Si trovano *in cucina.*	They are *in the kitchen.*
Domani mattina non vado *a scuola*, rimango *a casa.*	Tomorrow morning, I'm not going *to school*, I'm staying *at home.*

(B) In a number of verbal expressions such as:

avere caldo	be hot	**avere freddo**	be cold
avere fame	be hungry	**avere sete**	be thirsty
avere ragione	be right	**avere torto**	be wrong
avere voglia (di)	want to, feel like	**perdere tempo**	waste / lose time

(C) When listing things:

Devi comprare *latte, pane, burro, zucchero...*	You must buy *milk, bread, butter, sugar* . . .

(D) Before a noun in apposition to another noun [➤ 3e]:

***Roma, capitale* d'Italia, è ricca di storia.**	*Rome, the capital* of Italy, is full of history.

21d The Demonstrative Determiners 'This,' 'That'

Demonstratives are like a strong definite article. They refer to something very specific, usually indicating whether it is near to or far from the speaker in time and place. The demonstratives in Italian are:

- **questo** — *this* (near the speaker)
- **quello** — *that* (away from both the speaker and, possibly, the person addressed)

(i) Questo

Masculine

questo ragazzo	this boy
questi ragazzi	these boys

Feminine

questa ragazza	this girl
queste ragazze	these girls

(ii) *Quello*

You will see from the following examples that **quello** has forms like the definite article [➤21c(i)–(vi); and like the definite article, it changes form according to what follows it:

Masculine	
quel **ragazzo**	*that* boy
quei **ragazzi**	*those* boys
quello **studente**	*that* student
quel **bello studente**	*that* handsome student
quegli **studenti**	*those* students
quei **bei studenti**	*those* handsome students
Feminine	
quella **ragazza**	*that* girl
quelle **ragazze**	*those* girls
***quel'*isola**	*that* island
quelle **isole**	*those* islands

Le piace *questa* camicetta? — Sì, ma prima vorrei provare *quella* camicetta rossa che ho visto in vetrina.	Do you like *this* blouse? — Yes, but first I would like to try on *that* red blouse I saw in the window.

(iii) *Stesso / a / i / e* 'same'

È la *stessa* camicetta che pensavo di comprare.	It's the *same* blouse that I thought of buying.

Medesimo / a / i / e fulfills the same function as **stesso,** but it is used less frequently, especially in spoken Italian.

[For **questo** and **quello** as demonstrative pronouns ➤23j(i).]

21e *Unknown Individuals: The Indefinite Article 'A (An)' (Un, Uno, Una, Un')*

(i) *Un, uno*

Un and **uno** are the two masculine forms of the indefinite article. **Un** is used before words beginning with a consonant or vowel. **Uno** is used with words beginning with 1) **s-** *+ another consonant*; 2) **gn-, pn-, ps-, x-, z; y- / i-** *+ a vowel.* It follows exactly the same rules as the definite article **lo** [➤21c(iii)].

un amico	a friend
un regalo	a present
uno studente	a student
uno zio	an uncle

(ii) *Una, un'*

Una and **un'** are the feminine forms of the indefinite article. **Un'** is used in place of **una** in front of words beginning with a vowel:

una stanza	a room	**un'amica**	a friend

If the indefinite article is separated from its noun by an adjective, for example, then the choice of indefinite article depends on the adjective, according to the rules 21e(i – ii):

***uno* zio**	an uncle

but

***un* caro zio**	a dear uncle
***un'*amica**	a friend

but

***una* buon'amica**	a good friend

(iii) *Use*

When the indefinite article is used, we know what type of person or thing the noun refers to but not which specific individual or thing.

Per il mio compleanno, i miei genitori mi hanno regalato *un* orologio e *una* bicicletta.	For my birthday, my parents gave me *a* watch and *a* bicycle.

(iv) *Some other uses*

The indefinite article is also used:

(A) For emphasis:

Ho *una sete*!	I have *such a thirst*!

(B) To convey approximation:

Quant'è di qui all'autostrada? —*Un dieci* chilometri.	How far is it from here to the highway / motorway? —*About ten* kilometers / kilometres.

(v) *Omission of the indefinite article*

The use of the indefinite article in Italian is often much the same as in English, but there are a number of other occasions where it is not used.

(A) After **essere** 'be' and **diventare** 'become' with a noun complement denoting a profession, nationality, religion, or civil status, unless the noun is qualified by an adjective or other phrase.

Mio fratello, Gino, *è professore.* Tutti dicono che *è un professore eccezionale.* Quando era più giovane, voleva *diventare dentista. È* ancora *scapolo,* ma credo che la sua libertà stia per finire. Si è innamorato di una ragazza che ha conosciuto al mare durante le vacanze estive. Si chiama Barbara, ed *è americana.* Lei è *una bravissima giornalista.*	My brother, Gino, *is a teacher.* Everyone says that *he is an exceptional teacher.* When he was younger, he wanted *to become a dentist. He is* still *a bachelor*, but I think that his freedom is about to end. He has fallen in love with a girl he met at the seaside during the summer vacation / holidays. Her name is Barbara, and *she is American.* She *is a very good journalist.*

(B) In the following type of construction, composed of *verb + **da** + noun,* to convey 'in the manner of':

Ho fatto da interprete.	*I acted as an interpreter.*
Agisce da persona onesta.	*He behaves like an honest person.*
Ti sei comportato da vigliacco.	*You behaved like a coward.*

(C) After certain time expressions introduced by **da**:

***Da giovane*, ero un appassionato del calcio.**	*As / When a young man*, I was a soccer / football fan.
L'ho conosciuta *da studentessa.*	I knew her *as a student.*

(D) After **Che...!** 'What a . . . !' in exclamations:

Che bella giornata!	*What a beautiful day!*
Che peccato!	*What a shame!*

(E) Before **mezzo / a:**

un'ora e *mezzo*	an hour and *a half*
tre chili e *mezzo*	three and *a half* kilos

21f Unknown Quantities: The Partitive Article

In Italian **un, uno, una, un',** have no plural forms. To convey 'some' or 'any' you can use the partitive article (***di*** *+ the definite article* [➤21c(vii)]). There are occasions where no article is used in English where one would be required in Italian:

Quando fai la spesa non dimenticare di comprare *del prosciutto* e *della frutta*.	When you do the shopping, don't forget to buy *ham* and *fruit*.
Abbiamo *dello zucchero?*	Do we have *any sugar*?
Penso di sì. Comprami anche *delle cartoline e dei francobolli*.	I think so. Buy me *some postcards* and (*some*) *stamps* as well.
Mi puoi dare *dei soldi* perché non ne ho abbastanza?	Can you give me *some money* because I haven't got enough?

(i) Omission of the partitive article

(A) The partitive article is *always* omitted:

- In negative sentences before plural nouns:

***Non* ho *soldi*.**	I have*n't any money*.
***Non* hanno *figli*.**	They have *no children*.

- After the preposition **di**:

Ha bisogno *di riposo*.	He needs (*some*) *rest*.

Se perdo l'ultima corriera, posso sempre stare a casa *di amici*.	If I miss the last bus, I can always stay with *friends*.

(B) The partitive article *can be* omitted when there is no great emphasis on the idea of 'some' or 'any,' and the phrase is merely expressing an indefinite quantity of an article or product:

Non ti preoccupare, abbiamo *tempo*.	Don't worry, we have (*some*) *time*.
Per pranzo abbiamo mangiato *spaghetti*.	For lunch we had (*some*) *spaghetti*.
Hai *spiccioli*?	Do you have (*some/any*) *change*?

(ii) Other ways of expressing 'some' and 'any'

(A) The plural forms **alcuni** (masculine) and **alcune** (feminine):

Ho comprato *alcuni* libri e *alcune* riviste.	I have bought *some* books and *a few* magazines.

(B) Qualche:

Hai *qualche* rivista americana?	Have you *some (any)* American magazines?

Although **qualche** conveys a *plural* sense, it can *only be used with singular, countable nouns.*

(C) Un po' di:

Metti *un po' di* zucchero sulle fragole.	Put *a little (some)* sugar on the strawberries.
Per chi vuole, c'è ancora *un po' di* caffè.	For whoever wants it, there is still *a little* coffee.
Ho già risparmiato *un po' di* soldi per le vacanze di Pasqua.	I have already saved *a bit of* money for the Easter vacation / holidays.
Abbi *un po' di* pazienza.	Have *a little* patience.

Note: **Un po' di** is used with noncountable nouns, such as foods and abstract concepts.

(D) 'Any' in its widest sense ('any . . . whatsoever') is **qualsiasi** or **qualunque**:

I miei amici farebbero *qualsiasi* *(qualunque)* cosa per aiutarmi.	My friends would do *any*thing to help me.

21g Other Indefinite Determiners in Italian

In addition to the use of the indefinite and partitive articles above [▶21e, 21f], the following forms should be noted:

(i) Alcuno, nessuno

'No,' 'not any' are expressed by **alcuno** or **nessuno**. These words have the same rules of agreement as the indefinite article **un, uno, una, un'** [▶21e(i)–21e(ii)]. They can only be used with the *singular* of *countable* nouns. Like all negative words, if they follow the verb, the verb is preceded by **non**.

Non ho *nessuna/alcuna* difficoltà a capire il tuo italiano.	I have *no* difficulty in understanding your Italian.
Quando parli non fai nessun/alcun errore di grammatica.	When you speak you don't make *any* grammatical errors.

- As can be seen from the above examples, **alcuno** and **nessuno** are used for *emphasis*. If there is no great emphasis on the negative quantity of the article or product, then the quantifier is omitted.

Non ho difficoltà a capire il tuo italiano.	I have*n't any* difficulty in understanding your Italian.
Quando parli non fai errori di grammatica.	When you speak, you *don't* make *any* grammatical errors.

(ii) Altro/a/i/e

'Other', 'more' are expressed by the appropriate form of **altro**.

Se vuoi *altre* idee, devi comprarti un *altro* libro.	If you want *other* ideas, you must buy yourself an*other* book.

(iii) Ogni

Ogni 'each,' 'every,' exists only in this invariable singular form.

Vorrei andare in Italia *ogni* anno.	I would like to go to Italy *every* year.
L'anno scorso il nostro professore ha organizzato uno scambio e *ogni* membro della classe ci ha partecipato.	Last year our teacher organized an exchange and *every* member of the class took part in it.

- Like 'every' **ogni** can be used before numerals:

Il nostro professore va in Italia *ogni sei* mesi.	Our teacher goes to Italy *every six* months.

(iv) Tutto / a / i /e

'All' is expressed by the appropriate form of **tutto**.

***Tutti* i suoi parenti abitano nel sud d'Italia, e gli piace trascorrere *tutta* l'estate con loro.**	*All* his relatives live in the south of Italy, and he likes to spend *all* summer with them.

Note: The notion of 'every' can be expressed in two ways:

ogni anno	every year	**tutti gli anni**	every year

Care should be taken not to confuse the meaning of 'all' and 'every.'

Il mio professore va in Italia *tutti* gli anni. Una volta ci è rimasto *tutto* l'anno.	My teacher goes to Italy *every* year. Once he remained there *the whole (all)* year.

(v) Ciascuno

'Each,' 'every' can also be conveyed by **ciascuno**, which has forms like those of the indefinite article **un, uno, una, un.** [21e(i) – 21e(ii)].

***Ciascun* membro della classe ha deciso di partecipare allo scambio.**	*Each* member of the class has decided to take part in the exchange.

(vi) 'Both'

'Both' is translated by **entrambi/e, tutti e due/tutte e due,** or **ambedue.**

***Tutti e due* gli scambi ai quali ho partecipato finora sono stati stupendi.**	*Both* exchanges I have taken part in up to now have been wonderful.
***Entrambe/ambedue* le visite sono state utili da diversi punti di vista.**	*Both* visits were useful from various points of view.

(vii) Molto/a/i/e

The appropriate form of **molto** is used to express 'much,' many, 'a lot.'

Durante il nostro soggiorno in Italia non avremo *molto* tempo libero. Siccome ci fermiamo per solo una settimana, il professore preferisce organizzare *molte* gite.	During our stay in Italy we shall not have *much* free time. As we are there for only a week, our teacher prefers to organize *lots of* trips.

(viii) Troppo/a/i/e

Troppo means 'too much,' 'too many.'

Ci sono *troppe* cose da fare.	There are *too many* things to do.

(ix) Tanto/a/i/e

Tanto means 'so much,' 'so many.'

Ci sono *tanti* posti da vedere.	There are *so many* places to see.

(x) Parecchi / parecchie, vari / varie, diversi / e

'Several' can be expressed by **parecchi / parecchie, vari / varie,** or **diversi / e,** which are, of course, always plural.

Ho già letto *parecchi / vari / diversi* libri sulla regione che visiteremo.	I have already read *several* books on the region we shall be visiting.

Note: **Molto** 'very,' **troppo** 'too,' **tanto** 'so,' and **parecchio** 'rather (a lot)' / 'quite (a lot)' are also *invariable* adverbs [➤ 26b(ii)].

I libri che ho letto sono *molto* interessanti.	The books I've read are *very* interesting.

(xi) Poco / poca / pochi / poche

The appropriate form of **poco** is used to express, 'not much,' 'little,' 'a little,' 'few.' It is the opposite of **molto.**

Il professore è stato malato e perciò gli rimane *poco* tempo per organizzare tutto.	The teacher has been ill, and so he has *little (not much)* time left to organize everything.
Purtroppo, *pochi* colleghi sono in grado di aiutarlo.	Unfortunately, *few (not many)* colleagues are in a position to help him.

(Italian often prefers to use **poco** where in English we would say 'not much.')

Be careful to distinguish between **poco**, which has a negative connotation and means 'not much,' and **un poco di** [➤ 23l(i)], which means 'a little' / 'some' and has a more positive emphasis.

C'è *poco* tempo prima della nostra partenza.	There's *little (not much)* time before our departure.
Ho ancora *un po' di* tempo per ripassare quello che abbiamo fatto in classe.	I still have *a little* time to go over what we have done in class.

(xii) Certo / a / i / e

Certo means 'certain.'

Prima che partiamo farò uno sforzo per imparare *certi verbi* e *certe* espressioni.	Before we leave I shall make an effort to learn *certain* verbs and (*certain*) expressions.

(xiii) Tale / i

Tale means 'such,' 'such a (an).'

Per me, sarà la prima volta che avrò partecipato a un *tale* scambio.	For me, it will be the first time that I will have taken part in *such* an exchange.

(xiv) Quanto / a / i / e

Quanto means 'how much,' 'how many.'

Mi sono già dimenticato. Per *quanto* tempo restate in Italia?	I have already forgotten. For *how long* (*how much* time) are you staying in Italy?

(xv) Altrettanto / a / i / e

Altrettanto means 'as much,' 'as many.'

Durante il nostro soggiorno, visiteremo molte chiese e *altrettanti* musei.	During our stay, we shall visit many churches and *as many* museums.

(xvi) Più and meno

'More' is **più** and 'less' is **meno**. They are both invariable—that is, they never change—and generally present few problems in their use. 'More and more' / 'less and less' are **sempre più / sempre meno**.

Ogni anno ci sono *più* studenti che si interessano allo scambio con l'Italia.	Every year there are *more* students who are interested in the exchange with Italy.

Il nostro professore organizza scambi con altri paesi, ma c'è *meno* interesse. È un peccato perché ci sono *sempre più* studenti dagli altri paesi che vogliono venire da noi.	Our teacher organizes exchanges with other countries, but there is *less* interest. It's a pity because there are *more and more* students from other countries who want to come to us.

[For further uses of **più / meno** with comparatives ➤22f(i), 22f(iii).]

[For indefinite determiners in this section that can also be used as pronouns ➤23k(i).]

21h Ownership: Possessive Determiners

Possessives are used to show that the noun belongs to somebody or something. They take their form from the *possessor* and their gender and number from the *thing possessed*. The words 'belong' and 'possessor' are used loosely here: possessives are also used for all kinds of other relationships between people and things.

(i) Italian possessive determiners

Singular		***Plural***		
Masculine	*Feminine*	*Masculine*	*Feminine*	
il mio	**la mia**	**i miei**	**le mie**	my
il tuo	**la tua**	**i tuoi**	**le tue**	your (informal)
il suo	**la sua**	**i suoi**	**le sue**	his, her, its
il Suo	**la Sua**	**i Suoi**	**le Sue**	your (formal)
il nostro	**la nostra**	**i nostri**	**le nostre**	our
il vostro	**la vostra**	**i vostri**	**le vostre**	your (informal)
il loro	**la loro**	**i loro**	**le loro**	their
il Loro	**la Loro**	**i Loro**	**le Loro**	your (formal)

[These same forms are also used for the possessive pronouns ➤23l.]

***Il mio* desiderio è di parlare perfettamente l'italiano.**	*My* wish is to speak Italian perfectly.

Frequento un corso serale da quasi un anno. *La nostra* professoressa è bravissima, e *le sue* lezioni sono sempre interessanti. Purtroppo, non tutti gli studenti hanno il tempo per fare *i loro* compiti.	I have been attending an evening class for almost a year. *Our* teacher is very good, and *her* lessons are always interesting. Unfortunately, not all the students have the time to do *their* homework.

(ii) *'Your'*

Be careful to distinguish between the different words for 'your.' Which form you choose will depend on whom you are addressing. [For more details see also the corresponding forms of the subject pronouns ➤23b.]

Dove sei andato con *i tuoi* amici?	Where did you (**tu**) go with *your* friends?
Questa è *la Sua* macchina, signorina?	Is this *your* (**Lei**) car, Miss?

- The formal **il Suo, la Sua** is used when speaking to *one* person and **il Loro, la Loro** when addressing *more than one* person. (The same rule applies to the informal **il tuo, la tua,** etc. and **il vostro, la vostra.**)

***La Loro* camera è al quinto piano.**	*Your* room is on the fifth floor.

- The formal **Suo** and **Loro** have been written in capitals in the list of possessives, but it is fairly common nowadays to write them in small letters.
- **loro** is the one form that remains invariable. The gender and number of the 'thing' or 'person' possessed is indicated by the accompanying article.

(iii) *Avoiding ambiguity*

As **il suo** can mean 'his,' 'her,' 'your,' 'its,' and **il loro** 'their,' 'your,' it is not difficult to imagine that this could give rise to confusion and ambiguity, particularly in writing.

Maria legge *il suo* giornale.

This sentence could have *four* possible meanings:

—Maria is reading *her* newspaper. (another woman's)
—Maria is reading *his* newspaper.
—Maria is reading *your* newspaper.
—Maria is reading *her* (*own*) newspaper.

Fortunately, we rarely deal with sentences in isolation, but rather in a wider context, in which case the *possessor* of the newspaper would usually be obvious. Should there be a need to avoid ambiguity, however, then this can be achieved by using:

- **di** + the disjunctive pronoun [➤23h]:

Maria legge il giornale *di lui.*	Maria is reading *his* newspaper.
Maria legge il giornale *di lei.*	Maria is reading *her* newspaper.
Maria legge il giornale *di Lei.*	Maria is reading *your* newspaper. (polite form with a capital **L**)

- the adjective **proprio** 'own':

Maria legge il *proprio* giornale.	Maria is reading *her (own)* newspaper.

- the capital **S** when **suo** means 'your':

Maria legge *il Suo* giornale.	Maria is reading *your* newspaper.

Remember that the possessive determiners must agree in gender and number with the *thing or person possessed* and NOT with the *possessor.* Thus, in the above example the masculine singular form **il suo** must be used to agree with the masculine noun **il giornale.** English speakers sometimes get confused and use the feminine **la sua** because they are influenced by the fact that the possessor is a female ('her').

(iv) Possessive determiners and the definite article

You have already seen in the above examples that the possessive determiners are accompanied by the definite article **il, la, i, le,** and this is generally the case. There are many occasions when the definite article is replaced by another part of speech.

***un* mio parente**	*a* relative of mine
***questa* mia amica**	*this* friend of mine
***quel* nostro zio**	*that* uncle of ours
***alcuni* miei amici**	*some* of my friends / *some* friends of mine

***tre* tuoi conoscenti**	*three* of your acquaintances
***dei* loro colleghi**	*some* of their colleagues

(v) *Omission of the definite article*

There are a number of occasions when use of the definite article with the possessive is either omitted or optional:

(A) The definite article is omitted with family members and family relationships in the *singular*.

nostra zia	our aunt
tuo fratello	your brother

The article *must be used*, however:

- With *plural* forms of the above

***le* nostre zie**	our aunt*s*
***i* tuoi fratelli**	your brother*s*

- When the possessive determiner is **loro**

***mio* fratello**	*my* brother

but

***il loro* fratello**	*their* brother

- When the noun is qualified by *another adjective* in addition to the possessive

***mio* nipote**	*my* nephew

but

***il* mio *caro* nipote**	*my dear* nephew

- When the noun has a *suffix* [► 20k]

***nostra* sorella**	*our* sister

but

la* nostra sorell*ina	*our little* sister

(B) Use of the definite article is *optional* with terms of endearment such as **babbo, papà** 'dad,' **mamma** 'mom / mum,' **nonno** 'grandad,' and **nonna** 'grandma.'

mio babbo or **il mio babbo**	my dad

(C) The definite article is also omitted:

- With certain set expressions

Vado a casa loro.	I am going to their house.
Non è colpa mia.	It's not my fault.
Non sono affari tuoi.	It's none of your business.
Lasciamolo fare a modo suo.	Let's let him do as he wants / pleases.

- In exclamations

mamma mia!	my goodness!
amici miei!	my friends!
Dio mio!	my God! good heavens!

In both sets of examples you will have noticed that the possessive is placed *after* the noun.

- With particular expressions

a mio avviso / parere	in my opinion
a tua disposizione	at your disposal

[For omission of the definite article when **il mio,** etc., is used as a possessive pronoun ➤23b(iii).]

(vi) *Omission of the possessive determiner*

The possessive is not normally used with actions performed to parts of the body or clothing, where the indirect object pronoun [➤8e(iv), 23l(i)] identifies the possessor.

Mi* sono lavato *la faccia.	I washed *my face.*
Il signore *si* è tolto *il cappello.*	The gentleman took off *his hat.*

Neither is it required when the identity of the possessor is obvious from the context.

La ragazza ha chiuso *gli occhi.*	The girl shut *her eyes.*
Hai fatto *i compiti*?	Have you done *your homework*?

22 Describing Nouns: Adjectives

22a What Do Adjectives Do?

Adjectives describe nouns. They can be used either as part of a phrase containing a noun [➤22b] or in the predicate of the sentence [➤22c].

(i) Agreement of adjectives

Adjectives in Italian agree in gender and number with the noun(s) they describe.

(A) The many adjectives ending in **-o** have *four* forms: masculine singular and plural, feminine singular and plural.

il ragazzo italian*o*	the *Italian* boy
i ragazzi italian*i*	the *Italian* boys
la ragazza italian*a*	the *Italian* girl
le ragazze italian*e*	the *Italian* girls

Note: Adjectives of nationality are written with a small letter [➤2a(ii)].

(B) Adjectives ending in **-e** have the same ending for masculine and feminine singular. The plural is also the same for both genders and ends in **-i**.

il libro interessant*e*	the *interesting* book
i libri interessant*i*	the *interesting* books
la rivista interessant*e*	the *interesting* magazine
le riviste interessant*i*	the *interesting* magazines

(C) Adjectives ending in **-a** have the same ending for masculine and feminine singular. However, the masculine plural ends in **-i** and the feminine plural in **-e.**

il professore belg*a*	the Belgian teacher
i professori belg*i*	the Belgian teachers
la professoressa belg*a*	the Belgian teacher
le professoresse belgh*e*	the Belgian teachers

(D) Adjectives ending in **-one** have a feminine form in **-ona.** The plural endings are **-oni** and **-one,** respectively.

lo studente chiacchier*one*	the *talkative* student

gli studenti chiacchier*oni*	the *talkative* students
la studentessa chiacchier*ona*	the *talkative* student
le studentesse chiacchier*one*	the *talkative* students

(ii) *Adjectives that combine to form a single unit*

When two adjectives combine to form a single unit, the first remains unchanged but the second agrees in the normal way.

il programma *socioeconomico*	the *socioeconomic* program(me)
i programmi *socioeconomici*	the *socioeconomic* program(me)s

Care has to be taken when using these forms, since the spelling of the first adjective is often modified in some way; for example, the 'Italian-French agreement' is **l'accordo italo-francese.**

[For adjectives used as nouns ➤20i.]

(iii) *Agreement: Exceptions*

There is a small number of adjectives that are invariable, i.e., they have only *one* form irrespective of the gender or number of the noun they describe. They include the following:

(A) Some adjectives of color — these are adjectives of foreign origin or they exist as nouns in their own right.

il fiore *rosa*	the *pink* flower
i fiori *rosa*	the *pink* flowers
la giacca *blu*	the *blue* jacket
le giacche *blu*	the *blue* jackets
la maglia *viola*	the *purple* sweater
le maglie *viola*	the *purple* sweaters
la scarpa *marrone*	the *brown* shoe
le scarpe *marrone*	the *brown* shoes

(B) Adjectives ending in **-i**

un numero par*i*	an *even* number
i numeri dispar*i*	the *odd* numbers
la lotta impar*i*	the *unequal* struggle

22b *Accompanying the Noun: Attributive Adjectives*

Attributive adjectives form part of the same phrase as a noun, though sometimes the noun is *understood*, that is, left out because it is obvious [➤22b(vi)].

(i) *Normal position of adjectives*

The adjective normally follows the noun in Italian.

Un tè *freddo* per me e un bicchiere di vino *bianco* per Marco.	An *iced* tea for me and a glass of *white* wine for Marco.

- This goes especially for adjectives denoting nationality, religion, shape, color / colour, as well as past participles used adjectivally.

un amico *francese*	a *French* friend
un prete *cattolico*	a *Catholic* priest
una stanza *rettangolare*	a *rectangular* room
una camicia *bianca*	a *white* shirt
una casa *demolita*	a *demolished* house

However, a number of common adjectives normally precede the noun. Those marked with an asterisk below have irregular forms when they precede a noun [➤22d(i) – 22d(iii)].

bello*	**una bella giornata**	a beautiful day
buono*	**un buon riposo**	a good rest
breve	**una breve pausa**	a short break
brutto	**una brutta notizia**	bad news
cattivo	**un cattivo gusto**	a bad taste
giovane	**un giovane autista**	a young driver
grande*	**una grande casa**	a great / large house
grosso	**un grosso problema**	a big problem
largo	**un largo viale**	a wide avenue
lungo	**una lunga passeggiata**	a long walk
piccolo	**un piccolo giardino**	a small garden
vecchio	**una vecchia casa**	an old house

(ii) Even adjectives that normally precede a noun sometimes follow it. The change of position is important when one wishes to shift the emphasis and create other shades of meaning.

È un *piccolo* appartamento. **È un appartamento *piccolo.***	It's a *small* apartment / flat.

The positioning of the adjective after the noun emphasizes its *size*. Similarly, adjectives that are normally placed after the noun may precede it for emphasis.

Dobbiamo prendere una decisione *difficile*.	We have to make a *difficult* decision.
La *difficile* decisione che abbiamo preso è stata giustificata.	The *difficult* decision we made has been justified. *(greater emphasis)*

(iii) Adjectives that normally precede the noun *must* follow the noun when they are qualified by an adverb.

una *bella* ragazza	a *beautiful* girl
but	
una ragazza *molto bella*	a *very beautiful* girl
una *lunga* storia	a *long* story
but	
una storia *abbastanza lunga*	*quite* a *long* story

Note: If two or more adjectives are used with the same noun, they all keep their normal positions, but any that come together are joined by **e** 'and.'

una bella ragazza simpatica	a nice, beautiful girl
but	
una ragazza simpatica *e* intelligente	a nice, intelligent girl
una grande *e* bella casa	a big, beautiful house

(iv) A number of adjectives have a different meaning according to whether they precede or follow the noun:

alto	**l'alta marea**	high tide
	un uomo alto	a tall man
basso	**la bassa marea**	low tide
	un numero basso	a small / insignificant number
buono	**un buon attore**	a good / capable actor
	un vino buono	a good wine
caro	**un caro amico**	a dear friend
	un libro caro	an expensive book
cattivo	**un cattivo odore**	a bad / nasty smell
	una ragazza cattiva	a bad / wicked girl

certo	**una certa somiglianza**	a certain / some similarity
	una notizia certa	reliable news
diverso / vario	**diverse / varie volte**	various / several times
	riviste diverse / varie	different (not the same) magazines
dolce	**la dolce vita**	the good / sweet life
	l'acqua dolce	fresh (not salty) water
grande	**un grand'uomo**	a great man
	un uomo grande	a big / tall man
grosso	**un grosso errore**	a big / serious mistake
	un signore grosso	a big / portly gentleman
numeroso	**numerose famiglie**	numerous / many families
	famiglie numerose	large families
nuovo	**una nuova maglia**	another sweater (latest of a number)
	una maglia nuova	a new sweater
povero	**una povera famiglia**	a poor / unfortunate family
	una famiglia povera	a poor (not well-off) family
santo	**tutta la santa settimana**	all (blessed) week
	la Settimana Santa	Holy Week (before Easter)
semplice	**una semplice idea**	just / simply an idea
	un'idea semplice	a simple / uncomplicated idea
unico	**l'unica occasione**	the one (and only) opportunity
	un attore unico	a unique actor
vero	**un vero disastro**	a real disaster
	una storia vera	a true story

Generally speaking the adjectives in the above list have a *literal* meaning when they follow the noun and a more *figurative* meaning when they precede the noun. Many of these adjectives have a variety of meanings when used in other contexts, as you will find when you consult a dictionary.

(v) *Qualcosa, niente + di + adjective*

Qualcosa 'something' and **niente** 'nothing' combine with **di** before an adjective (which is always in the masculine singular form).

Hai fatto *qualcosa di bello* ieri sera?	Did you do *something nice* last night?
Non ho *niente di nuovo* da dirti.	I have *nothing new* to tell you.

(vi) *'Understood' noun*

When the noun is understood, the adjective continues to agree with it as if it were there.

Vuole provare queste scarpe marrone o *quelle nere*?	Do you want to try on these brown shoes or *the black ones*?

22c At a Distance: Predicative Adjectives

(i) What is a predicative adjective?

Predicative means *in the predicate* [➤4c]. These adjectives are usually the complement of the verb, that is, they are linked to the subject by a verb such as **essere** 'be,' **diventare** 'become,' **sembrare** 'seem.' Although separated from the noun they relate to, they nonetheless agree in number and gender exactly as when used attributively [➤22b].

Sono venuto a vivere in questa zona sei mesi fa. I dintorni sono veramente *belli*, il clima è *mite* e la gente è *simpatica*. Ora tutto è *tranquillo*, le strade sono *deserte*. Ma fra poco arriva l'estate e ho sentito dire che la zona diventa *affollata* di turisti. Forse non mi sembrerà più così *idillico*!	I came to live in this area six months ago. The surroundings are really *beautiful*, the climate is *mild*, and the people are *nice*. Now everything is *calm*, the streets are *deserted*. But summer will be here shortly, and I have heard that the area becomes *crowded* with tourists. Perhaps it will no longer seem so *idyllic* to me!

(ii) Agreement with more than one noun

When the same adjective describes two or more nouns of the same gender, it is plural and agrees with the common gender:

Oggi il teatro e il cinema sono *chiusi*.	Today the theater / theatre and the movie house / cinema are *closed*.
La panetteria e la macelleria sono *aperte*.	The baker's and the butcher's are *open*.

If the nouns in the same sentence are of different genders, the adjective is in the masculine plural:

La farmacia e il fioraio sono *aperti*.	The drugstore / chemist's and the florist's are *open*.

When an adjective precedes two nouns of different genders and is used to describe both, then it is possible to repeat the adjective and make it agree with its respective noun:

Ho visitato *molti* musei e *molte* chiese.	I visited *many* museums and (*many*) churches.

or the adjective is used with the first noun of the group and agrees with it:

Ho visitato *molti* musei e chiese.	I visited *many* museums and churches.

Although it would be normal not to repeat the adjective in cases where you have a series of nouns, it often makes more sense, and would be more correct to do so, when it is a question of two nouns of different gender or different number.

***Mio* fratello e *mia* sorella non vengono con noi.**	*My* brother and (*my*) sister are not coming with us.
Andiamo a trovare *mio* zio e *i miei* nonni.	We are going to see *my* uncle and *my* grandparents.

(iii) *Agreement with* ***si***

When the impersonal pronoun **si** 'one' [➤23d] is followed by a verb + adjective, then the adjective must always be in the masculine plural form.

Dopo una giornata di lavoro *si torna* a casa *stanchi.* Quando *si è giovani* non è un problema ma quando *si è vecchi* ...	After a day's work *you come back* home *tired.* When *you are young,* it's not a problem, but when *you are old. . . .*

(iv) ***Avere fame,*** *and so on*

A number of everyday expressions that in English are rendered by *'to be' + adjective* are expressed in Italian using ***avere*** (*not* ***essere***) + *noun.* They include:

avere caldo	be hot (referring to people)
avere fame	be hungry
avere freddo	be cold (referring to people)
avere paura	be afraid
avere ragione	be right
avere sete	be thirsty
avere sonno	be sleepy
avere torto	be right
avere vergogna	be ashamed

In these expressions, **caldo, fame, freddo,** and so on are nouns and therefore invariable: no agreement is required. However, adjectives that may accompany them, such as **molto** 'very,' must agree in the normal way.

Se hai *freddo* Daniela, mettiti la giacca.	If you are *cold* Daniela, put your jacket on.
Mamma, abbiamo molta *sete*.	Mom / Mum, we are *very thirsty*.

[For **avere** to express age ➤30e.]

(v) *Weather*

The same thing happens in weather expressions using **fa, c'è,** and such:

fa caldo	it's hot
fa freddo	it's cold
c'è la nebbia	it's foggy
c'è il sole	it's sunny
tira vento	it's windy

Non vado al mare a quest'ora perché *fa* troppo *caldo*.	I am not going to the seaside at this time because *it's* too *hot*.

Note: **Caldo** and **freddo** can be used both as nouns and adjectives.

22d Irregular Adjectives

There are a few adjectives that have irregular forms when they *precede* the noun. When they follow the noun they are formed regularly [➤22a(i)].

(i) Bello, quello

Bello 'beautiful' and the demonstrative determiner **quello** 'that' have forms like those of the definite article [➤21c(i)–21c(vi)].

Masculine singular	*Masculine plural*
bello	**begli**
bell'	**begli**
bel	**bei**
Feminine singular	***Feminine plural***
bella	**belle**
bell'	

un *bel* sorriso	a *beautiful* smile
dei *bei* bambini	some *beautiful* children
un *bell'*uomo	a *handsome* man
un *bello* specchio	a *beautiful* mirror
che *begli* occhi!	what *beautiful* eyes!
una *bella* ragazza	a *beautiful* girl
delle *belle* ragazze	some *beautiful* girls
una *bell'*arancia	a *fine* orange

[For the demonstrative determiner **quello** ➤21d(ii).]

(ii) Buono

Buono 'good' is irregular in the singular only and has forms like those of the indefinite article [➤21e(i–ii)].

un *buon* amico	a *good* friend
***buon* divertimento!**	have a *good* time!
un *buono* studente	a *good* student
***buona* fortuna**	*good* luck
una *buon'*attrice	a *good* actress

[**Alcuno** and **nessuno** also follow this same pattern in the singular ➤21g(i).]

(iii) Grande

Grande 'great,' 'large,' 'big,' may be shortened to **grand'** before nouns beginning with a vowel and **gran** before nouns beginning with a consonant, with the exception of nouns beginning with **s-** + another consonant, **z-, gn-, ps-,** and **x-**. However, the use of the complete form **grande** is now much more common.

una *grand'/grande* opportunità	a *great* opportunity
un *gran/grande* signore	a *great* gentleman

Note: The shortened form is used in expressions that convey *strong* feelings, such as:

Abbiamo un *gran* desiderio di tornare in Italia.	We have a *great* desire to go back to Italy.

(iv) Santo

Santo 'saint,' 'holy' has the following shortened forms when it precedes a noun:

- **sant'** before masculine and feminine nouns beginning with a vowel:

***sant'*Antonio**	*Saint* Anthony
***sant'*Anna**	*Saint* Anne

- **san** before masculine nouns beginning with a consonant other than **s-** + consonant:

***san* Paolo**	*Saint* Paul
***san* Giuseppe**	*Saint* Joseph

However, the complete form is used:

- before masculine nouns beginning with **s-** + a consonant:

***santo* Stefano**	*Saint* Stephen

- before feminine nouns beginning with a consonant:

***santa* Chiara**	*Saint* Claire

22e Plural Formation of Other Adjectives

There are a considerable number of adjectives that form their plurals in the same way as nouns [▶ 20h(iii)].

(i) -io

Adjectives ending in **-io** form their masculine plural in **-ii** when the **i** of **-io** is *stressed*, and in a single **-i** when *unstressed*.

stantio	**stant*ii***	stale
	but	
ampio	**amp*i***	wide

(ii) *-co, -go*

Masculine adjectives ending in **-co** and **-go** form their plural in **-chi** and **-ghi** when the stress falls on the *penultimate* syllable.

bianco	**bian*chi***	white
largo	**lar*ghi***	wide

An exception is:

greco	**greci**	Greek

Adjectives where the stress falls *before* the penultimate syllable generally form their plural in **-ci:**

magnifico	**magnifi*ci***	magnificent

An exception is:

carico	**carichi**	loaded, laden

Note: Since there are a number of exceptions to the rules governing the plurals of adjectives ending in **-co** and **-go,** it is always advisable to check the formation of the plural in a good dictionary.

(iii) *-ca, -ga*

Feminine adjectives ending in **-ca** and **-ga** form their plural in **-che** and **-ghe**.

magnifica	**magnifi*che***	magnificent
lunga	**lun*ghe***	long

(iv) *-cia, -gia*

Feminine adjectives ending in a consonant + **-cia** and **-gia** form their plural in **-ce** and **-ge**.

li*scia*	**li*sce***	smooth
selva*ggia*	**selva*gge***	wild

When these same endings are preceded by a vowel the plural ends in **-cie** and **-gie**.

rand*a*gia	**rand*agie***	stray

22f *'More' and 'Most': Comparative and Superlative*

Most (though not all) adjectives can be used to make comparisons: for this we use the *comparative* form. If we are comparing more than two people or things, then we use the *superlative*.

(i) *Comparative*

The comparative in Italian is formed by putting **più** 'more' before the adjective and, where necessary, **che** or **di** 'than' after it.

Ho due fratelli, Gino e Marco. Gino è *più giovane di* Marco. Gino è *più bravo* a scuola ma solo perché è *più diligente*. A Marco piace uscire quanto possibile e, in genere, è un tipo molto *più attivo di noi*.	I have two brothers, Gino and Marco. Gino is *younger than* Marco. Gino is *better* at school but only because he is *more diligent*. Marco likes to go out as much as possible and, generally, he is a much *more active* type *than we are*.

Note: **Di** is used before nouns (**di Marco**), pronouns (**di noi**), and numerals:

La settimana scorsa ha speso *più di* cinquecento dollari.	Last week he spent *more than* five hundred dollars.

Che is used before adjectives, adverbs, prepositions, participles, and infinitives.

Marco è più attivo *che passivo*.	Marco is more active *than passive*.
Quando fa i suoi compiti, li fa sempre più velocemente *che correttamente*.	When he does his homework, he always does it more quickly *than correctly*.
È un po' più diligente a scuola *che a* casa.	He is a bit more diligent at school *than at* home.
È più interessato allo svago *che motivato* dai suoi studi.	He is more interested in entertainment *than motivated* by his studies.
Per lui, è più importante uscire *che studiare*.	For him, it is more important to go out *than to study*.

When the comparison is between two nouns or pronouns that are complements or objects of the *same* verb, 'than' is expressed by **che** and not **di**:

Per lui, *è più importante lo svago che la scuola*.	For him, *entertainment is more important than school*.
I miei genitori *aiutano più me che lui*.	My parents *help me more than him*.

[For the use of the subjunctive after a comparative ➤ 16g.]

(ii) *Superlative*

The *superlative* is formed by using the *definite article + the comparative*, which may come before or after the noun, or may stand without the noun if it is understood. Note, however, that the article is *not* repeated when the adjective follows the noun.

Marco è *lo* studente *più dotato* ma Gino è *il più diligente.*	Marco is *the most gifted student,* but Gino is *the most diligent.*

- After a superlative, use **di** for 'in':

Marco è *il più dotato della* classe.	Marco is the *most gifted in* the class.

- Sometimes the preposition **fra** or **tra** [➤ 25c(ix)] is used in place of **di**:

Marco è *il più dotato fra/tra* tutti gli studenti della sua classe.	Marco is the *most gifted of* all the students in his class.

(iii) *Meno 'less,' 'least'*

The comparative and superlative forms introduced by **meno** 'less,' 'least' follow exactly the same patterns of formation and use as **più.**

Marco è senz'altro *meno ambizioso* di Gino, infatti penso che sia *il meno ambizioso* della sua classe.	Marco is certainly *less ambitious than* Gino, in fact I think he is *the least ambitious* in his class.

(iv) *Tanto ... quanto / così ... come*

When comparing people or things as equals, use either **tanto ... quanto ...** or **così ... come ...** 'as . . . as . . . ' or **non tanto ... quanto / non così ... come ...** 'not as / so . . . as . . .' in the negative.

Io sono *tanto diligente quanto* mio fratello Gino ma *non* sono *così ambizioso come* lui.	I'm as *diligent as* my brother Gino but I'm *not as/so ambitious as* he.

- **Tanto** and **così** are frequently omitted:

Io sono *diligente quanto* mio fratello Gino ma *non* sono *ambizioso come* lui.	I'm *as diligent as* my brother Gino but I'm *not as ambitious as* him.

Tanto and **quanto** are invariable when they qualify adjectives as in the example above. However, when they qualify nouns, they must agree in number and gender:

Nella mia classe ci sono *tanti ragazzi quante ragazze.*	In my class there are *as many boys as girls.*

(v) *-issimo*

To say something is *'very,' 'extremely,' + adjective,* you can add **-issimo** to the adjective after removing the final vowel. The **-issimo** ending agrees with the noun in the usual way. This form is known as the *absolute superlative.*

I miei compagni di scuola sono *simpaticissimi*, e facciamo *tantissime* cose insieme.	My school companions are *extremely nice*, and we do *a great many* things together.

- Remember that some adjectives need spelling adjustments before adding **-issimo**, for example, adjectives ending in **-co** and **-go** that form their plurals in **-chi** and **-ghi** [➤22e(ii)].

bianco	**bianc*hissimo***	very white
largo	**larg*hissimo***	very wide

- Adjective ending in **-io** drop both final vowels before adding **-issimo.**

vecchio	**vecchissimo**	very old

(vi) *Alternative forms to* ***-issimo***

Adjectives may also be emphasized:

- by placing an adverb such as **molto / assai** 'very,' **veramente** 'really,' **incredibilmente** 'incredibly,' in front of the adjective:

Sei *molto* gentile.	You are *very* kind.
Sono *assai* motivati.	They are *very* motivated.
Gino è *veramente* studioso.	Gino is *really* studious.
Suo fratello è *incredibilmente* pigro.	His brother is *incredibly* lazy.

- by means of a prefix such as **arci-, stra-, super-, ultra-:**

Come studente, Gino è *arci*contento.	As a student, Gino is *extremely* happy.
Frequenta una scuola *ultra*moderna.	He attends an *ultra*modern school.
Non è *super*intelligente, ma fa del suo meglio.	He is not *super*intelligent but he does his best.
I suoi genitori non sono *stra*ricchi, altrimenti l'avrebbero mandato a una scuola privata.	His parents are not *very* rich, otherwise they would have sent him to a private school.

- by repeating the adjective:

Abitiamo in una casa *piccola piccola.*	We live in a *very* small house.

- by adding another adjective that strengthens the meaning of the first:

Stamattina sono arrivato a scuola bagnato *fradicio.*	This morning I arrived at school *soaking* wet.
L'autobus era pieno *zeppo.*	The bus was *packed* full.
Ieri sera eravamo tutti stanchi *morti.*	Last night we were all *dead* tired.
Mia sorella non riesce a concentrarsi a scuola perché è innamorata *cotta.*	My sister can't concentrate at school because she is *head over heels* in love.

- by other expressions such as the following:

Abitiamo in campagna e in pieno inverno fa un freddo *da morire.*	We live in the country, and in the middle of winter it's *bitterly* cold.

Una vecchia zia abita con noi. È ancora molto vivace, ma è *sorda come una campana.*	An old aunt lives with us. She is still very lively but she's *as deaf as* a doorpost.

(vii) ***Più ... più ...*** *'The more . . . the more . . .'*

These express the consequences of doing something.

***Più* studio, *più* imparo.**	*The more* I study, *the more* I learn.

Meno ... meno ... 'the less . . . the less . . . ' is used in the same way. It is also possible to use a combination of these forms, as in the following example:

***Più* imparo, *meno* capisco.**	*The more* I learn, *the less* I understand.

[For comparative and superlative forms of adverbs ➤26b(iv).]

(viii) *Adjectives with two forms*

There is a small number of Italian adjectives that have irregular forms in addition to the regular ones:

	Comparative	*Superlative*	*Absolute superlative*
alto	**superiore**	**il superiore**	**supremo**
high	higher	the highest	very high
basso	**inferiore**	**l'inferiore**	**infimo**
low	lower	the lowest	very low
buono	**migliore**	**il migliore**	**ottimo**
good	better	the best	very good
cattivo	**peggiore**	**il peggiore**	**pessimo**
bad	worse	the worst	very bad
grande	**maggiore**	**il maggiore**	**massimo**
big	bigger	the biggest	very big
piccolo	**minore**	**il minore**	**minimo**
small	smaller	the smallest	very small

- There are some occasions where you can use either form of the comparative or superlative without affecting the meaning:

Questo vino è *buonissimo/ottimo.* Infatti, è *il migliore/il più buon* vino che abbia mai bevuto.	This wine is *very good.* In fact, it's *the best* wine I've ever drunk.

[For use of the subjunctive after a superlative ➤16f(iii).]

- In other cases, the different form gives rise to a different meaning:

Delle due case la nostra è *più grande.*	Of the two houses ours is *bigger.* (in size)
Il mio fratello *maggiore* si chiama Roberto.	My *older* (age) brother's name is Roberto.
Il costo dei danni causati dal maltempo è stato *maggiore* di quanto pensassimo.	The cost of the damage caused by the bad weather was *greater* (more substantial) than we thought.

Note: **Più piccolo** 'smaller' (in size) and **minore** 'younger' (in age) and 'lesser' (in importance) are used in a similar way to **più grande** and **maggiore.**

The other comparative and superlative forms listed can also be used in different contexts to convey various meanings. It is, therefore, worth consulting a good dictionary to study in greater depth the range of options available.

Note: Adjectives may be formed from the present participle [➤10c(iii)] and past participle [➤10f(ii)] of verbs.

Adjectives may also be used as nouns [➤20i].

22g Prefixes and Suffixes

(i) Prefixes

In English, we often make the opposite, usually the negative, of the adjective by using such prefixes as 'un-' or 'dis-', as in 'unable' or 'disorganized.' In Italian many opposites are formed by using the prefixes **in-, dis-,** and **s-**:

felice	happy	***in*felice**	*un*happy
accettabile	acceptable	***in*accettabile**	*un*acceptable
simile	similar, like	***dis*simile**	*dis*similar, unlike
occupato	employed	***dis*occupato**	*un*employed

fortunato	fortunate	***s*fortunato**	*un*fortunate
carico	loaded	***s*carico**	*un*loaded

As you can see from the examples, the English 'un-' can be conveyed in Italian by three different prefixes: **in-, dis-, s-.**

Do not attach prefixes to adjectives without first consulting a dictionary to ensure that the word really does exist.

Another fairly common way of making the opposite is the use of ***poco*** *+ adjective*.

Lei è *poco* motivata.	She's *un*motivated. (*not very* motivated)
Questi libri sono *poco* interessanti.	These books are *un*interesting.

Poco is always invariable in these constructions.

(ii) *Suffixes*

The meaning of some adjectives can be modified by suffixes. These include:

- the diminutives **-ino, -ello, -etto, -otto**:

caro	dear	**car*ino***	*pretty, cute*
cattivo	naughty	**cattiv*ello***	*rather* naughty
povero	poor	**pover*etto***	poor *thing*
vecchio	old	**vecchi*otto***	*rather* old, oldish

- the augmentative **-one**:

pigro	lazy	**pigr*one***	*very* lazy

Note: An augmentative — the opposite of diminutive — adds strength to the meaning of the adjective and conveys the idea of size. Remember that the feminine form is **-ona** and that there is often a negative connotation associated with this ending.

- **-accio**, which is used in a pejorative sense:

povero	poor	**pover*accio***	poor *wretch*

Note: Before adding the suffix remove the final vowel of the adjective.

As in the case of prefixes, it is safer to use the suffixes with adjectives you have seen or heard to avoid the risk of creating nonexistent words.

Representing Nouns: Pronouns

23a What Pronouns Do

The word *pronoun* means 'in place of a noun.' Pronouns are constantly used instead of nouns as a way of avoiding repetition. The types of pronoun discussed in paragraphs 23i to 23l below have corresponding determiners [➤21].

Pronouns take:

- their *gender* (masculine / feminine) and *number* (singular / plural) from the noun they refer to (although Italian has a number of 'neuter' pronouns, some of which are explained in paragraph 23g below);
- their *form* from the sentence they are in.

23b Personal Pronouns

These are the most neutral pronouns — they simply replace nouns without adding any further information. They may refer to the person(s) speaking (first person), the person(s) spoken to (second person), or the person(s) or thing(s) spoken about (third person).

(i) Subject pronouns

Singular		
First person	**io**	I
Second person	**tu**	you (informal)
	Lei	you (formal)
Third person	**lui (egli)**	he
	lei (ella)	she
	esso	it (masculine)
	essa	it (feminine)
Plural		
First person	**noi**	we
Second person	**voi**	you (informal)
	Loro	you (formal)
Third person	**loro (essi)**	they (masculine)
	loro (esse)	they (feminine)

Because the subject — the doer — of the action [▶ 4b] is contained in the verb ending in the Italian, the subject pronouns are only used for *emphasis, contrast*, or *to avoid confusion*, and *when they stand alone*. **Lei / Loro** are perhaps used more frequently, mainly because of the possible ambiguity over the shared third person verb endings, but also sometimes to emphasize deference to the person(s) addressed.

Cosa facciamo stasera?	What are we doing this evening?
— *Tu* puoi fare quello che vuoi, ma *io* preferisco stare a casa.	— *You* can do what you want, but *I* prefer to stay at home. (contrast between *you* and *I*)
Cosa fanno Gianni e Barbara?	What are Gianni and Barbara doing?
— *Lui* va a vedere la partita di pallacanestro, mentre *lei* va al cinema.	— *He* is going to the basketball game, while *she* is going to the movies / cinema. (contrast between *he* and *she*)
Perché non vai alla partita *anche tu*?	Why don't *you* go to the game *too*? (emphasis)
— *Io*, ma scherzi, sai che detesto lo sport.	— *Me*, you must be joking, you know that I hate sports. (subject stands alone without the verb)

Note: In the example **Perché non vai *anche tu*?** the subject pronoun **tu** is used for reasons of emphasis; but it must be used, anyway, after adverbs such as **anche, neanche.**

Non ci voglio andare *neanch'io*.	*I* don't want to go there *either*.

- Subject pronouns usually follow the verb when they are used for emphasis:

Se non vai *tu*, vado *io*.	If *you* don't go, *I* will.
— Chi parla?	— Who's speaking?
— Sono *io*, Barbara.	— It's *me*, Barbara.
— Ah, sei *tu*.	— Ah, it's *you*.

- It is a good idea to use the subject pronoun with the singular of the present subjunctive to avoid confusion, since the first three persons have an identical form [▶ 18c(ii),19].

Although the formal **Lei** and **Loro** 'you' have been listed under the second person, it is very important to remember that they not only take the third person of the verb, but that in all other functions they take *third person pronouns* and *possessives* [▶ 23b(ii), 23l, 21h(i)].

- **Egli/ella** 'he'/'she' and **esso/essa** 'it' are rarely used nowadays in speech. They have been replaced by **lui/lei**. Similarly, in the third person plural **essi/esse** 'they' have been replaced by **loro**. You will, however, come across these forms in the written language, *especially* in reference to inanimate nouns.

- The polite forms **Lei** and **Loro** are sometimes written with a small **l** in informal writing.

- **Formal and informal address**

In Italian it is very important to distinguish between the use of the informal **tu** and the formal **Lei. Tu** is used when addressing family, friends, children, and animals. You should use **Lei** in formal settings—at a bank, hotel, restaurant, travel agency—unless of course one of the employees is a friend of yours. A reasonable guideline is that people on a first name basis would use the informal **tu**, whereas people addressing one another by title—such as **signore, signora, signorina, dottore, professore**—would use **Lei.**

Foreigners often find themselves in a kind of dilemma when they first meet people of similar age. The safest thing to do is to use **Lei** until you are invited to do otherwise! (**Diamoci del tu.**—Let's use the **tu** form.) There is an increasing tendency in the spoken language to replace the formal plural **Loro** with **voi,** which is also of course the informal plural.

Come stai, Elena?—Bene grazie, e *tu*?	How are you Elena? —Well, thank you, and *you*?
Come sta, signora Bianchi? —Non c'è male grazie, e *Lei?*	How are you Mrs. Bianchi? —Not bad thank you, and *you*?
Elena e Marco, statemi a sentire un attimo, dove andate (*voi*) in vacanza quest'anno?	Elena and Marco, just listen to me for a moment; where are *you* going on vacation/holiday this year?
A che ora partono (Loro)/partite (voi)?	At what time are *you* leaving?

(ii) Direct object pronouns [➤8d]

Singular		*Plural*	
mi	me	**ci**	us
ti	you (informal)	**vi**	you (informal)
La	you (formal, masculine + feminine)	**Li**	you (formal, masculine)
		Le	you (formal, feminine)
lo	him, it	**li**	them (masculine)
la	her, it	**le**	them (feminine)

—Perché non vai al cinema con Barbara?—Danno lo stesso film della settimana scorsa e l'ho già visto. A proposito, Gianni e Barbara *ci* hanno invitato a pranzo domenica. *Mi* ascolti o no?—Certo che *ti* ascolto, e mentre stai in piedi spegni la televisione. —*L*'ho spenta cinque minuti fa.	—Why don't you go to the movies/cinema with Barbara? —They are showing the same film/movie as last week and I have already seen *it*. By the way, Gianni and Barbara have invited *us* to lunch on Sunday. Are you listening to *me* or not?—Of course I'm listening *to you*; and while you are up, turn off the television. —I turned *it* off five minutes ago.

Ascoltare means *'listen to'* and takes a direct object [➤ 8h(vii)].

• **Lo** and **la** elide (**l'**) before a vowel or **h**. Although elision is possible with **mi, ti, ci,** and **vi,** it happens less frequently. One notable exception with **ci** is of course the expression **c'è** 'there is.' Never elide the plural forms **li** and **le**.

[For agreement of past participle with direct object pronouns ➤ 11d(i).]

(iii) *Indirect object pronouns [➤ 8e]*

Singular		***Plural***	
mi	to me	**ci**	to us
ti	to you (informal)	**vi**	to you (informal)
Le	to you (formal)	**Loro**	to you (formal)
gli	to him, to it	**loro (gli)**	to them (masculine & feminine)
le	to her, to it		

• There is an increasing tendency to use **gli** for 'to them' in place of **loro** in the informal, spoken language. **Loro**, however, is still used in more formal situations as well as in the written language.

Loro is the one indirect pronoun that always follows a verb and can never be attached to an infinitive, gerund, imperative, or past participle [➤ 23b(iv)].

Ho detto *loro* che veniamo. or ***Gli* ho detto che veniamo.**	I told *them* that we are coming.

• Although the indirect object means 'to' or 'for' someone, in English this is not always clear, and care should be taken to use the correct object pronoun in Italian. It is helpful sometimes to put the word 'to' before the object. If this makes sense, then the object is *indirect.*

Dove hai messo la lettera che *ti* ho dato stamattina?	Where have you put the letter I gave *(to) you* this morning?

However, some verbs take an indirect object in Italian but not in English.

Perché non *mi* hai chiesto prima di accettare l'invito?	Why didn't you ask *me* before accepting the invitation?

[For other verbs that take an indirect object [➤8e(i)].

• When there is both an indirect and a direct object pronoun, with the exception of **loro** 'to them,' the indirect always precedes the direct [➤23b(v)].

Perché non *me* l'hai detto prima?	Why didn't you tell *(it to) me* before?

Note: 'It' is often omitted in English in sentences such as the one above, but Italian usually includes **lo / l'** to complete the sense. [For other examples ➤23g(i).]

(iv) *Position of object pronouns*

With the exception of **loro** all object pronouns immediately precede the verb.

Ma quando *ti* dico qualcosa non *mi* ascolti mai.	But when I tell *you* something you never listen to *me.*

• In compound tense forms the object pronoun comes before the auxiliary verb.

***Te* l'ho già detto due volte. — Non è vero, non *me* l'hai detto nemmeno una volta.**	I have already told *you* twice. — It's not true, you haven't told *me* even once.

Note also that in negative sentences the object pronouns still retain the same position immediately in front of the verb.

• Object pronouns are attached to the end of an infinitive after the final **-e** of the infinitive is removed. (For verbs modeled on **tradurre** 'translate' and **porre** 'put,' remove the final **-re** before attaching the object pronoun.)

Spero di veder*li* domani mattina.	I hope to see *them* tomorrow morning.

• With modal verbs [▶ 9] + infinitive, the object pronoun(s) can either be placed before the modal verb or be attached to the following infinitive.

***Gli* posso dire che hai un altro impegno.** or **Posso dir*gli* che hai un altro impegno.**	I can tell *them* that you have something else to do.

• With **stare / andare** + gerund [▶ 8k(i) – 8k(ii)] the object pronouns normally come before **stare / andare**, but it is also possible to attach them to the end of the gerund.

Cosa *mi* stavi dicendo? or (less common) **Cosa stavi dicendo*mi*?**	What were you saying *to me*?

The object pronouns must, however, be attached to both the simple and compound forms of the gerund when it stands alone.

Accettando*lo* (i.e., l'invito), avremo modo di conoscere i loro cugini che sono appena tornati dall'Italia.	By accepting *it* (i.e., the invitation), we shall have the opportunity to meet their cousins who have just returned from Italy.
Avendo*lo* accettato, non posso dire di no.	Having accepted *it*, I can't say no.

• Object pronouns must be attached to past participles standing alone:

Accettato*lo*, non posso dire di no.	Having accepted *it*, I can't say no.

and also to **ecco** 'here is' / 'here are,' 'there is' / 'there are.'

Ecco*li!*	There *they* are!
Ecco*mi!*	Here *I* am!

[For position of pronouns with imperative ➤15b(ii) – 15b(iii).]

(v) *Order of object pronouns*

When two object pronouns occur together, the *indirect* precedes the *direct.* The list below also includes the reflexive pronoun **si**, which will be dealt with in paragraph ➤23c. You will notice that **mi, ti, ci, vi,** and **si** become **me, te, ce, ve,** and **se** when they precede the direct object pronoun. **Gli** 'to him,' **le** 'to her,' and **Le** 'to you' (formal) become **glie** before combining with the direct object pronoun to give *one word.*

me lo	**me la**	**me li**	**me le**	**me ne**
te lo	**te la**	**te li**	**te le**	**te ne**
glielo	**gliela**	**glieli**	**gliele**	**gliene**
se lo	**se la**	**se li**	**se le**	**se ne**
ce lo	**ce la**	**ce li**	**ce le**	**ce ne**
ve lo	**ve la**	**ve li**	**ve le**	**ve ne**
se lo	**se la**	**se li**	**se le**	**se ne**

- When **me lo,** etc. precede the verb, they are written separately; but they too join to form one word when attached to an infinitive, gerund, past participle, and **ecco** [➤23b(iv) above].

Te lo* manderò, ma non posso mandar*telo subito.	I shall send *it to you*, but I can't send *it to you* immediately.

Glie combined with another third person direct object pronoun could mean 'to him' / 'her' or 'to you' (formal). Since there is a growing tendency to use **gli** in place of **loro,** especially in spoken language, then the meanings could also include 'to them' and 'to you' (formal plural). The person being addressed, however, is usually obvious from the context.

Hai detto a tuo fratello che è invitato a pranzo? — Si, *gliel'*ho detto.	Have you told your brother that he is invited to lunch? — Yes, I've told *him*.

- **Gli** also combines with **ne** [▶ 23f(i)] to become **gliene**:

***Gliene* ho parlato.**	I've spoken *to him about it.*

(vi) *'Redundant' object pronouns*

In spoken Italian noun objects, both direct and indirect, are often 'doubled' by the addition of the object pronoun, especially — but not necessarily — when the noun object precedes the verb.

***Questo invito*, non *lo* voglio rifiutare.**	I don't want to turn down *this invitation.*
Ma *a te*, cosa *ti* hanno detto esattamente?	But what did they tell *you* exactly?

23c ***Reflexive Pronouns***

(i) *Use of reflexive pronouns*

Reflexive pronouns are object pronouns that refer back to the subject of the sentence, as when you do something to yourself. In the first person (**mi** 'me,' **ci** 'us'), and the second person (**ti** 'you,' **vi** 'you' *informal*), Italian uses the normal personal object pronouns as reflexives. However, there is a special third person reflexive that is both singular and plural: **si**. This means 'himself,' 'herself,' 'itself,' 'themselves,' and also 'yourself,' and 'yourselves,' for **Lei** and **Loro**, which — remember! — use *third person pronouns.*

If you use the ordinary third person object pronouns **lo / la / li / le / gli,** etc. [▶ 23b(ii) – 23b(iii)], then the action is being done to someone or something else, not to the subject.

***Si* è comprata un bell'abito da sera.**	*She* bought *herself* a beautiful evening dress.
***Gli* ha comprato una cravatta.**	*She* bought *him* a tie.

***Si* è svegliato presto.**	*He* woke (*himself*) up early.
***L*'ha svegliata più tardi.**	*He* woke *her* up later.

Note: Actions performed to parts of one's own body or clothing are usually expressed by a reflexive verb rather than a possessive [▸ 21h(vi)].

***Mi* sono storto *la* caviglia.**	*I* twisted *my* ankle.
***Si* è lavata i capelli.**	*She* washed *her* hair.

(ii) 'Each other'

Plural reflexive pronouns (**ci, vi, si**) can also be used *reciprocally*, that is, when people do something not to themselves but to each other.

Che peccato che tuo fratello non possa venire a pranzo domenica; non *ci vediamo* da almeno due mesi, e chi sa quando è stata l'ultima volta che lui e i miei cugini *si sono incontrati*!	What a pity that your brother can't come to lunch on Sunday; *we haven*'t *seen each other* for at least two months, and who knows when he and my cousins last *met (each other)*.

Do not confuse reflexives with the words we use to emphasize that it was *the subject* that did something, not anyone else. To obtain this emphasis, simply use **stesso** 'self,' agreeing in gender and number, after the subject pronoun [▸ 23b(i)].

Ha accettato l'invito *lei stessa*.	She accepted the invitation *herself.*

23d The Indefinite Pronoun 'One'

(i) Si

To express the idea of the English indefinite pronoun 'one,' 'you,' 'we,' 'they,' 'people,' in a general sense, Italian normally uses the third person reflexive pronoun **si** with the third person singular of the verb.

***Si vede* che per tuo fratello domenica sarà impossibile.**	*One can see* that for your brother Sunday will be impossible.

Forse *si può* organizzare qualcos'altro. — Ma con lui, non *si sa* mai cosa fare.	Perhaps *we can* organize something else. — But with him, *you* never *know* what to do.

Care should be taken not to confuse the impersonal pronoun **si** 'one' with the **si passivante** [➤17e(i)].

- When used with a reflexive verb, **si** changes to **ci** to avoid repetition and confusion with the third person reflexive pronoun, which is also **si.**

***Ci* si abitua alla sua indecisione.**	*One* gets used to his indecision.

- When **si** is used with a compound tense [➤11b], the auxiliary is *always* **essere.** The past participle of verbs that are normally conjugated with **essere** is *always* in the plural.

***Si è detto che* i tuoi cugini torneranno in America alla fine delle vacanze.**	*People have said* that your cousins will be going back to America at the end of the vacation.
***Ci* si è abituat*i* alla sua indecisione.**	*One* has gotten used to his indecision.
Basta, *si* è tornat*i* sullo stesso discorso di prima.	That's enough, *we* have come back to the same subject of conversation as before.

Note: **Dire** 'say,' 'tell,' is normally conjugated with **avere**; **detto** is singular.

[For **si** + verb + *plural adjective* ➤22c(iii).]

- All object pronouns precede **si** with the exception of **ne** [➤23f(iii)], which follows it. **Si** becomes **se** when it precedes **ne.**

***Gli* si dice di essere un po' più socievole.**	People tell *him* to be a bit more sociable.
Dimmi a che ora devo venire domenica, e poi non se *ne* parla più.	Tell me at what time I have to come on Sunday, and then we won't talk *about it* anymore.

(ii) *Uno*

The indefinite pronoun **uno** is sometimes used in place of **si**.

Quando *uno* si comporta così è difficile.	When *one* (*someone*) behaves like that it's difficult.

The rules governing the use of **si** + compound tense, reflexive verb, etc., explained under ➤ 23d(i), *do not apply* when using **uno**:

23e The Pronouns Ci, Vi

*(i) **Ci** or **vi** 'there'*

In addition to their function as *object pronouns,* **ci** and, less frequently, **vi** are used as *adverbs* meaning 'there.'

Sei mai stata in America, Silvia? —No, non *ci* sono mai stata.	Have you ever been to America, Silvia?—No, I've never been *there.*

Note that very often no word for **ci** is present in English:

Ma spero di andar*ci* un giorno.	But I hope to go one day.

Ci is also used:

- to replace other adverbial expressions indicating location, such as 'in there,' 'by there':

I tuoi genitori sono *a casa*? —No, non *ci* sono, sono andati a trovare mia nonna. *Ci* passano ogni sera perché abita da sola.	Are your parents *at* home? —No, they're not, they've gone to see my grandmother. They drop *by* (*there*) every evening because she lives alone.

- to replace **a** + a noun or pronoun:

Penso ancora *alla indecisione* di mio fratello. *Ci* penso spesso. Non capisco perché voglia rinunciare *a questo invito.* —Lascialo stare, avrà i suoi motivi per rinunciar*ci.*	I'm still thinking *about* my brother's *indecisiveness.* I often think *about it.* I don't understand why he wants to decline *this invitation.* —Let him be, he must have his own reasons for not accepting *it.*

When used in this way, **a** can only refer to a thing or things, *never* to people. To refer to people use a disjunctive pronoun [➤23h]:

È strano perché pensa spesso a *loro.*	It's strange because he often thinks about *them.*

- to replace **a** + an infinitive or an entire phrase:

Allora non sei riuscita *a convincerlo.*—No, purtroppo, non *ci* sono riuscita.	So you didn't manage *to convince him.*—No, unfortunately, I didn't.
Forse si è abituato *a stare a casa.*—Hai ragione, *ci* si è abituato.	Perhaps he's gotten used *to staying at home.*—You're right, he's gotten used *to it.*

- in a number of more idiomatic expressions to convey meanings such as 'about,' 'of,' 'to,' 'on,' 'from it':

Dimmi, cosa *ci* posso fare?	Tell me, what can I do *about it*?
—Non *ci* capisco più niente.	—I can't make any sense *of it* any-more.
Per quanto riguarda quell'altra faccenda, *ci* penserò io.	As for that other matter, I shall see *to it.*
—Ma ti ho detto che puoi contare sul mio aiuto.	—But I told you that you can count on my help.
Lo so che *ci* posso contare.	I know that I can count *on it.*
—Se vendi il tuo appartamento adesso, cosa *ci* guadagni?	—If you sell your apartment/flat now, what do you gain *from it*?
Il doppio di quello che ho pagato.	Double what I paid for it.
—Non *ci* credo.	—I don't believe *it.*
Comunque, i soldi non *c'*entrano!	However, money doesn't come *into it*!

- in some other idiomatic expressions in combination with **la**:

Questo appartamento è troppo grande per me, c'è sempre tanto lavoro e non *ce la* faccio.	This apartment/flat is too big for me, there is always so much work to do and I can't manage.
Mia sorella *ce l'*ha sempre con me.	My sister is always angry with me.

- with **avere** in expressions like:

Hai il mio indirizzo?—No, non *ce* l'ho.	Have you got my address?—No, I haven't.
***Ce* le hai tu le foto del mio appartamento?—Sì, *ce* le ho.**	Have you got the photos of my apartment/flat?—Yes, I have.

Ci in such expressions is for purposes of reinforcement, as **l'ho** and **le ho** on their own sound rather odd.
[**Ci** becomes **ce** in front of another object pronoun ➤ 23b(v).]

Note also:

***Ci* ho sonno.**	I am tired.
***Ci* hai fame?**	Are you hungry?

This is a *very colloquial* use of **ci** that you will come across in the spoken language but that should not be used in writing.

(ii) *Position*

When it is used in combination with other pronouns, **ci** comes first [➤ 23b(v)]. However, it comes after **mi** and **ti**.

Se vai da Gianni domani sera, ti *ci* vedrò.	If you go to Gianni's tomorrow evening, I shall see you *there*.

[For position when used on its own ➤ 23b(iv).]

Note: In place of **ci** meaning 'there' it is possible to use **lì** or **là**. These must *never* be attached to a verb form.

Se vai da Gianni domani sera, ti vedrò lì.	If you go to Gianni's tomorrow evening, I shall see you *there*.

23f *The Pronoun* Ne

(i) ***Ne*** *replaces* ***di***

The pronoun **ne** replaces **di** (or one of its forms) + a noun or pronoun. Given the range of uses of **di** in Italian, **ne** covers a wide range of meanings such as 'of him'/'of her'/'of them,' 'of it'/'of this'/'of that,' 'some,' 'any.'

Come sta tua zia? — Da quando è andata a vivere a Venezia non *ne* so niente.	How is your aunt? — Since she went to live in Venice I know nothing *about her*.
Ma ti avrà mandato almeno una cartolina? — No, nemmeno una, ma non voglio parlar*ne*.	But she must have sent you at least a postcard? — No, not even one, but I don't want to talk *about it*.
Ma può darsi che stia male, cosa *ne* pensi? Cambiando il discorso, hai comprato dei fiori per il compleanno di tua sorella? — No, non *ne* ho comprati, vado a comprar*ne* subito.	But maybe she's ill / sick, what do you think (*about it*)? Changing the subject, have you bought some flowers for your sister's birthday? — No, I haven't bought *any*, I shall go and buy *some* at once.

(ii) *With expressions of quantity*

Ne often appears with expressions of quantity as a great number of them are followed by **di**.

Se vai dal fioraio, compra due mazzi di fiori, uno per te e uno per me. — Va bene, *ne* compro due.	If you go to the florist's, buy two bunches of flowers, one for you and one for me. — All right, I'll buy two (*of them*).
Quanti soldi hai? — *Ne* ho abbastanza.	How much money do you have? — I have enough (*of if*).
Se passi dal mercato, compra delle banane. — *Ne* comprerò due chili.	If you go by the market, buy some bananas. — I'll buy two kilos (*of them*).

(iii) *Other uses*

Ne is also used:

- with an adverbial function, meaning 'from there' / 'from here':

Quando *ne* torni, ti faccio un bel caffè.	When you come back (*from there*), I shall make you a nice coffee.

- on occasions to replace **di** + an entire phrase or sentence, particularly after verbs like **dimenticarsi** 'forget' and **rendersi conto** 'realize,' which are followed by **di**.

Sapevi che volevo vendere il mio appartamento, vero?—Sì, me l'avevi detto una volta, ma poi me *ne* sono dimenticata.	You knew that I wanted to sell my apartment / flat, right?—Yes, you had told me once, but then I forgot *about it.*
Ti rendi conto che avrai difficoltà a venderlo adesso? —Sì, comincio a renderme*ne* conto.	You realize that you will have a hard time in selling it now?—Yes, I'm beginning to realize (*it*).

As the above examples illustrate, **ne** is required in Italian, where in many cases in English its equivalent is absent or understood.

Note: **Ne** could be similarly used with a number of the verbs listed under 8h(ii).

[For agreement of **ne** with the past participle in compound tenses ➤ 11d(i).]

(iv) *Position*

Ne follows other object pronouns, including reflexives:

Te *ne* vai adesso?	Are you off now?
Non dimenticare, comprame*ne* due chili.	Don't forget, buy two kilos *of them* for me.
Sono già le undici e non *ce ne* siamo accorti!	It's eleven o'clock already, and we didn't realize it!

[For position when used on its own ➤ 23b(iv).]

23g Neuter Pronouns

(i) *Lo*

Apart from its more frequent use as 'him' / 'it,' **lo** is also used as a neuter object or complement in cases where English would omit it or perhaps use 'so' or even 'one.'

Mio fratello è incapace di prendere una decisione.—*Lo* so, me *l'*hai detto cento volte.	My brother is incapable of making a decision.—I know *(it)*, you've told me *so* a hundred times.

Vuole diventare chirurgo, ma non *lo* diventerà mai.	He wants to become a surgeon, but he will never become *one.*
Pensa di essere un tipo molto estroverso, ma non *lo* è.	He thinks he's a very extrovert type but he isn't (*one*).

(ii) *'It'*

The English impersonal subject pronoun 'it' has no real equivalent in Italian, since the subject is contained in the verb ending. There are, however, plenty of impersonal verbs, such as weather expressions like **fa freddo** 'it's cold' and expressions such as **è difficile** 'it is difficult.' These are dealt with fully in paragraph 8g.

23h Prepositions and Personal Pronouns: Disjunctive Pronouns

Disjunctive means here *not related directly to the verb.* These pronouns are sometimes also called *prepositional* pronouns, since their main use is after prepositions.

Singular		*Plural*	
me	me	**noi**	us
te	you (informal)	**voi**	you (informal)
Lei	you (formal)	**Loro**	you (formal)
lui	him	**loro**	them (masculine & feminine)
lei	her		
esso/essa	it	**essi/esse**	them

(i) Note that except for **me** and **te,** the form is the same as that of the subject pronouns in 23b(i).

Non posso venire *con te.* Devo andare da mia nonna perché due volte alla settimana faccio la spesa *per lei.*	I can't come *with you.* I have to go to my grandmother's because twice a week I do the shopping *for her.*

There are some prepositions that require an additional preposition — **di** — before a disjunctive pronoun. They include the following:

contro	against	**dentro**	inside
dietro	behind	**dopo**	after
fra / tra	among, between	**senza**	without
sopra	above, upon	**sotto**	under, below
su	on, above	**verso**	towards

Conta molto *su di me.*	She depends a lot *on me.*
Dice sempre che non ce la farebbe *senza di me.*	She is always saying that she couldn't manage *without me.*

Note: **Di** is sometimes omitted after **fra / tra**.

Remember that disjunctive pronouns are used after verbs that take a prepositional object [➤8h].

(ii) *Other uses*

Disjunctive pronouns are also used:

- for emphasis, in which case they replace an object pronoun:

***A lei*, non piace uscire la sera.** (emphatic) **Non le piace uscire la sera.** (unemphatic)	*She* doesn't like going out in the evening.
Ma quando io avevo dei problemi, lei aiutava *me.* (emphatic) **Ma quando io avevo dei problemi, lei mi aiutava.** (unemphatic)	But when I had problems, she used to / would help *me.*

- whenever the verb has two or more direct or indirect objects:

Delle volte quando vado da mia nonna aiuto *lei* e *i suoi vicini,* che sono anziani anche loro. (two *direct* objects)	Sometimes when I go to my grandmother's I help *her* and *her neighbors / neighbours,* who are also elderly.
Do una mano *a lei* e *a loro.* (two *indirect* objects)	I help *her* and *them.*

- after **di, che, tanto ..., quanto ... / così ..., come ...,** in comparisons [➤22f(i), 22f(iii), 22f(iv)]:

Comunque, aiuto più lei *che loro.*	However, I help her more *than them.*
Mia nonna non è così attiva *come loro.*	My grandmother is as active *as they.*
I miei genitori fanno molto più *di me.*	My parents do much more *than I.*

- in exclamations after some adjectives:

Fra poco andiamo in vacanza. — *Beati voi!*	— Shortly we are going on vacation / holiday. — *Lucky you!*
Io, invece, non andrò da nessuna parte. — *Povero te!*	Whereas I shall be going nowhere. — *Poor you!*

Note: Disjunctive pronouns plus **stesso /a / i /e** are used to convey the emphatic forms 'myself,' 'yourself,' etc.

Pensi solo a *te stesso.*	You think only of *yourself.*

(iii) Sé

There is also a third person reflexive [> 23c(i)] disjunctive pronoun **sé**, which means 'him' / 'himself,' 'her' / 'herself,' 'itself,' 'oneself,' 'themselves,' 'yourself,' 'yourselves' (**Lei / Loro**). It is used after prepositions when the object of the preposition is the same person as the subject.

Mia nonna non può fare tutto da *sé.*	My grandmother can't do everything by *herself.*
Forse questo problema che ha tuo fratello si risolverà da *sé*.	Perhaps this problem that your brother has will resolve *itself.*

This pronoun is often used together with **stesso**. When this happens, **sé** is written without the acute accent.

A volte, mi fa arrabiare perché pensa solo a *se stesso.*	At times, he makes me angry, because he only thinks of *himself.*

Be careful not to confuse the emphatic use of **me stesso, te stessa,** etc. with the use of reflexive pronouns [> 23c(i)]:

Mi sono tagliato.	I've cut myself. (the 'myself' is conveyed by the reflexive pronoun **mi**)

23i 'Which One?': Interrogative Pronouns

These are question words listed in paragraphs 6d(i) to 6d(iii).

(i) Chi 'Who?' 'Whom?'

- **Chi?** is used for 'who?' 'whom?' as subject, direct object, and object of a preposition. The preposition must *always* precede **chi**; and it may not come at the end of the clause, as it often happens in English. **Chi** is invariable.

***Chi* ha telefonato? — Una ragazza.**	*Who* phoned / rang? — A girl.
***Con chi* voleva perlare?**	To *whom* did she want to speak?
— Non lo so, è caduta la linea.	— I don't know, I was cut off.
***Chi* hai incontrato alla festa?**	*Whom* did you meet at the party?
***A chi* hai prestato il tuo ombrello?**	To *whom* did you lend your umbrella?

(While *whom* is now largely restricted to formal language in English, its inclusion here is intended to be helpful in distinguishing between the subject and the object form.)

In spoken Italian it is fairly common to put the preposition and pronoun after the verb.

Voleva parlare con chi?	Who did she want to speak to?

- **Di chi...?** 'Whose?'

***Di chi* è questa giacca?**	*Whose* jacket is this?
***Di chi* sono queste scarpe?**	*Whose* shoes are these?

Do not confuse this with the word **cui** meaning 'whose,' which is a relative pronoun and is not used to ask questions [➤23m(v)].

(ii) Cosa / che / che cosa? 'What?'

Cosa, che, or **che cosa** are used for 'what?' as subject, direct object, or object of a preposition (which must precede it).

***Cos'*hai fatto?**	*What* have you done?
***Che* è successo?**	*What* has happened?
***A che cosa* stai pensando?**	*What* are you thinking *about*?
***Con che cosa* posso pagare se sono al verde?**	*What* do I pay *with* if I am broke?

Note that it is possible to elide **Cosa** (**Cos'**) but never **Che**.

Remember that you can only use **che,** not **cosa** or **che cosa** as an interrogative adjective [➤21b]. So, for example, 'What type/sort of . . . ?' would be **Che tipo/genere di . . .?**

(iii) *Quale/quali? 'Which one(s)?'*

Quale 'which one' and the plural **quali** 'which ones' can refer to both people and things.

Ho comprato due riviste. *Quale* vuoi leggere?	I've bought two magazines. *Which one* do you want to read?
Abbiamo riviste dappertutto; non possiamo tenerle tutte. Allora, *quali* buttiamo via?	We have magazines everywhere; we can't keep them all. So *which ones* shall we throw out?

Note that **quale** is shortened to **qual** before the verb **essere**. The **-e** is *not* replaced by an apostrophe.

***Qual* è la tua rivista preferita?**	*Which* is your favorite/favourite magazine?
***Quale* dei tuoi amici ti ha prestato questa videocassetta?**	*Which* of your friends lent you this video?

Qual also means 'what' in sentences such as 'what is the . . . ?'

***Qual* è il tuo motivo per tenere tutte queste riviste?**	*What* is your reason for keeping all these magazines?

(iv) All the interrogative pronouns referred to above [23j(i) – 23j(iii)] are used in exactly the same way in indirect speech:

Non so *chi* ha telefonato.	I don't know *who* called/rang.

Dimmi *cosa* vuoi.	Tell me *what* you want.
Mi ha chiesto *quale* volevo leggere.	He asked me *which one* I wanted to read.

23j Pointing and Showing: Demonstrative Pronouns

Demonstrative pronouns are used to point out or emphasize things—the equivalent in English being 'this one,' 'that one,' 'these,' / 'those (ones).' They are usually used to convey whether something is near to or far from the speaker, though sometimes this distance is mental rather than physical.

(i) *Forms*

The demonstrative pronouns in Italian are **questo** 'this' and **quello** 'that.' Like adjectives ending in **-o** [➤22a(i)] they agree in number and gender with the noun they stand for.

Quale colore preferisce, *questo* o *quello?*	Which color / colour do you prefer, *this one* or *that one*?
Di chi sono tutte queste riviste? —*Queste* sono le mie e *quelle* sono le tue.	Whose are all these magazines? —*These* are mine and *those* are yours.

To emphasize further the notions of proximity and distance, **qui / qua** 'here' and **lì / là** 'there' are added after the demonstrative pronoun. These, therefore, could be added to both of the above examples.

Quale colore preferisci, questo *qui* o quello *lì?*	Which color / colour do you prefer, this one *(here)* or that one *(there)*?

- **Qui / qua** and **lì / là** can follow nouns as well as the pronouns **questo** and **quello**:

Preferisco questo *colore qui.*	I prefer this *color / colour (here).*

- **Questo** and **quello** also function as neuter pronouns:

Di chi è *questo?*	Whose is *this*?
Di chi è *quello?*	Whose is *that*?

• **Quello** and **questo** are used to convey 'the former' and the 'latter,' respectively. The appropriate form of **il primo** and **il secondo** can also be used.

Le mie due sorelle, Daniela e Rosaria, si sono iscritte all'università: *questa / la seconda* ha scelto di fare la storia dell'arte e *quella / la prima* la medicina.	My two sisters, Daniela and Rosaria, have enrolled at the university: *the latter* has chosen to do history of art and *the former*, medicine.

• **Quello** (*not* **questo**) + the preposition **di** is used in the following type of construction:

Il corso che ha scelto Daniela sarà più lungo di *quello di* Rosaria.	The course that Daniela has chosen will be longer than Rosaria'*s*.

The Italian **quello di** 'that of' is the way of expressing the English apostrophe + **s** ('s). The masculine form of the pronoun **quello** replaces the masculine noun **il corso**.

[For 'those who . . .,' 'all those who . . . ' ➤ Relative pronouns 23m(viii).]

(ii) Ciò 'that'

Ciò 'that' is an invariable neuter pronoun used to refer to something previously mentioned. However, **questo** is preferred here in spoken Italian.

***Ciò / Questo* mi sembra impossibile.**	*That* seems impossible to me.

23k 'How Much?' 'How Many?': Pronouns of Quantity

Some *quantifiers* refer to the whole or none of something, others to some part or some members of it.

(i) Quantifier pronouns

The following list includes most of the *quantifier pronouns* used in Italian. Many resemble closely the quantifier determiners [➤ 21f, 21g].

alcuni / e	some, a few
altrettanto / a / i / e	as much, as many
altro / a	other, something else, anything else
altri / e	others
ambedue, entrambi / e, tutti / e e due	both
certi / e	some
chiunque	anyone
ciascuno / a	each one
diversi / e, vari / varie	several, a number of
molto / a	much, a lot
molti / e	many, a lot
nessuno / a	no one
niente / nulla	nothing
ognuno / a	everyone, everybody
parecchio / a	quite a bit, a lot
parecchi / parecchie	several, quite a few
un poco (di)	a little (of), a bit (of)
poco / a	little, not much
pochi / e	few, not many
qualcosa / qualche cosa	something
qualcuno	someone
quanto / a?	how much?
quanti / e?	how many?
tale / i	someone, person
tanto / a	so much
tanti / e	so many
troppo / a	too much
troppi / e	too many
tutto / a	all, everything
tutti / e	all, everybody
uno / a	one, someone, somebody

***Qualcuno* è venuto a riparare la televisione? — No, non è venuto *nessuno*.**	Has *anyone* come to repair the television? — No, *no one* came.
Ma quando guardavo dalla finestra, ho visto *uno* suonare alla casa di fronte.	But when I was looking out of the window, I saw *someone* ring the doorbell / ringing at the house opposite.
E poi? — E poi *niente, nessuno* è venuto ad aprire e quel *tale* è andato via.	And then? — And then *nothing, no one* came to open the door and the *person* went away.

C'era *qualcosa* che volevi guardare?
Was there *something* you wanted to watch?

È ora di buttare via quel televisore, ci è già costato *parecchio* per le riparazioni, *troppo* infatti. In fin dei conti, quanti programmi interessanti ci sono da vedere? *Pochi.*
It's time to throw that television set away, it's already cost us *quite a lot* for repairs, *too much* in fact. When it comes down to it how many interesting programs / programmes are there to see? *Not many.*

***Certi* sono interessanti, *altri* meno.**
Some are interesting, *others* less so.

Ieri sera, quando la televisione funzionava ancora, abbiamo guardato due film, *uno* era bello e l'*altro* no ma, come me, tu hai guardato *tutti e due* fino alla fine.
Last night, when the television was still working, we watched two movies / films, *one* was good and the *other* not; but just like me, you watched *both* right to the end.

Ma solo perché non avevo *altro* da fare.
But only because I didn't have *anything else* to do.

Ma va', guardi sempre *tutto*.
Come on, you always watch *everything*.

***Ognuno* ha i suoi difetti.**
Everyone has his faults.

(ii) *Negative pronouns*

Negative pronouns such as **niente, nulla,** and **nessuno** need **non** before the verb when they follow it [▶ 27a(ii)], but not when they precede it. **Non** is not needed when the verb is preceded by **senza** 'without' [▶ 27a(v)].

Lunedì sono andato a letto *senza guardare niente.*
On Monday I went to bed *without watching anything.*

(iii) *'Anyone'*

Care should be taken with the equivalent of 'anyone.' 'Not . . . anyone' is, of course, the same as 'no one' **nessuno.** Although different in English, 'someone' and 'anyone' in the sense 'is anyone / someone there?' are both **qualcuno** in Italian. However, 'anyone' in the very wide sense of 'anyone at all' is **chiunque: chiunque avrebbe fatto la stessa cosa** 'anyone would have done the same thing.'

This same distinction applies to 'not . . . anything / nothing' **niente,** and to 'is there anything / something . . . ?' **qualcosa.**

C'è *qualcosa* da bere?	Is there *anything / something* to drink?

Note that 'anyone . . . who' is **chi...** [▷ Relative pronouns 23m(viii)].

Be careful not to confuse the pronoun quantifiers with their adjectival equivalents. Compare the following examples:

Ho *molti* amici.	I have *many* friends.
***Molti* di loro sono italiani.**	*Many* of them are Italian.

In the first example **molti** is an adjective and is not followed by the preposition **di**. In the second example **molti** is a pronoun and is normally followed by **di** in front of a noun or its equivalent. This same rule applies to most of the pronoun quantifiers listed above under 23k(i).

23l Ownership: Possessive Pronouns

Possessive pronouns are unique in that they represent two different nouns at once: the *possessor* and the *thing possessed.* Like possessive determiners they take their *form* from the *possessor*, and their *gender* and *number* from the *thing possessed.* Take care not to confuse the two: one person can own several things — which means that the possessive pronoun will be the *masculine or feminine plural* form — and several people can be joint owners of one thing — which means that the possessive pronoun will be *masculine or feminine singular.*

The possessive pronouns in Italian have identical forms to the possessive adjectives [▷ 21h(i)].

Remember that the third person singular pronoun **il suo,** etc. can mean 'his,' 'hers,' 'its,' as well as 'yours' (formal). The third person plural **i loro,** etc. can mean 'theirs' and 'yours' (formal). In formal writing **suo** and **loro** are often found with an initial capital letter.

Use

Possessive pronouns are normally used with the definite article:

Questa è la mia macchina; qual è *la tua?*	This is my car; which is *yours*?
La mia* è più bella *della tua.	*Mine* is nicer than *yours.*

The article is sometimes omitted when the pronoun comes after the verb **essere**:

Mamma mia, quanti regali! — Allora, questo è *tuo*, questo è *suo*, quello lì è *vostro* e questo qua è *mio*.	Goodness me, what a lot of presents! — Now then, this is *yours*, this is *hers*, that is *yours*, and this one is *mine*.

The article is generally retained for emphasis and to underline the idea of ownership.

This last example shows the distinction between **tuo** — singular and for one person — and **vostro** — plural and for more than one person. Remember that although **suo** means 'hers' in this context, the masculine form is used because it refers to **regalo**.

'*Mine*,' etc. is not to be expressed by the possessive pronoun in expressions such as the following:

uno dei *miei* amici / un *mio* amico	a friend of *mine*
una delle *nostre* zie / una *nostra* zia	an aunt of *ours*

In these examples, **miei, mio, nostre, nostra,** are possessive *adjectives*.

23m Relative Pronouns

(i) Use

A relative pronoun relates or links a noun to a clause that closely follows it and that defines or comments on it. The noun is known as the *antecedent*, and the clause introduced by the relative pronoun is called a *relative clause* [➤5b].

Il film *che* abbiamo visto era sensazionale.	The movie / film *that* we saw was sensational.

In the above sentence, the relative clause is **che abbiamo visto,** and its function is to give more information about **il film**. The relative pronoun is **che,** in this case the object of **abbiamo visto**.

Beware especially of the fact that in English, relative pronouns can take a variety of forms, and are often omitted altogether: **il film che abbiamo visto** can be expressed in English as 'The movie / film that we saw' or 'The movie / film which we saw' or 'The movie / film we saw.' This variety of alternatives does not exist in Italian, and the relative pronoun *must never be omitted.*

(ii) *Che*

Che as a relative pronoun means 'who,' 'whom,' 'which,' and 'that.' It is used, therefore, as both a subject and an object. It is invariable.

Sono andato al cinema con due persone *che* conosco molto bene: Marco, *che* lavora in banca con me, e Sonia *che* è appena rientrata dopo un viaggio in Africa.	I went to the movies / cinema with two people (*whom*) I know very well: Marco, *who* works at the bank with me, and Sonia *who* has just returned after a trip to Africa.

(iii) *Il che*

When the relative pronoun refers to an idea or a sentence, i.e., not to a preceding noun, then the neuter pronoun **il che** must be used.

Il divo del film muore alla fine, *il che* ci ha sconvolto.	The star of the movie / film dies at the end, *which* shocked us.

It wasn't *the end* that upset them, but *the fact that the star dies.*

(iv) Preposition + *cui*

When the relative pronoun follows a preposition, you must *never* use **che**. Use the invariable pronoun **cui**.

Dove danno il film *di cui* ci hai parlato?	Where are they showing the movie / film *that* you spoke to us *about*?

Conosco molto bene le due persone *con cui* sono andato.	I know the two people (*whom*) I went *with* very well.

In both of the above examples you see that in English the preposition comes later on in the relative clause. In Italian, the preposition *must precede* the relative pronoun. Remember also that English often omits the relative pronoun whereas this is *not possible* in Italian.

Note the following useful expressions:

il motivo / la ragione *per cui* ...	the reason *why* . . .
il momento / il giorno *in cui* ...	the moment / the day *when* . . .
per cui ...	so (that), and so . . .

Avevamo sentito dire che la fine era un po' triste, e questo era il motivo *per cui* mia sorella non voleva venire con noi.	We had heard that the ending was a little sad, and that was *the reason why* my sister didn't want to come with us.
La fine era un po' triste, *per cui* mia sorella ha deciso di non venire.	The ending was a little sad, *and so* my sister decided not to come.

(v) *Definite article +* ***cui***

'Whose,' 'of whom,' 'of which,' is conveyed by placing **cui** between the definite article and the noun.

Il film, *il cui* regista mi è completamente sconosciuto, ha avuto un successo strepitoso.	The movie / film, *whose* director is completely unknown to me, has been an outstanding success.
Mi pare un regista per *le cui* idee simpatizzo.	He seems (to be) a director *whose* ideas I go along with.

Il cui, etc. is strictly a determiner, but it is more appropriate to deal with it here.

(vi) ***Il quale***

It is possible to replace **che** or **cui** with the relative pronoun **il quale**, which has the following forms:

il quale (masculine singular)	**i quali** (masculine plural)
la quale (feminine singular)	**le quali** (feminine plural)

Il quale, etc. is seldom used in place of **che** as a subject or object. It is used:

- particularly after prepositions, and often therefore as a substitute for **a cui, di cui,** etc. The same examples as those in paragraphs (iv) and (v) above illustrate this point:

Dove danno il film *del quale* ci hai parlato?	Where are they showing the movie/ film *that* you spoke to us about?
Conosco molto bene le due persone *con le quali* sono andato.	I know the two people (*whom*) I went *with* very well.
Il film, il regista *del quale* mi è completamente sconosciuto, ha avuto un successo strepitoso.	The movie/film, *whose* director is completely unknown to me, has been an outstanding success.
Mi pare un regista per le idee *del quale* simpatizzo.	He seems (to be) a director *whose* ideas I go along with.

- to avoid ambiguity:

L'amica di Marco, *la quale* non conosco molto bene, non è potuta venire con noi.	Marco's friend, *whom* I don't know very well, couldn't come with us.

La quale here obviously refers to **l'amica**. However, this is only useful when there is one masculine and one feminine noun.

(vii) Quello che, quel che, ciò che

Quello che, quel che, and **ciò che** convey the English 'what [that which].' All three relative pronouns refer here to things and not to persons. It does not matter which form you use.

Non voglio che mi racconti *quello che* è successo alla fine.	I don't want you to tell me *what* happened at the end.
***Ciò che* succede alla fine è molto triste.**	*What* happens at the end is very sad.

Note: **Quello che** 'the one who' also refers to people.

Chi è Marco?—È *quello che* lavora in banca.	Who is Marco?—He is *the one who* works in the bank.

To convey 'everything,' 'all that,' place **tutto** before **quello che,** etc.:

Se mi racconti *tutto quello che* è successo dall'inizio alla fine, non avrò bisogno di andare a vedere il film.	If you tell me *everything that* happened from beginning to end, I won't need to go and see the movie / film.

(viii) Chi

Chi can convey a whole range of meanings such as 'he / she who,' 'the one(s) who,' 'people who,' 'those who,' 'whoever,' 'anyone who.' Although it can be used in a plural sense, the verb *must always be in the singular.*

***Chi* va a vedere questo film non sarà deluso.**	*Anyone who* goes to see this movie / film will not be disappointed.
Se non vuoi sapere quello che succede alla fine, è meglio non chiedere a *chi* l'ha già visto.	If you don't want to know what happens at the end, it is better not to ask *people who* have already seen it.
***Chi* impara tutte queste regole grammaticali sarà premiato.**	*Those who* learn all these grammar rules will be rewarded.

Chi is found in a number of proverbs:

***Chi* dorme non piglia pesci.**	The early bird catches the worm.
***Chi* va piano va sano e va lontano.**	Slow and steady wins the race.

- 'Those who' can also be expressed by **coloro che** and **quelli che,** which take a plural verb:

***Coloro che vanno* a vedere questo film non *saranno* delusi.**	*Those who* go to see this movie / film *will* not *be* disappointed.

Note: **Chi** tends to be preferred to the more formal **coloro**.

- To express 'all those who' place **tutti** in front of **coloro che** or **quelli che**:

***Tutti quelli che* avranno studiato dettagliatamente questo capitolo saranno stanchi morti.**	*All those who* have studied this chapter in detail will be dead tired.

24 Giving Vent to Your Feelings: Exclamations and Interjections

24a Exclamations

Exclamations express emotions such as delight, anger, surprise, or fear. The standard exclamations are introduced by words normally used as interrogatives, and may be created with whatever vocabulary is appropriate.

- Before a noun phrase **Che** is the standard device:

Che bella sorpresa!	What a lovely surprise!
Che peccato!	What a pity!
Che spavento!	What a fright!
Che delusione!	What a disappointment!
Che barba!	What a bore!
Che fregatura!	What a rip-off!
Che schifo!	How disgusting!
Che scemo!	What an idiot!

- **Che** + adjective is also very common:

Che bello!	How nice / lovely!
Che freddo!	Isn't it cold!
Che triste!	How sad!

- The following type of construction is even more emphatic:

Che bravo che sei!	How good you are!
Che pignolo che sei!	How fussy you are!
Che brutte abitudini che hai!	What bad habits you have!
Che pigrone che sei!	What a lazy bones you are!

- 'How' + adjective or adverb can also be rendered by **Come** + verb + adjective or adverb:

Come siete gentili!	How kind you are!
Come sei buffo!	How funny you are!

Come suona bene il pianoforte!	How well she plays the piano!
Come mangiano male!	How badly they eat!

- 'What a lot of . . . !' is **Quanto ...** !

Quanta gente!	What a lot of people!
Quanto lavoro!	What a lot of work!
Quanto hanno bevuto!	What a lot they have drunk!

- '(Just) look how . . . !' is **Guarda (un po') come ... !** + verb:

Guarda come piove!	Look how it's raining!
Guarda un po' come mi parla!	Just look how he speaks to me!

24b Interjections

Interjections range from words or short phrases that are real exclamations to the gamut of noises associated with emotions.

- Some are reactions to the senses — sadness, pain, taste, smell, sound, sight — and are barely words:

***Ah*, povero ragazzo!**	*Oh*, poor boy!
***Ahi*, mi fai male!**	*Ouch*, you're hurting me!
***Eh*, non c'è più speranza!**	*Oh*, there's no hope left!
***Puah*, che puzza!**	*Ugh*, what a smell!

- Some express boredom, resignation, doubt:

***Uffa*, che scocciatura!**	*Ouf*, what a bore!
***Bah*, cosa ci posso fare io!**	*Ah well*, what can I do about it!
***Boh*, penso di sì!**	*Ah*, I think so!

Note that some interjections such as **ah** and **eh** can communicate different feelings in different contexts. It is worth remembering also that it is not always easy, or even possible, to express in English certain interjections used in Italian. Their meaning usually becomes more obvious in a real life situation as many interjections are accompanied by gestures.

- Some express surprise or disbelief:

Davvero!	Really!
Ma come?	But how?/What do you mean?

Ma dai!	Come off it!
Eh!	Phew! Did it really!
Mamma mia!	Goodness gracious!
Ma insomma!	For heaven's sake!
Ma no!	Really! / You don't say!
Ma via!	Go on!

- Some express pleading or exhortation to action:

Per l'amor di Dio!	For goodness sake! / For heaven's sake!
Coraggio!	Don't be afraid! / Cheer up!
Dai! / Su! / Andiamo!	Come on!

- Some contain a warning or instruction:

Aiuto!	Help!
Attenzione!	Attention please! / Mind! / Look out!
Avanti!	Come in! / Move forward! / Go on!
Fermo!	Stop! / Stay where you are! / Hold it!
Fuori!	Get out!
Giù le mani!	Hands off!
Occhio!	Mind! / Watch out!
Silenzio!	Quiet! / Hush!
Smettila!	Stop it!
To'! / Tieni!	Here you are!
Voce!	Speak up!

- Some express reactions such as indignation or disappointment:

Neanche per sogno!	Not on your life!
E allora?	So what?
Accidenti! / Maledizione!	Damn!

- Others pleasure or joy:

Bravo!	Well done! / Bravo!
Fantastico!	Marvelous! / Wonderful! / Splendid!
Magnifico!	Wonderful! / Brilliant!
Stupendo!	Super! / Great!

Note: Like all languages, Italian too has its fair range of swearwords. A good current dictionary will no doubt provide a fair selection of those you may require, but you should be careful about how you use them!

E

LINKING AND MODIFYING MEANINGS: PREPOSITIONS AND ADVERBIAL EXPRESSIONS

25 Prepositions and Their Uses

25a *What Does a Preposition Do?*

A preposition is a connecting word, that is placed in front of a noun or pronoun to relate it to the rest of the sentence.

25b *Prepositional Phrases Linked to Verbs*

A prepositional phrase can be linked to a verb in two ways.

(i) *Free-standing adverbial expressions*

The prepositional phrases may be a free-standing adverbial expression [➤27] that modifies or extends the meaning of the verb by answering questions such as **Quando?** 'When?'/ **Dove?** 'Where?'/ **Come?** 'How?' [➤6d(vi) – 6d(viii)].

Quando sono partiti i tuoi parenti? — *Verso le sette.*	When did your relatives leave? —*Around seven o'clock.*
Dove pensano di fermarsi stasera? — *Vicino alla frontiera.*	Where are they thinking of stopping tonight? — *Near the border.*
Come viaggiano? — *In macchina.*	How are they traveling? — *By car.*

(ii)

Certain common prepositions link particular verbs to the following noun phrases [➤8h] or to the infinitive of another verb [➤8j]. (See the paragraphs mentioned for details.)

(iii) *Prepositional phrases*

Prepositions like ***di, con,*** and ***a*** are frequently used in Italian to create prepositional phrases with the value of an adjective [➤3b, 25c(iv)], a relative clause [➤25c(vi)], or an adverb [➤27b(ii)].

Chi era quella signora *di mezza età con i capelli ricci*? — Era mia zia.	Who was that *middle-aged* lady with *curly hair*? — She was my aunt.

Perché zoppicava? — Da quando si è rotta la gamba, cammina *a stento.*	Why was she limping? — Ever since she broke her leg, she has *difficulty* walking.

(iv) *Verbs after prepositions*

The only part of the verb that can follow a preposition is the infinitive [➤10a(iv)].

Volevano partire di buon mattino *per evitare* l'ora di punta.	They wanted to leave early in the morning *(in order) to avoid* the rush hour.
Hanno fatto colazione *prima di partire.*	They had breakfast *before setting off.*

(v) *Verbs + prepositions; adjectives, adverbs, nouns + prepositions*

A, di, and sometimes **per** are frequently used as fixed links following particular verbs [➤8j].

Abbiamo cercato *di* convincerli *a* rimanere ancora qualche giorno. A un certo punto stavano *per* cambiare idea, ma alla fine...	We tried *to* convince them *to* stay another few days. At some point they were *about to* change their minds, in the end . . .

- Many nouns and some adjectives are linked to a following infinitive by **di**.

Si capisce la loro decisione *di* partire presto con la speranza *di* evitare gli ingorghi stradali.	You can understand their decision *to* leave early in the hope *of* avoiding the traffic jams.
Saranno contenti *di* tornare a casa.	They will be happy *to* get back home.

[For adverbs linked to a following infinitive by **da** ➤25c(iii).]

25c Common Prepositions and Their Use

Because prepositions are used in a variety of ways, with considerable variation of meaning both within and between languages, it is generally easier to learn them in context—that is, in association with particular expressions, fixed phrases, or defined uses. The meaning in English is often the least reliable clue to the choice of the appropriate preposition in Italian. Prepositions in Italian can be simple, of one word; or compound, of two or more words joined to the following noun or pronoun with ***a*** or ***di***.

(i) *The simple prepositions* ***a, da, di, in, su, per, con***

The prepositions **a, da, di, in, su, per,** and **con** are among the most frequently used in Italian and will therefore be dealt with in some detail. **A, da, di, in,** and **su** combine with the definite article to form one word [▶ 21c(vii)].

(ii) *A*

- Destination, location, direction, position ('to,' 'at,' 'in,' 'on'):

andare a casa	to go home
andare a scuola	to go to school
stare a letto	to stay in bed
stare a casa	to stay at home
a Milano	to / at / in Milan (**a** before names of towns / cities)
voltare a destra, a sinistra	to turn right / left
la prima strada a destra / sinistra	the first street on the right / left
alla televisione	on television
alla radio	on the radio
al sole	in the sun
all'ombra	in the shade
all'aperto	outdoors, in the open

- Time, age, distance, speed, measure, price ('at,' 'in,' 'until,' 'by'):

all'una	at one o'clock
alle otto	at eight o'clock
a mezzanotte	at midnight
lavorare dalle sei alle dieci	to work from six to ten
all'alba	at dawn
a luglio	in July
a Natale / Pasqua	at Christmas / Easter

una volta al giorno / alla settimana / al mese / all'anno	once a day / a week / a month / a year
a presto!	see you soon!
a stasera!	see you this evening!
a trent'anni	at the age of thirty
abitare a tre chilometri dalla stazione	to live three kilometers / kilometres from the station
viaggiare a duecento chilometri l'ora	to travel at two hundred kilometers / kilometres an hour
vendere al chilo	to sell by the kilo
questi dischi si vendono a ventimila (lire)	these records are being sold at twenty thousand (lire)

- Method, means, manner, use ('by,' 'on,' 'in,' 'with'):

fatto a mano	handmade
scrivere a matita	to write in / with a pencil
a piedi, a cavallo	on foot / on horseback
ad alta / a bassa voce	in a loud / soft voice
ai ferri / alla griglia	grilled
una cotoletta alla milanese	a cutlet Milanese style
un panino al prosciutto	a ham roll
a braccia aperte	with open arms
imparare a memoria	to learn by heart
chiudere a chiave	to lock
una barca a vela	a sailboat
una cucina a gas	a gas range
un motore a reazione	a jet engine

- Added detail or features:

una giacca a doppio petto	a double-breasted jacket
una maglia a strisce	a striped sweater
una televisione a colori	a color / colour television

- After ordinals [➤28b(i)], **solo, unico,** and some adjectives:

Erano i primi ad arrivare e gli ultimi a partire.	They were the first to arrive and the last to leave.
Il solo a dire qualcosa.	The only one to say something.
Siamo pronti a mangiare.	We are ready to eat.
Ma non siamo disposti a lavare i piatti.	But we are not willing to wash the dishes.

Note that **ad** often replaces **a** before a word beginning with a vowel — see the first example above — and *especially* if the word begins with the letter **a**.

- After the verb **giocare** in talking about games:

giocare a calcio	to play soccer / football
giocare a carte	to play cards

- In some invocations:

al fuoco!	fire!
al ladro!	stop thief!

- Other uses:

a prima vista	at first sight
a perdita d'occhio	as far as the eye can see
un senatore a vita	a senator for life
a poco a poco	little by little
a due a due	two by two

[For **a** with other adverbial expressions ➤27b(ii).]

- With verbs taking an indirect object in Italian but not in English:

assomigliare a	look like

[For other examples ➤8h(i).]

(iii) *Da*

- Origin, movement 'from' / 'to' / 'by' / 'through' a place:

venire da Bari	to come from Bari
arrivare da Venezia	to arrive from Venice
uscire dal negozio	to go / come out of the store / shop
andare dal dentista	to go to the dentist's
passare da Bologna	to go through / via Bologna
uscire dalla finestra	to go out through the window

Note: It is worth comparing the use of **da** and **di** in the following constructions:

***Da* dove vieni? — Vengo *da* Bari.**	Where do you come *from*? — I come *from* Bari.
but	
***Di* dove sei? — Sono *di* Bari.**	Where are you *from?* — I'm *from* Bari.

- At someone's place, in someone's town or country:

abitare dai genitori	to live with one's parents
cenare dai nonni	to have dinner at one's grandparents'
da loro si mangia bene	at their house you eat well
da noi non c'è questo problema	we haven't got this problem (in our country)

- Purpose:

un abito da sera	an evening dress
un cavallo da corsa	a racehorse
una sala da giochi	a game room
una camera da letto	a bedroom
una macchina da cucire	a sewing machine
un costume da bagno	a bathing suit / costume
un bicchiere da vino	a wineglass

Note: 'A glass of wine' is **un bicchiere di vino.**

- Necessity, obligation:

la roba da lavare	things to wash / be washed
cose da fare	things to do / be done
lettere da scrivere	letters to write / be written

- After adverbs such as **molto, troppo, tanto, poco,** and the indefinite pronouns **qualcosa** and **niente**:

molto / troppo / tanto / poco da fare	a lot / too much / so much / little (not much) to do
qualcosa da bere	something to drink
niente da mangiare	nothing to eat

- Description:

l'uomo dal naso storto	the man with the crooked nose
la ragazza dagli occhi verdi	the girl with the green eyes
la casa dalle persiane nere	the house with the black shutters

- Manner, worthy of:

comportarsi da galantuomo	to behave like a gentleman
mascherarsi da infermiera	to dress up (disguise oneself) as a nurse
un comportamento da gentiluomo	gentlemanly behavior / behaviour
una vita da cani	a dog's life

- After passive verbs [➤17c]:

Molte case sono state distrutte dall'uragano.	Many houses have been destroyed by the hurricane.
Questo libro è stato scritto da un mio amico.	This book was written by a friend of mine.

- Price value:

un biglietto da cinquanta mila lire	a fifty-thousand-lire ticket
una gonna da novantamila lire	a ninety-thousand-lire skirt

- Cause:

morire dalla fame	to die of hunger
tremare dal freddo	to tremble with cold

- Time, age:

Imparo l'italiano da tre mesi.	I have been learning Italian for three months.
Pioveva da tre giorni.	It had been raining for three days.
Da giovane non praticavo nessuno sport.	When I was young, I didn't play any sport.
Da studente la mia materia preferita era la matematica.	As a student my favorite / favourite subject was mathematics.

[For use of tenses after **da** ➤12a(iv), 13b(viii).]

- Note also the following expressions:

cieco da un occhio	blind in one eye
sordo da un orecchio	deaf in one ear

Never elide **da** before a vowel—for example, **fare *da* interprete** 'to act as interpreter.'

(iv) Di

- Possession, definition, specification:

la casa di mio fratello	my brother's house
il treno delle nove	the nine o'clock train
il professore d'italiano	the Italian teacher
il direttore dell'ufficio	the office manager
una vista del mare	a view of the sea

un uomo di mezza età	a middle-aged man
un bambino di sei mesi	a six-month-old baby
l'isola di Capri	the island of Capri

- After many expressions of quantity:

una bottiglia di vino	a bottle of wine
una fetta di pane	a slice of bread
un grappolo d'uva	a bunch of grapes
un mazzo di fiori	a bouquet of flowers
migliaia di turisti	thousands of tourists
un paio di volte	a couple of times

- In partitives, i.e., to express 'some,' 'any,' 'of,' 'of the' [➤21f]:

del pane	some bread
uno di loro	one of them
una delle riviste	one of the magazines

- Material, contents:

una borsa di pelle	a leather bag
una camicia di cotone	a cotton shirt
una lattina di birra	a can of beer
una medaglia d'argento	a silver medal
un sacchetto di plastica	a plastic bag
una scatola di fiammiferi	a box of matches

- With a number of expressions of time:

di giorno	by day, in the daytime
di pomeriggio	in the afternoon
di sera	in the evening
di notte	at night, during the night
d'estate	in summer
d'inverno	in winter
alle otto di mattina	at eight in the morning / at 8:00 a.m.

- In adverbial expressions of manner:

essere di buon / cattivo umore	to be in a good / bad mood
ridere di cuore	to laugh heartily
uscire di corsa	to run out (of a place)
vestire di nero	to dress in black

- After certain adjectives:

lieto di **conoscerLa**	*pleased to* meet you
un paese ***ricco di*** **materie prime**	a country *rich in* raw materials
un libro ***povero di*** **idee**	a book *lacking in* ideas
non essere ***responsabile del*** **proprio comportamento**	not to be *responsible* for one's own behavior / behaviour
un camion ***carico di*** **legno**	a truck / lorry *loaded with* wood

- Origin, motion from a place:

sono di Parma	I am from Parma
la gente del Sud	the people from the South
uscire di casa	to leave the house
uscire di strada	to go off the road

- After **qualcosa, niente,** when followed by an adjective:

qualcosa di interessante	something interesting
niente di speciale	nothing special

- Other uses:

conoscere qualcuno di persona / di vista / di nome	to know someone personally / by sight / by name
dare del tu / del Lei a qualcuno	to address someone with the **tu / Lei** form
ho detto di sì / no	I said yes / no
penso di no	I think not
spero di sì	I hope so

[For use of **di** after comparatives ➤22f(i); after superlatives ➤22f(ii); after verbs ➤8h(ii).]

(v) In

- 'To' or 'in' a place

andare in città	to go to town
andare in banca	to go to the bank
lavorare in ufficio	to work in an office
abitare in periferia	to live on the outskirts
abitare in montagna	to live in the mountains

Note: **In** is similarly used with countries, continents, regions, and large islands.

andare in Italia / in Europa / in Calabria / in Sicilia	to go to Italy / Europe / Calabria / Sicily

- Transportation

andare in macchina / in treno / in aereo / in pullman / in bicicletta	to go by car / train / plane / coach (bus) / bike

- With many expressions of time:

in gennaio	in January
nel 1999 (millenovecento-novantanove)	in 1999
in primavera / in autunno	in spring / in the fall / autumn
nel Cinquecento	in the sixteenth century
arrivare in anticipo / in ritardo	to arrive early / late
il pullman è arrivato in orario	the bus / coach arrived on time
ho finito il lavoro in un'ora	I finished the work in one hour (duration, i.e., 'one hour' is *how long it took to complete the work*)

- Manner:

camminare in punta di piedi	to (walk on) tiptoe
guardare in silenzio	to watch in silence
parlare in dialetto	to speak in dialect
parlare in fretta	to speak quickly
vivere in pace	to live in peace

- Other uses:

eravamo in cinque	there were five of us
essere bravo in lingue	to be good in / at languages
essere debole in scienze	to be weak in / at sciences
la parola non viene in mente	the word doesn't come / spring to mind
se fossi in te	if I were you
siamo in pochi	there are only a few of us
stare in piedi	to stand

(vi) Su

- Place, position:

il ponte sul fiume	the bridge over the river
una città sul mare	a city by the sea

Il giornale è sul tavolo.	The newspaper is on the table.
L'appartamento dà sul parco.	The apartment / flat overlooks the park.

- Approximation:

essere sulla settantina	to be around seventy

Il viaggio costerà sulle centomila lire.	The journey will cost about one hundred thousand lire.
Peso sui settanta chili.	I weigh approximately seventy kilos.

- 'About,' 'on,' 'concerning':

informarsi sulla situazione politica	to find out about the political situation
una conferenza sulla musica classica	a lecture about classical music
una lezione sul Rinascimento	a lesson on the Renaissance

- 'Out of':

otto su dieci	eight out of ten

- Other uses:

l'abbiamo letto sul giornale	we read it in the newspaper
i pantaloni fatti su misura	made-to-order pants / trousers
prendere qualcuno sul serio	to take someone seriously

(vii) Per

- Movement 'to' / 'through' / 'around' a place

partire per la Spagna	to set off for Spain
passare per la Francia	to go through France
camminare per la città	to walk round the town

- With a number of expressions of time:

Ho studiato per tre ore.	I studied for three hours.
Devo fare questo per domani.	I have to do this for / by tomorrow.
Si fermeranno per due settimane.	They will stay for two weeks.

- 'Because of,' 'out of':

Per il freddo, ho deciso di stare a casa.	Because of the cold, I decided to stay at home.
L'abbiamo fatto per curiosità.	We did it out of curiosity.

- '(Intended) for,' '(in relation) to':

Questo regalo è per te.	This present is for you.
È alto per la sua età.	He's tall for his age.

- 'By,' 'by means of':

Le ho comunicato la notizia per telefono.	I told her the news by phone.
Ti manderò le informazioni per posta.	I shall send you the information by mail / post.

- Purpose:

Ho deciso di fare il corso per migliorare il mio italiano.	I decided to do the course (in order) to improve my Italian.
D'inverno devo sempre usare la crema per le mani.	In winter I always have to use hand cream.

- Mathematical calculations:

cinque per cinque	five times five
dividere per due	divide by two

- Other uses:

andare su / giù per le scale	go up / down the stairs
fare qualcosa per scherzo	do something as a joke
per caso	by chance
per favore / per piacere / per cortesia	please
per fortuna	fortunately
prendere qualcuno per il braccio	take someone by the arm
stare per	be about to [➤ 8c]
uno per volta	one at a time

(viii) Con

- 'With'

Non usciamo più con loro.	We are not going out with them again.

- 'Towards':

Si sono comportati male con noi.	They behaved badly towards us.

- Description:

la ragazza con i capelli corti	the girl with the short hair
la signora con gli occhiali	the lady with the glasses

- 'With,' 'in view of':

Come facciamo a studiare con questo caldo?	How can we study with this heat?

- 'With,' 'despite':

Con tutti i suoi problemi finanziari, è sempre di buon umore.	Despite all his financial problems, he is always in a good mood.

- Transportation:

viaggiare con la macchina / con il treno	to travel by car / by train

- Manner:

accettare l'invito con piacere	to accept the invitation with pleasure
agire con prudenza	to act wisely
fare le cose con calma	to do things calmly

- Other uses:

con mia grande sorpresa	to my great surprise
con nostro grande sollievo	to our great relief

(ix) *Other simple prepositions*

Those marked with an asterisk take the preposition **di** before a disjunctive pronoun [➤23h(i)]. This same rule also applies to **su**, dealt with under 25c(vi) above.

attraverso	across	**mediante**	by means of
circa	about, regarding	**nonostante**	in spite of
contro*	against	**presso***	near, with
dentro*	inside	**salvo**	except, barring
dietro*	behind	**secondo**	according to
dopo*	after	**senza***	without
durante	during	**sopra***	above, upon
eccetto	except (for)	**sotto***	under, beneath
fra / tra*	among, between	**tramite**	through, by means of
lungo	along	**tranne**	except
malgrado	in spite of	**verso***	towards, around

Siamo partiti *verso* le dieci di sera. Abbiamo viaggiato *durante* la notte. *Salvo* imprevisti, speriamo di arrivare alla nostra destinazione domani pomeriggio. *Malgrado* la distanza che dobbiamo percorrere, abbiamo in mente di fare il viaggio *senza* sosta. Siamo in quattro e, *tranne* Marco, sappiamo tutti guidare.

We set off *around* ten in the evening. We traveled *during* the night. *Barring* mishaps, we hope to arrive at our destination tomorrow afternoon. *Despite* the distance we have to travel, we intend to make the journey *without* stopping. There are four of us and, *except for* Marco, we can all drive.

*(x) Compound prepositions with **a***

accanto a	next to, beside
davanti a	in front of
di fronte a	opposite, facing
dirimpetto a	opposite
fino / sino a	up to, until
in cima a	at the top of
incontro a	towards
in fondo a	at the end of, at the bottom of
in mezzo a	in the middle of
insieme a	along with, together
in testa a	at the head of
intorno a	around
quanto a	as for

riguardo a	regarding
rispetto a	regarding, compared to
vicino a	near

La nostra casa è *accanto a* un bar che rimane aperto *fino a* tardi. *Di fronte al* bar c'è un locale notturno che chiude *intorno alle* due di notte. Molti giovani, quando escono dal bar o dal locale notturno, si fermano *in mezzo* alla strada a parlare. Delle volte si mettono a cantare proprio *davanti alla* mia finestra—ho una camera al pianterreno. *In fondo alla* strada c'è un grandissimo parco. Perché non vanno lì a parlare, e poi non danno fastidio a nessuno? *Rispetto all'*anno scorso la situazione va sempre peggiorando.	Our house is *next to* a bar that stays open *until* late. *Opposite* the bar there is a nightclub that closes *around* two a.m. Many young people, when they leave the bar or nightclub, stop *in the middle of* the street to talk. Sometimes they start singing right *in front of* my window—I have a room on the ground floor. *At the end of* the street there is a huge park. Why don't they go there and talk, and then they won't bother anyone? *Compared to* last year the situation is getting worse and worse.

*(xi) Compound prepositions with **di***

a causa di	because of, on account of
a favore di	in favor/favour of
a seconda di	according to
ad eccezione di	with the exception of
fuori di	outside, out
invece di	instead of
nel mezzo di	in the middle of
per mezzo di	by means of
per via di	by means of, because of
prima di	before

***Per via degli* esami che darò fra poco, devo studiare giorno e notte *ad eccezione* del sabato, l'unico giorno in cui non faccio nulla.**	*Because of the* exams that I shall be taking shortly, I have to study day and night *with the exception of* Saturdays, the only day when I do nothing.

Invece di **studiare, esco con i miei amici, e non vado mai a letto *prima di* mezzanotte. Sabato scorso sono stato *fuori di* casa tutto il giorno.**	*Instead of* studying, I go out with my friends, and I never go to bed *before* midnight. Last Saturday I was *out of* the house all day.

Note: Occasionally **fuori** is used without **di:**

Mio fratello è *fuori* città.	My brother is *out of* town.

(xii) Compound prepositions with ***da***

fin / sin da	ever since, (as) from
lontano da	far from
lungi da	far from

Non abitiamo *lontano dal* centro. *Fin da giovane* mi è sempre piaciuta questa città. I miei genitori pensano di traslocarsi in campagna, ma io sono *lungi dal* fare una cosa del genere.	We don't live *far from* the center / centre. *Ever since* I was young, I have always liked this town. My parents are thinking of moving to the country, but I wouldn't *dream of* (am far from) doing such a thing.

26 Types of Adverbial Expression

26a *What Is an Adverbial Expression?*

(i) Adverbial expressions (often shortened to *adverbials*) mainly answer the questions listed in paragraphs 6d(vi) to 6d(x). We say that they modify meanings because they complete, alter, or even contradict them. They may modify the meanings of verbs, adjectives, or of the whole sentence. Adverbial expressions can take the form of a single word, a phrase, or a complete clause with its own verb.

Te lo spiegherò.	I shall explain it to you.
Te lo spiegherò *dopo.*	(afterwards: *adverb*)
Te lo spiegherò *dopo la conferenza.*	(after the lecture: *adverbial phrase*)
Te lo spiegherò *quando la conferenza sarà finita.*	(when the lecture is over: *adverbial clause*)

Each of these three adverbials performs the same sort of function, of modifying the meaning of **Te lo spiegherò** by adding information, in this case about when the action will happen. The word **dopo** is itself an adverb, but the adverbial phrase and the adverbial clause are simply groups of words performing the same role.

[For more detail on adverbial clauses ➤5a(ii).]

(ii) *Adverb + adjective/adverb*

Adverbs can modify verbs, as in the above illustration, but also adjectives and other adverbs.

È *molto* facile da capire.	It's *very* easy to understand. (**molto** modifies the adjective **facile**)
Capiscono *molto* facilmente.	They understand *very* easily. (**molto** modifies the adverb **facilmente**)

26b Formation of Adverbs

(i) *Adverbs formed from adjectives [➤22]*

Most of these adverbs answer the question **Come?** 'How?'

The majority of adverbs in Italian (as in English) are formed from adjectives, by adding **-mente** to the *feminine* form of the adjective. Thus, for adjectives ending in **-o** [➤22a(i)] the formation is as follows:

Adjective	*Feminine*	*Adverb*	
lento	**lenta**	**lentamente**	slowly
onesto	**onesta**	**onestamente**	honestly
sincero	**sincera**	**sinceramente**	sincerely

- There are some exceptions to the above rule, and they include:

benevolo	**benevolmente**	benevolently
leggero	**leggermente**	lightly
malevolo	**malevolmente**	malevolently
violento	**violentemente**	violently

- An adjective ending in **-e** [➤22a(i)] forms its adverb by adding **-mente**:

breve	**brevemente**	briefly
cortese	**cortesemente**	politely
recente	**recentemente**	recently

- Adjectives ending in **-le** and **-re** drop the final **-e** before adding **-mente**:

facile	**facilmente**	easily
normale	**normalmente**	normally
particolare	**particolarmente**	particularly
regolare	**regolarmente**	regularly

The final **-e** is not dropped, however, when the **-le** and **-re** are preceded by another consonant:

folle	**follemente**	madly
acre	**acremente**	bitterly

- Some adverbs are formed from their adjectives in a completely irregular way:

buono	good	**bene**	well
cattivo	bad	**male**	badly

migliore	better	**meglio**	better

(ii) *Alternatives to adverbs formed from adjectives*

- Adjectives are used as adverbs in a range of fixed expressions:

abitare lontano / vicino	live far away / nearby
andare forte	go fast
costare caro	cost a lot of money (dearly)
lavorare sodo	work hard
mirare alto	aim high
parlare chiaro	speak clearly
parlare piano	speak quietly
picchiare sodo	hit hard
stare fermo	keep still
tagliare corto	cut short
tenere duro	stand fast
vestire leggero	dress lightly

- In formal style, adjectives sometimes replace adverbs, they must then agree with the subject of the verb [▶22c(i)]

Si avviarono verso casa *lenti* e *silenzi*osi.**	They set off for home *slowly* and *silently*. (Slow and silent, they . . .)

- There is a small number of adverbs that end in **-oni**:

bocconi	flat on one's face
carponi	on all fours
ciondoloni	dangling, hanging
ginocchioni	on one's knees
a tastoni	gropingly

- As the addition of **-mente** makes some adverbs rather long and clumsy, Italian often resorts to using an advervial phrase [▶26a(i)] using **con** or another suitable preposition + noun or **in un modo** (masculine), **in una maniera** (feminine) + adjective [▶22a].

La gente ha reagito *con calma, pazienza* e *in silenzio.* **La gente ha reagito *in un modo calmo, paziente* e *silenzioso.*** **La gente he reagito *in una maniera calma, paziente* e *silenziosa.***	The people reacted *calmly, patiently*, and *silently*.

(iii) *Other adverbs*

Many of the most common adverbs—especially those answering the questions **Quando?** 'When?' and **Dove?** 'Where?'—are not formed from adjectives. These are often short words such as **già** 'already,' **fuori** 'outside,' **giù** 'down,' **dietro** 'behind' [➤27]. In many cases also, common words are used as adverbs, prepositions, adjectives, pronouns, and / or conjunctions in different settings.

Abitiamo *vicino.*	We live *nearby*. (adverb)
Abitiamo *vicino alla* stazione.	We live *near* the station. (preposition)
La mia amica abita nella città *vicina.*	My friend lives in the *nearby* town. (adjective)
I nostri *vicini* sono molto gentili.	Our *neighbors* are very kind. (noun)
Ho fatto *poco* lavoro.	I've done *little* work. (adjective)
Ne ho fatto *poco.*	I've done *little*. (pronoun)
Ho finito *poco* fa.	I finished *a short while ago.* (adverb)

An adverb is an invariable part of speech. When the same word is used as an adjective, then it must agree in gender and number with the noun it describes [➤22a(i)]. This point is illustrated by two of the examples above, i.e., **Abitiamo *vicino*** and **nella città *vicina***. In the first example **vicino** is an adverb, and in the second example it functions as an adjective.

(iv) *Comparison of adverbs*

The comparative and superlative of adverbs in Italian are formed in much the same way as for adjectives [➤22f] by the use of **più..., il più..., meno..., il meno...**

Adverb	*Comparative*	*Superlative*
facilmente	**più facilmente**	**il più facilmente**
easily	more easily	most easily
	meno facilmente	**il meno facilmente**
	less easily	least easily

Not all adverbs have a comparative and superlative form. Those that do are mainly adverbs of manner described under 26b(i) above, with the exception of adverbs ending in **-oni** and a few adverbs of time and place such as **spesso** 'often,' **tardi** 'late,' **presto** 'early,' **lontano** 'far,' **vicino** 'near.'

Siete arrivati presto.—Sì ma siamo partiti *più presto* del previsto. Gli altri arriveranno *più tardi.* Come sapete, abitano il più lontano dal centro–città.

You have arrived early.—Yes, but we set off *earlier* than expected. The others will arrive *later.* As you know, they live *furthest* from the center / centre of town.

- As with adjectives, a small number of adverbs have irregular comparatives and superlatives:

Adverb	*Comparative*	*Superlative*	*Absolute superlative* (see (v) below)
bene	**meglio**	**il meglio**	**ottimamente / benissimo**
well	better	the best	very well
male	**peggio**	**il peggio**	**pessimamente / malissimo**
badly	worse	the worst	very badly
molto	**più**	**il più**	**moltissimo**
very, much	more	the most	very much
poco	**meno**	**il meno**	**pochissimo**
little	less	the least	very little

Quando il mio amico italiano parla con me al telefono, capisco *poco.* Se comincia a parlare in inglese, capisco *meno*—a dire il vero capisco *pochissimo.*

When my Italian friend speaks with me on the telephone, I understand *little.* If he begins to speak in English, I understand *less*—to tell the truth I understand *very little.*

Se riesco a mettere insieme tre parole, il mio amico mi fa sempre complimenti e dice che parlo *benissimo;* ma vorrei parlare molto *meglio.*	If I manage to string three words together, my friend always pays me compliments and says that I speak *very well;* but I would like to speak much *better.*

- Note the expression **il più / il meno** + adverb + **possibile**:

Abbiamo cercato di arrivare *il più presto possibile.*	We tried to arrive *as early as possible.*

- Note the use of **di più / di meno** 'more' / 'less,' 'most' / 'least' in the following type of construction:

Dei due film questo mi è piaciuto *di più / di meno.*	Of the two movies / films I liked this one *more / less.*
Quale film ti è piaciuto *di più / di meno?*	Which movie / film did you like *most / least?*

(v) The absolute superlative

This is simply an *emphatic* form of the adverb. It has two forms. Adverbs such as **spesso, tardi, presto, lontano,** and **vicino** add **-issimo** after removing the final vowel — the absolute superlative of adjectives is formed in the same way [➤22f(v)]:

spesso	**spessissimo**	very often
tardi	**tardissimo**	very late
presto	**prestissimo**	very early
lontano	**lontanissimo**	very far
vicino	**vicinissimo**	very near

Adverbs ending in **-mente** form the absolute superlative by adding **-mente** to the feminine singular superlative of the corresponding adjective:

facile	**facilissima**	**facilissimamente**	very easily

Note: This form of the absolute superlative is seldom used, but the same meaning can be expressed by placing **molto** or **assai** 'very' before the adverb.

Abbiamo seguito *molto/assai* facilmente tutte le direzioni.	We followed all the directions *very* easily.

26c Suffixes

There are a few adverbs whose meaning can be modified by suffixes:

bene	well
benino	quite well
benone	very well
male	badly
maluccio	not too well
poco	little
pochino	rather little
tardi	late
tardino	rather late

Stamattina mi sentivo *maluccio* e sono andato in camera per sdraiarmi. Adesso mi sento *benone.*	This morning I was feeling *rather poorly,* and I went to my room to lie down. Now I feel *very well indeed.*
Non c'è da meravigliarsi dato che ieri sera hai mangiato *pochino,* hai bevuto *mezzo* litro di vino e sei andato a letto *tardino.*	It's not surprising given that last night you ate *rather little,* you drank half a liter/litre of wine, and you went to bed *rather late.*

[For positions of adverbs ➤27e.]

27 What Adverbial Expressions Do

27a Negative Expressions

(i) *Making a verb negative*

To make a verb negative **non** is placed immediately before it. It can only be separated from the verb by object pronouns [➤ 23b(ii)–23b(vi), 23c].

Non mangio* la carne. *Non la mangio.	I *don't eat* meat. I *don't eat it.*

(ii) *Negative expressions*

If any negative expression follows the verb in Italian, **non** must be placed before the verb. **Non**, however, is *not required* if the negative expression comes first [➤ 27a(iv)], or it stands on its own without a verb [➤ 27a(vi)], or the verb is preceded by **senza** 'without' [➤ 27a(v)].

Most, though not all, negative expressions are adverbials; and it is convenient to list all of them here, since the above rule applies to them all.

no	no
non	not
non ... mai	never, not ever
non ... niente	nothing, not anything
non ... nulla	nothing, not anything
non ... affatto	not . . . at all
non ... per niente	not . . . at all
non ... mica	not . . . at all
non ... più	no more, no longer, not any more, not any longer
non ... da nessuna parte	nowhere
non ... né ... né	neither . . . nor
non ... neanche	not even
non ... nemmeno	not even
non ... neppure	not even

non ... nessuno	nobody, not anybody; not . . . any, no
non ... alcuno	not any, no

Note: **Niente** and **nessuno** are pronouns [➤23k(i)].
Alcuno and **nessuno** also function as determiners [➤21g(i)].

Quest'estate *non* vado *da nessuna parte*. *Non* ho *nessuna* voglia di uscire con questo caldo. I miei amici *non* capiscono *affatto* perché preferisco stare a casa. Abito a due passi dal mare, ma *non* vado *neppure* a fare il bagno. Sono proprio pigro. *Non* faccio *niente*. Mi chiedono sempre di andare da qualche parte con loro la sera, ma *non* vado *mai*. *Non* voglio andare *né* al cinema *né* in discoteca.

This summer I am *not* going *anywhere*. I have *no* wish to go out in this heat. My friends do*n't* understand *at all* why I prefer to stay at home. I live a stone's throw from the sea, but I do*n't even* go for a swim. I am really lazy. I do *nothing*. They are always asking me to go somewhere with them in the evening, but I *never* go. I do*n't* want to go *either* to the movies / cinema *or* the disco.

- The position of the negative expression is the same with infinitives and imperatives, i.e., **non** before and the second half of the negative expression after the verb:

Preferisco *non* fare *niente*.	I prefer to do *nothing*.
***Non* chiedergli *più*.**	*Don't* ask him *any more / again*.

(iii) *Negatives in compound tenses*

In compound tenses the negatives **mai**, **più, affatto, mica, neanche, nemmeno, neppure,** can either precede or follow the past participle:

Dopo l'ultima volta, *non* mi hanno *più* chiesto / *non* mi hanno chiesto *più* di uscire con loro.	After the last time, they *didn't* ask me to go out with them *anymore / again*.

- The negatives **niente, nulla, nessuno, per niente, da nessuna parte,** come after the past participle:

***Non* sono andato *da nessuna parte*, e *non* ho fatto *niente* di speciale.**	I did*n't* go *anywhere*, and I did *nothing* special.

In English it is possible to express a negative idea using a verb in different ways:

I went *nowhere.*	I did*n't* go *anywhere.*
I did *nothing.*	I did*n't* do *anything.*

These alternatives do not exist in Italian. In fact, in Italian it is perfectly correct in a number of cases to use two or more negatives in one sentence.

The following combinations are possible:

non ... mai da nessuna parte
non ... mai più
non ... mai nessuno
non ... mai niente
non ... più niente / nulla
non ... più nessuno

Non* faccio *mai niente.	I *never* do *anything.*
***Non* ho *più niente* da dire.**	I have *nothing more* to say.
Durante il mese di luglio la mia famiglia *non* va *mai da nessuna parte.*	During the month of July, my family never goes anywhere.
Se continui a criticarmi, *non* farò *mai più niente.*	If you go on criticizing me, I shall *never* do *anything again.*
Quando abbiamo ospiti, mia sorella *non* dice *mai niente* a *nessuno.*	When we have guests, my sister *never* says *anything* to *anyone.*

(iv) *Negatives preceding the verb*

The negatives **nessuno** and **niente / nulla** can be the subject of a verb:

***Nessuno* ha telefonato.**	*No one* called / rang.
***Niente* è successo.**	*Nothing* has happened.

The negatives **mai, né ... né, neppure, nemmeno, neanche**, can also precede the verb:

***Né* mia sorella *né* mio fratello vanno in vacanza quest'anno.**	*Neither* my sister *nor* my brother is going on vacation / holiday this year. (note that the verb must be plural in Italian)
***Mai* in vita loro sono stati a casa nel mese di luglio.**	*Never* in their life have they been at home in July.
***Nemmeno* una volta sono rimasti a casa durante questo periodo.**	*Not even* once have they remained at home during this period.

Non is omitted when the negative precedes the verb [27a(ii)].

(v) *Senza* 'without'

Many of the negative expressions are used after **senza,** very often after an infinitive. **Non** is always omitted:

senza dire niente	without saying anything
senza vedere nessuno	without seeing anyone
senza mangiare più niente	without eating anything else
senza alcun dubbio	without any doubt

(vi) *Negatives without a verb*

Many negative expressions can stand entirely on their own or with words other than verbs:

Che cosa hai imparato? — *Non* molto.	What have you learned? — *Not* much.
Hai detto qualcosa? — *No, niente.*	Did you say something? — *No, nothing.*
Ti hanno dato del lavoro scritto da fare a casa? — Un giorno sì e uno *no.*	Did they give you some written work to do at home? — Every other day.

Ti è piaciuto il posto? — *Nient'affatto.*	Did you like the place? — *Not in the least.*
Non ci vuoi tornare allora? — *Mai più.*	You don't want to go back there then. — *Never again.*
***Neanch*'io!**	*Neither* do I!

Note also:

spero di *no*	I hope *not*
penso / credo di *no*	I think / believe *not*
vuoi uscire o *no?*	do you want to go out or *not*?

(vii) ***Non ... che*** *'only'*

Non ... che 'only' is used without the value of a negative:

***Non* ho *che* un fratello.**	I have *only* one brother.

It is much more common, however, to use either **solo, solamente,** or **soltanto** 'only' in place of **non ... che**.

Ho *solo* un fratello.	I have *only* one brother.

- Note the use of **non ... che** in the following type of construction with **fare** + **altro**:

***Non* ha fatto *altro che* piovere.**	It has done *nothing but* rain.
***Non* fai *altro che* fumare.**	You do *nothing but* smoke.

27b ***Other Adverbs and Adverbial Phrases***

These answer various questions

(i) ***Quando?*** *'When?': time[**➤6d(vi)**]*

adesso / ora	now
al momento / in questo momento	at the present time
ancora	still, yet, again
a poco a poco	little by little
attualmente	at the present time
a volte	sometimes

qualche volta	sometimes
una volta	once
allora	then, at that time
a quel tempo	at that time
di buon'ora	early
di tanto in tanto	from time to time, occasionally
di quando in quando	from time to time
domani	tomorrow
dopodomani	the day after tomorrow
dopo	after, afterwards
d'ora in poi	from now on
finora	up to now, so far
fra poco	shortly
già	already
ieri	yesterday
ieri mattina	yesterday morning
ieri sera	yesterday evening, last night
l'altro ieri	the day before yesterday
improvvisamente	suddenly
ad un tratto	suddenly
tutt'ad un tratto	all of a sudden
infine	finally, in the end
intanto	meanwhile
nel frattempo	meanwhile
in passato	in the past
nel primo pomeriggio	in the early afternoon
mai	never, ever
oggi	today
oggi / questo pomeriggio	this afternoon
oggi a otto	in a week's time, a week today
ogni tanto	every now and again
ormai / oramai	by now, by then, by this time
per il momento	for the moment, for the present
poco fa	a short while ago
poi	then, next
presto	soon, early, quickly
prima	before, beforehand
prima o poi	sooner or later
proprio adesso	right now
raramente	rarely
recentemente / di recente	recently
ultimamente	lately, recently

sempre	always
quasi sempre	almost always
spesso	often
stamattina	this morning
stasera	this evening
stanotte	tonight, last night
subito	at once, immediately
tardi	late

Ci alziamo *sempre* molto presto anche se andiamo a letto *tardi*. *Stanotte* ho dormito poco perché ero preoccupato per mia figlia che ha perso *di recente* il suo posto di lavoro. Ha cercato *subito* un altro lavoro, ma *finora* non ha trovato niente. *Attualmente*, c'è molta disoccupazione. *Prima*, c'era molto lavoro ma *poi*, *improvvisamente*, la situazione è peggiorata. Ci dispiace tanto per nostra figlia che si sposerà *fra poco*. *Prima o poi* ci sarà una ripresa economica, ma *per il momento* dobbiamo tutti stringere la cinghia.

We *always* get up very *early*, even if we go to bed *late*. *Last night* I didn't sleep much, because I was worried about my daughter who *recently* lost her job. She *immediately* looked for another job, but *up to now* she has found nothing. *At the present time*, there is a lot of unemployment. *Before* there was lots of work, but *then*, *suddenly*, the situation got worse. We feel so sorry for our daughter, who will be getting married *shortly*. *Sooner or later* there will be an economic recovery, but *for the moment* we shall all have to tighten our belts.

(ii) ***Come?*** *'How?': manner, methods and means [► 6d(viii)]*

a fatica	with difficulty
(andare) a gonfie vele	(be) successful
a malincuore	reluctantly, unwillingly
a stento	barely, hardly, with difficulty
a tutto gas	at full speed, flat out
alla leggera	lightly, thoughtlessly
alla meglio	as best one can
(pagare) alla romana	(go) Dutch / halves
al passo	at walking pace
a rotta di collo	at breakneck speed
bene	well
abbastanza bene	quite well

(vedere qualcuno) di buon occhio	(look on someone) favorably / favourably
di male in peggio	from bad to worse
male	badly
per caso	by chance
in autobus	by bus
in pullman	by coach / bus
in treno	by train
in macchina / tassì	by car / taxi
in aereo	by plane
in bicicletta	by bicycle

Ho l'impressione che la situazione vada *di male in peggio*. L'anno scorso la ditta per la quale lavorava mia figlia andava *a gonfie vele*. Nel giro di pochi mesi tutto è cambiato. Mia figlia ha perso il suo lavoro e mentre prima stava *abbastanza bene*, adesso tira avanti *alla meglio*. Fa uno sforzo per prendere tutto *alla leggera* ma non è così facile.

I have a feeling that the situation is going *from bad to worse*. Last year the firm my daughter worked for was *successful*. In the space of a few months everything has changed. My daughter has lost her job, and whereas before she was *quite well-off*, now she keeps going *as best she can*. She makes an effort to take everything *lightly*, but it's not so easy.

(iii) ***Dove?*** *'Where?': place [**➤ 6d(vii)**]*

altrove	elsewhere
dappertutto	everywhere
da qualche parte	somewhere
da qualunque parte	anywhere
davanti	in front
dentro	in, inside
dietro	behind
di sopra	upstairs
di sotto	downstairs
fuori	outside
giù	down
indietro	behind
intorno	around
laggiù	down there
lassù	up there

lì / là	there
lontano	far away
qua e là	here and there
quaggiù	down here
quassù	up here
qui / qua	here
sopra	up, on, above
sotto	under, below
su	on, up
vicino	near, nearby

A mia figlia piace abitare *qui* e, anche se fosse possibile trovare lavoro *altrove*, non vorrebbe andare a vivere da *qualunque parte*. Siamo molto contenti che abiti *vicino*.	My daughter likes living *here;* and even if it were possible to find work *elsewhere*, she wouldn't want to go and live *anywhere*. We are pleased that she lives *nearby*.

- A number of these adverbs also function as prepositions [➤25c(viii) – 25c(xi)].

(iv) ***Quanto?*** *'How much?': degree [➤6d(ix)]*

abbastanza	enough, quite
altrettanto	as much
appena	hardly, scarcely, just
assai	very
meno	less
molto	a lot, much, a great deal
moltissimo	very much
parecchio	quite a lot
più	more
più o meno	more or less
piuttosto	rather
poco	little, not much
pochissimo	very little
pressappoco	approximately, roughly, about
quanto	how much
un poco / un po'	a little, a bit
sempre meno	less and less
sempre più	more and more
su per giù	more or less, roughly, about

tanto	so much
troppo	too much

È *piuttosto* difficile trovare lavoro in questa zona. Adesso che stiamo attraversando questa crisi economica c'è *sempre meno* lavoro. Quando lavorava, mia figlia guadagnava *parecchio*, se mi ricordo bene, *pressappoco* tre milioni di lire al mese, e il suo ragazzo guadagnava *altrettanto*.

It is *rather* difficult to find work in this area. Now that we are going through this economic crisis there is *less and less* work. When she was working, my daughter earned *quite a bit*, if my memory serves me right, *about* three million lire a month, and her boyfriend earned *just as much*.

(v) ***Perché?*** *'Why?': reasons [➤6d(x)]*

di conseguenza	consequently
perciò	therefore

La situazione attuale è *perciò* molto preoccupante.

The present situation is *therefore* very worrisome.

(vi) *Adverbs of certainty and doubt*

appunto	precisely
certo / certamente	certainly
davvero	really
esatto / esattamente	exactly
forse	perhaps
ovviamente	obviously
probabilmente	probably
quasi	almost
senz'altro	certainly
senza dubbio	undoubtedly
sì	yes
sicuro / sicuramente	certainly, surely
veramente	really

***Forse* mia figlia cambierà idea e andrà altrove in cerca di lavoro.**

Perhaps my daughter will change her mind and will go elsewhere in search of work.

***Senz'altro* troverà qualcosa. Qui è diventato *quasi* impossibile trovare un lavoro stabile.**	She will *certainly* find something. Here it has become *almost* impossible to find a permanent job.

27c The Position of Adverbs in the Sentence

(i) Verb + adjective/adverb

When an adverb modifies an adjective or another adverb, it is placed immediately in front of it as in English:

***molto* importante**	*very* important
***veramente* difficile**	*really* difficult
***quasi* subito**	*almost* immediately

(ii) Verb + adverb

Adverbs that express certainty or doubt normally precede the verb:

***Certamente,* non sarà facile.**	It will *certainly* not be easy.
***Probabilmente,* le faranno sapere qualcosa domani.**	They will *probably* let her know something tomorrow.

- Many adverbs of time tend to come before the verb:

***Stamattina* ha scritto parecchie lettere.**	*This morning* she wrote several letters.

However, it is not possible to give a hard-and-fast rule, since adverbs are sometimes placed after the verb to create a different emphasis:

***Domani* andrà a parlare con qualcuno.**	*Tomorrow* she will go and speak to someone.
Andrà *domani* a parlare con qualcuno.	She will go and speak to someone *tomorrow*.

In the first example **domani** simply indicates when the action will take place. The placing of **domani** after the verb in the second example stresses the point that the action will take place 'tomorrow' and not 'in two weeks' or 'a month,' for example.

- Most adverbs, however, follow the verb they qualify:

Quando parlano *lentamente*, capisco *benissimo* ma se parlano *in fretta*, capisco *pochissimo*.	When they speak *slowly*, I understand *very well*; but if they speak *quickly*, I understand very *little*.

(iii) *Compound tenses*

In the case of compound tenses, the adverb usually follows the past participle:

Quando hanno parlato *lentamente* ho capito benissimo.	When they spoke slowly, I understood *very well*.

However, some commonly used adverbs such as **già** 'already,' **appena** 'just,' and **mai** 'ever' are placed after the auxiliary:

Sono *appena* arrivati.	They have *just* arrived.
Abbiamo *già* mangiato.	We have *already* eaten.
Sei *mai* stato in Italia?	Have you *ever* been to Italy?

F

USING NUMBERS

Numerals

28a Counting: Cardinal Numbers

The cardinal numbers in Italian are:

1	uno (una)	22	ventidue
2	due	23	ventitré
3	tre	28	ventotto
4	quattro	30	trenta
5	cinque	31	trentuno
6	sei	38	trentotto
7	sette	40	quaranta
8	otto	50	cinquanta
9	nove	60	sessanta
10	dieci	70	settanta
11	undici	80	ottanta
12	dodici	90	novanta
13	tredici	100	cento
14	quattordici	101	centouno
15	quindici	200	duecento
16	sedici	300	trecento
17	diciassette	1.000	mille
18	diciotto	2.000	duemila
19	diciannove	10.000	diecimila
20	venti	100.000	centomila
21	ventuno		

1.000.000	un milione
1.000.000.000	un miliardo
1.000.000.000.000	un bilione

As can be seen from the above table, the cardinal numbers in Italian are fairly straightforward, though the following points should be borne in mind:

(A) Uno has a feminine form, and it follows the rules of the indefinite article [➤21e] when it precedes a noun.

un libro	one book (*or* a book)
una rivista	one magazine (*or* a magazine)
uno studente	one student (*or* a student)

(B) Zero takes the plural **due zeri, tre zeri**.

(C) The plural of **mille** is **mila**:

mille lire
duemila studenti

(D) Milione, bilione, miliardo, have plural forms **(milioni, bilioni, miliardi)** and require the preposition **di** before a following noun:

tre milioni di abitanti
cinque miliardi di dollari

They do not require the **di** when followed by another number:

duemilionicinquecentomila lire

Numbers such as the one above can be separated by **e**:

duemilioni e cinquecentomila lire.

All other numbers are invariable:

quattro bambini, quattro bambine
duecento, trecento

(E) When **uno** and **otto** are part of numbers above twenty and below one hundred, then the final vowel of **venti, trenta,** etc., is omitted:

ventuno, trentotto, settantuno, novantotto, etc.

(F) Tre has an accent with compound numbers:

ventitré, duecentotré, etc.

(G) In Italian a period/full stop is used to separate thousands, and a comma to separate decimal points. The opposite applies in English [➤2b(vii)].

5.000	5,000
2,83	2.83

(H) In spoken Italian it is quite common to use abbreviated forms, particularly to indicate the hundreds above a thousand:

settemila e tre = settemila e trecento

This form could lead to confusion as **settemila e tre** can be interpreted as 7003; but if you hear this said at a market or in a shop, for example, then you can be sure that it means 7300.

28b Arranging in Order: Ordinal Numbers

(i) The ordinal numbers — **primo** *'first,' etc. — are adjectives [► 22] and must agree in gender and number with the noun(s) they qualify. The most commonly used ordinal numbers are:*

primo	first
secondo	second
terzo	third
quarto	fourth
quinto	fifth
sesto	sixth
settimo	seventh
ottavo	eighth
nono	ninth
decimo	tenth

The remainder of the ordinal numbers are formed by removing the final vowel of the cardinal number and adding **-esimo.**

undicesimo, dodicesimo, ventesimo, centesimo, millesimo, etc.

(ii) Ordinal numbers generally precede the noun except in the case of monarchs and popes:

la prima volta	the first time
il secondo giorno	the second day
l'undicesimo secolo	the eleventh century

but

Enrico ottavo	Henry the Eighth, Henry VIII
Pio nono	Pius the Ninth, Pius IX

Note: From the 'thirteenth' to the 'twentieth century' there is an *alternative* form in Italian:

il Duecento / il tredicesimo secolo	the 13th century (the 1200s)
il Trecento / il quattordicesimo secolo, etc.	the 14th century (the 1300s)
il Novecento / il ventesimo secolo	the 20th century (the 1900s)

The alternative form, written with a capital letter, is used particularly when referring to art, history, literature, etc. It is also possible to use Roman numerals:

nel XIV secolo	in the 14th century

(iii) *Ordinal numbers can be written in two ways: I, II, or 1º, 1ª, 2º, 2ª, etc.*

The ordinal number is *only* used with the first day of the month. Thereafter, cardinal numbers are used.

il primo agosto, but **il 2 (due) agosto,** etc.

28c Sharing Out: Fractions

(i) *The most commonly used fractions are:*

un quarto	a quarter
tre quarti	three quarters
un terzo	a third
due terzi	two thirds
mezzo / la metà	half

(ii) *All other fractions are formed using ordinal numbers:*

un quinto	a / one fifth
tre quinti	three fifths

(iii) *'Half' as an adjective is* ***mezzo,*** *which agrees with the noun it refers to:*

mezzo litro di vino	half a liter / litre of wine
mezza bottiglia di rosso	half a bottle of red (wine)

Following a noun, the same rule applies, and it is linked by **e**:

una tazza e mezza	a cup and a half
un litro e mezzo	a liter / litre and a half

'Half' as a noun is **la metà**:

Ho già speso la metà del mio stipendio.	I have already spent half my salary.
Sono riuscito a fare la metà del mio lavoro.	I have managed to do half my work.

(iv) *Where the fraction is followed by a noun, the two are linked by* ***di:***

tre quarti della popolazione	three quarters of the population

un terzo di questo gruppo	a third of this group
un quinto del mio tempo libero	a fifth of my free time

28d Grouping and Estimating: Collective Numbers

Italian has a few collective numbers that are useful for giving an *approximate* number. They are all joined to the following noun by **di:**

un paio	a couple, a pair
una decina	about ten
una dozzina	a dozen
una quindicina	about fifteen
una ventina	about twenty
una trentina	about thirty
un centinaio	about a hundred
centinaia	hundreds
un migliaio	about a thousand
migliaia	thousands
milioni	millions

Ieri c'erano *migliaia di* macchine in città. Per arrivare a casa ho impiegato *un paio di* ore, un viaggio che normalmente faccio in *una trentina di* minuti.	Yesterday there were *thousands of* cars in town. To get home it took me *a couple of* hours, a journey I normally make in *about thirty* minutes.

[To express approximation, see also 25c(vi).]

29 Telling Time

To ask the time, the standard questions are **Che ora è?** or **Che ore sono?**

There are two ways of giving the time: the conversational way, and the one used for timetables of trains, buses, and airlines.

29a Time: The Conversational Style

È l'una.	It's one o'clock.
Sono le due.	It's two o'clock.
Sono le tre.	It's three o'clock.
È l'una e cinque.	It's five past / after one.
Sono le due e dieci.	It's ten past / after two.
Sono le tre e un quarto.	It's a quarter past / after three.
Sono le tre e quindici.	It's three fifteen.
Sono le quattro e mezzo / mezza.	It's half past four.
Sono le quattro e trenta.	It's four thirty.
Sono le cinque meno un quarto.	It's a quarter to / before five.
Sono le quattro e quarantacinque.	It's four forty-five.
Sono le sette meno cinque.	It's five to / before seven.
Sono le sei e cinquantacinque.	It's six fifty-five.
È mezzogiorno.	It's midday.
È mezzanotte.	It's midnight

- For **l'una** 'one o'clock' the verb is singular, and the feminine form is used because **ora** is understood. For the remainder of the other hours (from two to twelve), the verb is plural; and **le due,** etc. are feminine plural, **ore** being understood.

29b Time: The Timetable Style

When using this style the words such as **un quarto** and **mezzo** are discarded in favor of figures, given according to the 24-hour clock.

le nove e quindici	09:15
le diciassette e trenta	17:30 (5:30 *p.m.*)

- At a particular time is **all'una, alle due,** and so forth.

A che ora parte il treno? **—*Alle* quattordici e venti.**	At what time does the train leave? —*At* 14:20 (two-twenty).

- There is no Italian equivalent of 'a.m.' and 'p.m.' Where necessary, use **di / della mattina, di / del pomeriggio, di sera, di notte**.

Partiamo alle otto *della mattina* e speriamo di arrivare alle due *del pomeriggio*.	We are leaving at eight *a.m.* and we hope to arrive at two *p.m.*
L'ultima volta che abbiamo fatto lo stesso viaggio, siamo partiti alle dieci *di sera* e siamo arrivati alle tre *di notte*.	The last time we made the same journey, we left at ten *in the evening* and arrived at three *in the morning*.

- The following are useful:

Il negozio è chiuso *dalle* 12.30 *alle* 14.30.	The shop is closed *from* 12:30 *to* 14:30 (2:30 p.m.).
La libreria è aperta *fino alle* 20.30.	The bookstore is open *until* 8:30 p.m.
Arrivano *verso* (*circa*) le nove.	They are arriving *about* nine.
Devo essere a casa *per* le dieci.	I must be at home *by* ten.
***È ora di* mangiare.**	*It's time* to eat.
Che ora *fai*?	What time *do you have?*
Sono le due *passate*.	It's *past* two.
Alle undici *precise*.	At eleven o'clock *sharp*.
Il mio orologio è *avanti di cinque minuti*.	My watch is *five minutes fast*.
Il mio orologio è *indietro di tre minuti*.	My watch is *three minutes slow*.
Ci vediamo *fra poco*.	We shall see each other *soon*.
Si sono trasferiti a Firenze due mesi *fa*.	They moved to Florence two months *ago*.

[For adverbs and adverbial phrases of time ➤27b(i).]

The Calendar

Unless they start the sentence, days and months in Italian are written with a small letter [▶2a(ii)].

With the exception of **la domenica** 'Sunday,' the days are masculine. The months of the year are all masculine.

30a Days of the Week

lunedì	Monday
martedì	Tuesday
mercoledì	Wednesday
giovedì	Thursday
venerdì	Friday
sabato	Saturday
domenica	Sunday

'On Monday' is **lunedì,** 'on Mondays' is **il lunedì.**

Note also:

oggi	today
ieri	yesterday
l'altro ieri	the day before yesterday
domani	tomorrow
dopodomani	the day after tomorrow
sabato prossimo	next Saturday
lunedì scorso	last Monday
stamattina	this morning
oggi pomeriggio	this afternoon
stasera	this evening
stanotte	tonight, last night

Stanotte ho dormito male perchè avevo mangiato troppo.	I slept badly last night because I had eaten too much.

30b Months and Seasons

gennaio	January
febbraio	February
marzo	March
aprile	April
maggio	May
giugno	June
luglio	July
agosto	August
settembre	September
ottobre	October
novembre	November
dicembre	December
la primavera	spring
l'estate	summer
l'autunno	fall / autumn
l'inverno	winter
nel mese di gennaio / a gennaio / in gennaio	in January
all'inizio di / ai primi di febbraio	at the beginning of February
a metà (di) luglio	in the middle of July
alla fine di agosto	at the end of August

'In spring,' 'in the fall / autumn,' is ***in*** **primavera and *in* autunno;** but with 'summer' and 'winter' **di** is also possible and is used to indicate an habitual action.

D'estate vado al mare, ma d'inverno vado a sciare.	In summer I go to the seaside, but in winter I go skiing.

30c Dates

The ordinal number **il primo** [▶28b(i)] is used for the first day of each month and the cardinal numbers [▶28a] for all the other days. Sometimes **di** 'of' follows the number, but it is not essential. When writing a date in a letter heading, the definite article is omitted.

il primo (di) marzo	March 1st / 1 March
but	
il due aprile	April 2nd / 2 April
il ventun novembre	November 21st / 21 November

il trentuno ottobre	October 31st / 31 October

These would normally be written **il 1° marzo, il 2 aprile, il 21 novembre, il 31 ottobre**. Note that **ventuno** and **trentuno** tend to drop the **o** with months beginning with a consonant.

Note **l'otto maggio** (**l'8 maggio**) and **l'undici settembre** (**l'11 settembre**), as both numbers begin with a vowel.

'On' a date is expressed by simply using the definite article.

Quando arrivano? — *Il* nove giugno.	When are they arriving? — *On* June 9th.

- Some useful expressions to note:

Che data è oggi? — È il 15 dicembre.	What is the date today? — It is the fifteenth of December.
Quanti ne abbiamo (del mese)? — Ne abbiamo cinque.	What day is it today? — It's the fifth.
Che giorno è oggi? — È mercoledì.	What day of the week is it today? — It's Wednesday.
In che giorno siete liberi?	On what day are you free?

30d Years

Years are expressed using the cardinal numbers preceded by the definite article.

il 1990 (millenovecentonovanta)	1990
il 2000 è un anno bisestile	2000 is a leap year

To express 'in,' use **in** + the definite article (**nel**).

In che anno sei nato? — Sono nato *nel* 1972 (millenovecentosettantadue).	In what year were you born? — I was born *in* 1972.

When the complete date is written out, the article is omitted before the year.

Sono nato il 14 marzo, 1955.	I was born on March 14th / March 14, 1955.

Years are frequently shortened in everyday speech:

Ho cominciato ad imparare l'italiano nel '79 (settantanove).	I started to learn Italian in '79.

Note also the way of expressing decades:

Mi è sempre piaciuta la musica degli anni '80 (ottanta).	I have always liked the music of the 80s.

30e Age

Age is expressed in Italian using the verb **avere** + number + **anni**:

Mia sorella ha diciassette anni.	My sister is seventeen.

Anni would normally be omitted in response to the question 'How old are you?'

Quanti anni hai? Sedici (or **ne ho sedici**).	How old are you? Sixteen (*or* I am sixteen).

[For the use of **ne** to replace a noun ➤23f.]

Note the following expressions to convey approximate age:

Il mio collega ha *una trentina di anni*.	My colleague is *around thirty*.
Mia zia è *sulla sessantina*.	My aunt is *about sixty*.
Mio cognato è *sui quarant'anni*.	My brother-in-law is *about forty*.

- Note also:

un dodicenne	a twelve-year-old boy
una ventenne	a twenty-year-old girl

This form can only be used with the numbers from eleven upwards. Remove the final vowel of the cardinal number and add **-enne.**

G
INDEX

Index

N.B. Cross-references are to chapters and paragraphs

T